THE

LAST ECONOMIC SUPERPOWER

THE RETREAT OF GLOBALIZATION,
THE END OF AMERICAN DOMINANCE,
AND WHAT WE CAN DO ABOUT IT

JOSEPH P. QUINLAN

NEW YORK   CHICAGO   SAN FRANCISCO
LISBON   LONDON   MADRID   MEXICO CITY   MILAN
NEW DELHI   SAN JUAN   SEOUL   SINGAPORE
SYDNEY   TORONTO

The **McGraw·Hill** Companies

1 2 3 4 5 6 7 8 9 10   DOC/DOC   1 9 8 7 6 5 4 3 2 1 0

ISBN 978-0-07-174283-2
MHID   0-07-174283-2

Library of Congress Cataloging-in-Publication Data

Quinlan, Joseph P.
  The last economic superpower : the retreat of globalization, the end of American dominance, and what we can do about it / by Joseph P. Quinlan.
    p. cm.
  Includes bibliographical references and index.
  ISBN 978-0-07-174283-2 (alk. paper)
  1. International economic relations. 2. International trade. 3. International finance. 4. Economic history—20th century. 5. Economic history—21st century. 6. United States—Economic policy. 7. United States—Foreign economic relations. I. Title.
  HF1359.Q56 2011
  337—dc22

                                                                    2010029776

To my best friend,
Karen Ann

And the little guy,
Katahdin Robertson

Contents

Acknowledgments   vii

INTRODUCTION   The Beginning of the End   ix

CHAPTER 1   Globalization's Comeback   1

CHAPTER 2   The Gathering Storm   27

CHAPTER 3   Financial Armageddon and the Retreat of Globalization   53

CHAPTER 4   Speeding toward a Messy Multipolar World   83

CHAPTER 5   A Handicapped Giant: Causes and Consequences   119

CHAPTER 6   The Twilight of Europe and Japan   143

CHAPTER 7   Flexing Their Muscle—The New Power Brokers in Action   173

CHAPTER 8   The Coming Economic Cold War   211

CHAPTER 9   Globalization Reincarnated   241

Notes   267

References   275

Index   279

Acknowledgments

This book was made possible by the energy, enthusiasm, and encouragement of my agent, Matthew Carnicelli. It was Matthew's vision and gentle prodding that helped me focus my mind and put my fingers to keyboard, turning various proposals into a reality. I am very much in debt to one of the best agents in the business.

I am also enormously grateful to the people of McGraw-Hill. I was very fortunate to have worked with Knox Huston and Jane Palmieri during the editing process—many thanks to both. And thanks to Lydia Rinaldi, Mary Glenn, and Gary Krebs of McGraw-Hill for their part in bringing this project to fruition.

At US Trust, I am indebted to Chris Hyzy, John Santelli, and Kimberly O'Neil for getting the book launched. I am especially grateful to Jessica Martin, a friend and colleague, and one of the best young minds on Wall Street.

Over the past year, I had the very good fortune to have worked with John Paine, and I wish to acknowledge his deft hand in shaping the content and message of this book. I also benefited enormously from the insights, experience, and encouragement of Kati Suominen of the German Marshal Fund in Washington, DC.

A special thanks to Isaiah "Al" Litvak at Florida Atlantic University for his invaluable comments on the manuscript. I am indebted to Jeff Lande as well for his interest in the book.

Finally, I owe much gratitude to a family that has learned when to ask and not to ask about "the book." To PJ, Brian, and Sarah—you are the inspiration that drives me to do what I do. That is equally true of Corrie and the little guy, Katahdin. To Bo and Lydia—thanks for putting up with me during your time at the house. For better or worse, you are family. And to my wife and best friend, Karen, I will say it again: you are simply the best. Thank you. This one is for you.

The Beginning of the End

The last economic superpower went bust in September 2008. The financial tsunami that swept over Wall Street that month not only laid waste to venerable institutions like Lehman Brothers and battered the reputations of Goldman Sachs, Morgan Stanley, and other financial stalwarts, but the "Made in America" crisis also undermined the capacity and credibility of the world's last economic superpower—the United States. After years of living beyond its means and after amassing mountains of debt, the music finally stopped for a country that had long set the tune for the global economy and grown accustomed to standing at the pinnacle of the global economic order.

The epic U.S. housing boom and bust—and all the sordid auxiliary details associated with subprime mortgages and toxic derivatives—culminated in one of the worst financial crises in U.S. history. As fear and panic spread in September 2008, the world watched in stunned horror as U.S. banks folded, shotgun corporate marriages were hastily arranged on Wall Street, and the free-market-touting U.S. government was forced to bail out or take control of one financial institution after another. More worrisome, the pain was not contained to the United States. Given the financial hardwiring of the global economy, the after-shocks of Wall Street's financial meltdown spread far and wide, inflicting pain on tiny villages in Norway, German banks, Spanish homeowners, South Korean utilities, and many other parties. In the ensuing months, global economic activity collapsed. World trade and investment plunged, while the rate of global unemployment soared, triggering a mad scramble among governments "to do something" to stave off another Great Depression.

It was a humbling and humiliating moment for the United States—the chief architect of the global economy and long-time champion of globalization. In the quarter century leading up to the financial crisis, most of the world had few qualms with a global economy largely groomed and managed by the West, principally the United States. Most of the world also had little resistance to the central tenets of globalization—namely industry deregulation, unfettered global capital flows, trade and investment liberalization, and the primacy of the private sector. This acceptance was underwritten by superior results. From the early 1980s forward, the global economy experienced a blessed period of muted inflation, low unemployment, and infrequent and shallow recessions. Global trade and investment rose sharply over this period. The integration of China, India, and Russia into a world economic order structured and headed by the United States helped lift millions out of poverty. There were periodic financial crises during this period, but they were never at the core of the global economy—or the United States.

As the last decade rolled on, the U.S. economy seemed to be indestructible, quickly rebounding from the dot-com bust early in the decade and then the shocking events of 9/11. Against this backdrop, the world became more and more dependent on the

U.S. consumer in particular and the U.S. economy in general for growth. Early in the 2000s, the United States, with just 4.5 percent of the global population, accounted for nearly one-fifth of total world imports. Such was the outsized influence of the U.S. consumer on the rest of the world. Meanwhile, with the world's largest and deepest capital markets, Wall Street was at the epicenter of global finance and set the tune for the global capital markets. Concurrently, Japan's economic might continued to fade in the first decade of this century, while Europe struggled to generate sustained growth. China was emerging but had yet to arrive. America was the world's sole economic superpower as the new century commenced.

Those days have passed, however. The events of September 2008 not only decimated the portfolios of investors all over the world but the "Made in the U.S." financial debacle also demolished America's ability and authority to lead the global economy. As details have emerged of lax U.S. financial regulations, bogus credit ratings, sloppy risk management, excess risk taking by U.S. households and Wall Street firms, these unflattering truths, juxtaposed against the crumbling finances of the U.S. government, have converged to jeopardize the long-term growth of the U.S. economy and undermine the global attractiveness of the U.S.-led capitalist model. The world no longer dances to the tune of the United States. The U.S.-centric global economy of the past three decades is being reshaped. New economic powers are on the ascent—led by nations like China, India, Brazil, and Turkey, for instance—with these emerging players less inclined to follow the global rules laid out by the United States and the West. The developing nations, or "the Rest," have their own ideas about how the global economy should be managed.

The financial crisis of 2008 was a circuit breaker—the global financial meltdown broke the supposed inexorable advance of free-market capitalism, throttled the primacy and influence of global finance, and undermined the economic superpower status of the United States. In another sense the crisis accelerated a number of key long-range trends that were already in motion before the crisis struck. The relative economic decline of the developed nations and the rising influence of the emerging markets in general and China in particular were fast-forwarded by the crisis and have, in turn, accelerated the move toward a less U.S.-centric, more multipolar world.

This new world will be more complex, fluid, and disruptive, notably for the architects and standard bearers of the postwar economic system: the United States, Europe, and to a lesser extent Japan. In the years ahead, global power and influence will be more diffused among nations and regions, making it more challenging to coordinate and craft solutions to pressing global problems. The era in which a handful of nations could meet for a weekend and set the global economic agenda for the rest of the world is over. The new era will require far-reaching adjustments for those nations in decline and for those on the ascent. Becoming more acclimated to a new multipolar world will challenge not only nations but also key postwar multilateral institutions like the United Nations Security Council, International Monetary Fund, World Bank, and other Western-dominated institutions that have long held sway over global economic governance. Invariably, these institutions will have to yield more to the aspirations of the developing nations and their strategic interests in order to remain relevant.

In the end, as the following pages discuss, the financial crisis of 2008 was a tipping point. A messy multipolar world is upon us, one that will further erode the economic superpower status of the United States and one if improperly handled that will result in an economic cold war between the developed and developing nations. The latter represents the worst-case scenario. A more benign and favorable outcome could still emerge from the crisis if the United States, Europe, China, India, Brazil, and others can foster a climate of cooperation and agreement. Globalization is in retreat but need not cease to exist if the main economic players in a multipolar world can forge commonalities and subsume national interests for the global good. That is a tall order but not an impossible outcome.

PLAN OF THE BOOK

Chapter 1 discusses the rise of globalization since the collapse of the Bretton Woods system and highlights how globalization was kick-started by the liberalization of global capital markets. Money makes the world go round, and as capital flows became less constrained and more liberated over the past quarter century, the globalization of the real economy took hold. Cross-border trade and investment soared as the world economy, lead by the United States, was stitched closer together.

Well before the great financial meltdown of 2008, however, multiple warning signs suggested that all was not well with the uber-charged U.S. economy. The key metrics that were flashing red are examined in Chapter 2, while the financial meltdown and its aftershocks are the main topics of Chapter 3.

The messy, multipolar world of today is examined in Chapter 4. This chapter discusses five seismic trends that will test America's ability to adapt and thrive in the world of tomorrow: the advent of the G-20 as the world's new steering committee; the shift in the "commanding heights," or the rise of the state at the expense of the private sector; the rise and accelerating pace of regionalism; the arrival of Brazil on the global stage; and

China's economic emergence and the implications for the mainland and the world economy.

Chapter 5 examines the exhausted finances of the United States. A creditor nation in the mid-1980s, America is now the world's largest debtor nation, a situation that will greatly handicap the U.S. economy and its global influence for a long time to come. How did we get here? What caused America's finances to implode during the first decade of this century? America looks more and more like a financial cripple owing to the untimely convergence of two wars, the financial crisis of 2008, and soaring entitlement liabilities. The bill from each one of these factors, according to various estimates, is at least $1 trillion, and counting.

The fading appeal of Europe and Japan, and the implications for the United States, is the subject of Chapter 6. The twilight of Europe and Japan and their diminished capacity to affect the global agenda is just as important as the much told story of the rise of China and India. Their decline coupled with America's increasingly exhausted resources means that the most important forces that had been driving globalization forward for the past three decades have been crippled, leaving the fate of globalization much in doubt. America's ability to shape the global agenda in economics, foreign affairs, and other key multilateral issues has been increasingly compromised by politically weak and economically stagnant allies who have in turn lost faith in America's ability to lead.

Chapter 7 highlights and discusses the new power brokers in action—or how states like China, Brazil, and others are reconfiguring and reshaping the global economy. The chapter analyzes how the world's most critical inputs—natural resources, capital, and labor—are under the increasing control of the developing nations, and the mounting tensions that are expected to arise as a result of these circumstances. In particular, the chapter examines the new mindset and goals of corporations from the developing nations, many of which are determined to increase their market presence in the United States and Europe. Global mergers and acquisitions are no longer the exclusive domain of the developed nations; new corporate players from Brazil, Turkey, and India, for instance, are spreading their corporate wings, creating a great deal of angst and anxiety in the West. Simultaneously, at the precise moment that many Western firms need access to the markets and resources of China, Brazil, India, and other emerging markets, the latter have become a great deal pickier and choosier about foreign direct investment from the West. In the end, consumers, natural resources, capital, talent—most of the critical inputs to economic growth now lie outside the control of the United States, an unfavorable turn that has helped undermine America's economic superpower status. There is nothing "super" about an economy that is overly dependent on other people's oil and natural resources, deep in debt to the rest of the world, and increasingly reliant on emerging market consumers in the face of stagnant and mature markets at home.

Chapters 8 and 9 peer into the future and discuss the two paths before the United States and the world economy. Given the dramatic changes that have overcome the economies of the West and the Rest, we face two potential scenarios: the first scenario centers on an economic cold war between rich, developed nations and poor, developing nations.

In this first scenario, the subject of Chapter 8, the United States and the developed nations, rather than adjust to a new global landscape and accept their diminished relative role in the world economy, deny reality and cling to the old order. The policies and structures of the past, however, are unacceptable to the developing nations who feel that the time has long passed for the rich to lead and the poor to follow. As a result, tensions rise between a U.S.-led developed nations bloc and a China-led developing nations cohort. Growing worker discontent and rising nationalism and xenophobia in both the developed and developing nations trigger various forms of protectionism, entangling the global economy in a web of regulations and cross-border barriers that inhibit the unfettered flow of people, goods, and capital.

Economic nationalism becomes rampant around the world. Defending globalization becomes the best way to lose political legitimacy and power at home. Tensions reach a breaking point, and an economic cold war breaks out, fragmenting the global economy and all but ending the current phase of globalization. In this world, global reregulation replaces deregulation. The private sector takes its cue from the public sector—politicians— rather than the market. Banks effectively become utilities, or risk-averse institutions whose principal mandate is to support the local and national economy. Cross-border capital flows are restricted; capital is again "caged," hindering growth in world trade and investment. Multinationals are politically browbeaten to become more local, less global at home, while given the cold shoulder overseas, impairing their global reach and their global earnings. This, along with a rise in tit-for-tat trade and investment protectionism, leads to a reduction in global trade and investment. Consumers are big losers, with rising trade barriers and the hoarding of resources resulting in higher prices for food, energy, and other staples. Global capital markets swoon as investors take cover. All told, the global economy sputters to a halt and enters a prolonged period of slow or no growth.

The second scenario, the subject of Chapter 9, is the reincarnation of globalization. Under this scenario, the West and the Rest come to recognize their mutual interdependence and move down the path of mutual cooperation, not competition, on a number of fronts. With an effective G-20 governing the global economy, with the United States and Europe accepting and adapting to their diminished role in the world, and with key developing nations becoming real global stakeholders, a new era of globalization is possible. Joint global stewardship will be required—not just between the United States and China, but also from Europe, Russia, Brazil, and key nations in Africa and the Middle East.

While the financial crisis of 2008 has thrown parts of globalization into reverse and undermined the economic superpower status of the United States, a more robust and inclusive global economy could still emerge in the years ahead. We have reached the end of globalization as determined and designed by the United States but not the end of globalization if America and the West can embrace a new configuration with different characteristics—Chinese, Indian, Brazilian, Egyptian, and many others. This represents a significant challenge to a country that likes to think of itself as "indispensible," and one that is long accustomed to sitting at the head of the table, giving orders, not taking them.

The challenges in front of China, India, Russia, and other key developing nations are no less daunting. Having arrived on the global stage, are these nations ready to assume the mantle of global leadership? Will they be willing to subordinate national self-interests for the good of the global common good when it comes to tackling weighty global issues like climate change, the proliferation of nuclear weapons, and aid and development for the world's poorest nations? The answers to these questions are unclear. What is clear is that the aftershocks of the global financial crisis present a golden opportunity for the world's leaders to recast, reinvent, and reenergize globalization.

Only time will tell whether or not the world economy is heading for an economic cold war or about to chart a new course toward greater globalization. *The Last Economic Superpower* lays bare the challenges in front of the United States. How the story ultimately ends remains to be discovered.

Globalization's Comeback

The decamping of the state from the commanding heights marks a great divide between the twentieth and twenty-first centuries.

—DANIEL YERGIN AND JOSEPH STANISLAW,
The Commanding Heights

Disillusionment can be a great motivator. Make enough people miserable, drain their hopes for the future, sap their confidence, and the result is an ideal prelude for change. During the 1970s the United States suffered two oil shocks, soaring prices, two economic recessions, declining productivity, and the demoralizing effects of stagflation—high inflation-cum-high unemployment. Against this ugly backdrop, the political and economic scars the decade left on the United States were deep enough to set off a global revolution.

The seminal event that started the 1970s downturn came from halfway around the world. Up until the early 1970s, the United States had been the unchallenged leader of the free world, and times were so good after World War II that the 1950–1973 period is often referred to as the "golden era." As the label implies, the two decades following the war were a time of strong global growth and development thanks to U.S. economic aid and leadership (a.k.a., the Marshall Plan), and the successful rebuilding of war-torn Europe and Japan. By the time the 1970s rolled around, all the major economic players before the war had recovered from the ravages of conflict.

The good times ended when a group of developing nations decided to exert their collective might against the West. On October 16, 1973, the Organization of Petroleum Exporting Countries (OPEC) announced that it was raising the price of oil by 70 percent. This body blow from the Middle East suddenly upended a near quarter century of prosperity and growth for the United States and many other nations. Soaring oil prices stunned the fossil-fuel-dependent West and brought economic growth in the United States and beyond to a grinding halt.

In the ensuing months, prices soared, and the unemployment lines lengthened. Those weren't the only lines. Soon long lines of cars were winding into gasoline stations across the nation, an outcome of gasoline shortages. To make ends meet, many U.S. households that had grown comfortable with a single wage earner found they needed two incomes to keep up with the rising price of food, energy, and other staples. Relatively tame over the 1960s, the U.S. inflation rate surged from 3.4 percent in 1972 to more than 12 percent by 1974. Not surprisingly, investors took fright of the shifting economic landscape, and by the end of that year, the Dow Jones Industrial Average was down by roughly 40 percent from the levels at the end of 1972.

In such an environment, the misery index—a figure that simply combines the rate of inflation with the unemployment rate—gained national prominence. The index spiked to nearly 18 percent in 1975 as prices continued to soar and the number of idle workers increased. Jimmy Carter pounded the point over and over during the campaign of 1976, helping him win the presidency.

Popular discontent stoked skepticism over the government's role in the marketplace, undermining support for government management of the economy. Strict industry regulations, wage and price controls, state-owned enterprises, and various industrial policies—these state-led initiatives were discredited as the 1970s dragged on. The Nixon presidency would be remembered by some as the "last liberal administration,"[1] a rap on its aggressive pursuit of wage and price controls and the creation of new government agencies like the Environmental Protection Agency and the Occupational Safety and Health Administration. The administrations of Presidents Ford and Carter did not fare any better when it came to creating the environment for real economic growth. Taken as a whole, the 1970s turned out to be the weakest decade of growth in the post–World War II period.

Worse was to come. A second oil shock erupted in 1979, after Iran, a major oil producer, was taken over by religious fundamentalists. The flow of oil from the country was halted, and even when the oil spigot opened again, the flow was intermittent. The U.S. economy was staggered yet again. The misery index reached an all-time peak of 20.36 percent in 1980. President Carter found the tables turned on him that year, when Ronald Reagan also found the misery index a convenient rallying cry. Rarely had a decade started on such a sour economic note. And the pain lingered. The U.S. economy contracted in 1980, faintly recovering the following year before sliding back into recession again in 1982.

The point of maximum pain came in November of that year, when the employment rate soared to a postwar record of 10.8 percent. Not since the end of World War II had so many Americans been on the dole. And not since the end of World War II had the U.S. economy taken such a hit, with the economy contracting by nearly 2 percent in 1982. Against this backdrop, the championing of state-directed prosperity had reached a point of no return. Times were ripe for change.

THE SHIFT IN THE COMMANDING HEIGHTS

A silver lining would emerge from the miserable performance of the U.S. economy in the 1970s. The rocky times spawned a new mindset about economic policies not only in the United States but also in Europe. The 1980s brought a new way of thinking about the role of the state in the economy. In the most basic terms, market failures could be blamed on government failures. A consensus formed around the idea that governments and bureaucrats were no longer capable stewards of the economy. That idea opened the door to a radical rethinking about the relationship between government and the marketplace. The new cause needed a flag bearer and it found two: Margaret Thatcher and Ronald Reagan. As Reagan would famously remark, "The best minds are not in government. If any were, business would hire them away."

Starting in the United Kingdom, swiftly embraced in the United States, and adopted to some degree by key countries around the world, control of the most important components of the economy, or the "commanding heights" as Vladimir Ilyich Lenin put it, shifted in a way that would have made the communist leader red with anger—from the state to the private sector. Starting in the early 1980s, a counterrevolution kicked in—policies were crafted that favored the deregulation of domestic industries, the privatization of state enterprises, and the liberalization of international trade and investment. During this era giants in the telephone and airline industries in the United States were deregulated, while across the pond Britain privatized British Telecom and British Gas. Smaller government was the rallying cry, entailing lower tax rates and less regulation. Beginning in the early 1980s and continuing through the 1990s, free-market capitalism was gradually embraced, cross-border capital flows soared, global trade and investment flourished, and globalization made a stunning comeback.

The global economy set the course for a quarter century of almost unprecedented prosperity following the severe economic downturn of the early 1980s. Around the world, increased competition, greater cross-border openness, privatization of state enterprises, and industry deregulation became guiding economic norms. The developed nations—with the United States at the forefront—led the way in promoting the primacy of the free markets. In heavily state-run parts of the world, socialists and communists alike joined in jettisoning the "visible hand" of the government for the "invisible hand" of the markets. Privatization and deregulation meant the hiving off of hundreds of businesses that used to be government-owned or government-controlled. State-owned banks, utilities, steel mills, and other companies were all put up for sale around the world. The effect, broadly speaking, was to greatly reduce the involvement of the public sector in the economy.

Led by the United States, the global economy was woven together by rising cross-border trade, investment, and capital flows. At first, globalization's return rested on deepening cross-border ties among the United States, Europe, and other developed nations—or the West. Beyond the developed nations, however, globalization's roots gradually spread to other countries and regions of the world. China's tilt toward the West in the late 1970s would gradually unlock one of the largest markets in the world. Under Mikhail Gorbachev, political opening (glasnost) and economic restructuring (perestroika) took hold in the Soviet Union, eroding the underpins of the Communist Empire and helping to bring the Berlin Wall crashing down in 1989. Since the weight of failed communist bloc economic policies had brought Eastern European satellite countries to ruin, most of them eagerly embraced the principles of the free market. Under the pressure of its declining balance of payments, India revamped its inward-looking economic policies in 1991, gradually freeing its state-run industries from the onerous restrictions imposed by the state since its 1947 revolution. Various Latin American countries reformed their economies during the 1990s, most notably Brazil as it broke free of military dictatorship. Around the world, free-market capitalism emerged superior to the bankrupt socialist model.

By the end of the 1990s, the second great age of globalization was in full bloom. In order to understand why it was the second, some historical perspective is needed. The first age of globalization had occurred during the period that stretched from 1870 right up to the eve of World War I. This was a period of buoyant global growth, robust trade, and strong cross-border flows of investment. Money flowed freely around the world, although most of this capital flowed from the United Kingdom, France, and Germany to less developed nations in the Americas, Asia, and Africa. As pernicious as imperialism was, trade for the first time spanned the globe at a level that far surpassed all that had come before. John Maynard Keynes famously captured the mood of the times with this passage from his *Economic Consequences of the Peace*, penned in 1919:

> What an extraordinary episode in the economic progress of man that age was which came to an end in August 1914! The inhabitant of London could order by telephone, sipping his morning tea in bed, the various products of the whole earth, in such quantity as he might see fit, and reasonably expect their delivery upon his doorstep; he could at the same moment and by the same means adventure his wealth in the natural resources and new enterprises of any

quarter of the world, and share, without exertion or even trouble, in their prospective fruits and advantages; or he could decide to couple the security of substantial municipality in any continent that fancy or information might recommend.

World War I, however, would end the first age of globalization, and nor would globalization be revived after the war. Europe, the main agent of the first flowering of world trade, was too indebted to the United States to do much more than scramble to stay afloat, and the United States largely turned its back on the world. The economic shocks in Weimar Germany would keep the rest of Europe uneasy, and the U.S. stock market crash in 1929 sounded the death knoll of what was remaining of the era's economic expansion. The disastrous run on major European banks that followed in 1931 and collapse in global trade would plunge the world into depression. While the U.S. economy expanded by more than 40 percent between 1933 and 1937, tax increases and spending cuts helped push the economy back into recession in 1938. It was World War II that ultimately pulled the world out of recession, with the United States emerging as the leader of the capitalist world. Seizing upon their imperialist masters' weakness, Europe's far-flung colonies, through riots and armed struggles, would fight their way to independence in the decades following the war.

In the rise of the second age of globalization, those colonies have become integral players in the expansion of world prosperity. The holy trinity of deregulation, privatization, and trade and investment liberalization has raised world output, bolstered global trade and investment, and lifted millions out of poverty in India, China, and other developing nations. The economic numbers vividly illustrate the tale. Between 1983 and 2007, the global economic pie expanded from roughly $12 trillion to over $55 trillion. World exports of goods and services soared from $2.2 trillion to over $17 trillion during the same period; reflecting the deep nature of globalization, world merchandise exports as a percentage of world gross domestic product (GDP) hit a postwar peak of 26 percent in 2008. The stock of outward foreign direct investment surged from $ 616 billion in 1983 to over $16 trillion in 2007. Meanwhile, per capita incomes in the developing nations gradually rose, notably in developing Asia and parts of Latin America. Global stock market capitalization surged from $2.2 trillion in 1985 to a peak of nearly $59 trillion in October 2007. Numbering just around 20 in 1990, the number of stock markets in the developing markets topped 68 in 2009.

This era of prosperity has been marked by bumps along the way, to be sure. However, recessions in the United States became less frequent and shorter in duration. Periodic financial crises came and went without much lasting damage to the forward momentum of globalization. The Mexican peso crisis in 1982, the U.S. stock market crash of 1987, the U.S. savings and loans crisis in the late 1980s, the concurrent boom and bust of Japan's property market, and the 1997 Asian financial crisis—all these events roiled the financial markets at the time but were quickly brushed aside as one-off events. By the 1990s, so fine-tuned was the U.S. economic growth engine that many on Wall Street talked of the "Goldilocks economy," or an economy not-too-hot, not-too-cold. Others spoke of the "great moderation"—or a propitious backdrop of steady economic growth, low inflation, and infrequent recessions. This relative calm was quite different from the stagnant growth-cum-rising prices of the 1970s, and given this radical turn of events, the consensus was that free-market capitalism was the best wealth-generating system ever concocted, with the Anglo-Saxon model at the forefront.

As part of this consensus, the battle between the state and the marketplace was unequivocally over, and the marketplace was declared the clear winner. Indeed, so decisive was the shift in "the commanding heights" that in the last decade of the twentieth century, experts began predicting the end of the nation-state and governments subordinated to the markets. Francis Fukuyama famously proclaimed "the end of history." So powerful were the market forces sweeping the world that any state or government that stood in the way would ultimately end up as "road kill."[2]

Underlying all of globalization's success was one vital ingredient: the unfettered cross-border flow of capital. To understand how capital was unshackled from the chains of regulation in the 1950s and 1960s, one has to go back further than Thatcher and Reagan. A better starting point is with a most unlikely revolutionary: Richard Nixon.

THE FOUNDING FATHER OF MODERN GLOBALIZATION

The legacy of Richard Nixon is replete with seminal events—the Vietnam War, détente with China, and of course, the deception of Watergate. Nixon's legacy, however, is rarely associated with the advent of globalization and the rise of the free markets. Yet Nixon's decision on August 15, 1971, to abandon the gold standard—effectively ending the Bretton Woods system put in place following World War II—would set the world economy and financial markets on a different path in the ensuing decades. As Martin Wolf of the *Financial Times* pointed out, "The abandonment of the Bretton Woods system of fixed, but adjustable, exchange rates in the 1970s marked the beginning of a new global economy."[3] In effect, financial globalization was born.

Prior to Nixon's momentous decision, the U.S. greenback acted as the world's reserve currency. The buck was backed by gold, meaning that the United States was committed to exchanging gold for dollars at a fixed rate of $35 per ounce. For a quarter century this system had worked very well. Along with the rise of the West came the expansion of global multilateral institutions that promoted global trade and investment, including the World Bank, the International Monetary Fund, and the General Agreement on Trade and Tariffs (GATT).

The system worked as long as foreign claims matched the size of U.S. gold reserves. Late in the 1960s, however, the fixed exchange rate came under increasing strain. Rising government spending on the Vietnam War and the costs associated with the Great Society program of the Johnson administration stoked inflation and encouraged speculative attacks on the dollar. Efforts were made by both the United States and its trading partners to shore up the dollar but to no avail.

As Europe and Japan healed from the ravages of war, they made rising exports to the United States the key to their recovery, and as a result their dollar holdings gradually exceeded the U.S. stock of gold. This important shift, along with rising inflation, slowly eroded confidence in the U.S. dollar and America's commitment to the Bretton Woods system. The system rested on the belief that the dollar's value was "as good as gold." But in 1971, the United States posted its first annual trade deficit since World War I, sparking fears about America's dwindling gold reserves and loss of global competitiveness. With the political and economic costs mounting, President Nixon capitulated in August 1971 by "closing the gold window," thereby effectively ending the Bretton Woods system.

At the same time, Nixon imposed a temporary surcharge on a host of imports, but neither the downward adjustment in the U.S. dollar (with the dollar declining by roughly 10 percent a few months after the buck was delinked from gold) nor the tax on imports did much to improve the competitiveness of the United States. While the U.S. trade balance swung to a modest surplus in 1973, the pendulum swung in the other direction the following year thanks to the spike in world oil prices and the attendant jump in U.S. oil imports. The United States posted a trade deficit of $4.3 billion in 1974, beginning a string of annual trade deficits that continues virtually uninterrupted to this day.[4]

The disintegration of Bretton Woods ushered in a new world of floating exchange rates and greater cross-border capital mobility—a vastly different world from the tight controls after World War II. For more than two decades, the global capital markets had remained "caged."[5] That is how the chief architects of Bretton Woods—Britain's John Maynard Keynes and America's Harry Dexter White—wanted it. Both men believed that capital controls were required to help eliminate the economic volatility and financial anarchy of the years between the two world wars. The Great Depression had spawned an extensive web of global capital controls as one nation after another attempted to insulate themselves from the economic wreckage around it. Trade and overseas capital were heavily regulated; indeed, by the eve of World War II, according to the World Bank, global capital flows had dried up.[6]

Keynes and White considered cross-border flows "speculative" and "destabilizing." Accordingly, the short-term movement of capital across borders was tightly controlled. Bank activities were largely restricted to the domestic economy. Interest rates were capped. The use of import licenses to protect local industries helped suppress capital mobility. In some countries, tourists traveling overseas were limited to how much local currency they could take out of the country. Not surprisingly, these strictures did not afford banks or financial institutions much in the way of international profits. Accordingly, while U.S. banks were considered among the largest in the world in 1960, of the 13,000 plus banks in the United States, only 8 had their own permanent foreign operations.[7]

Yet with the end of the gold standard in 1971 and the subsequent shift toward floating exchange rates in 1973, capital now had the opportunity to roam the world to find the best returns. Management guru Peter Drucker spoke of "an enormous mass of 'world money'" unleashed by floating exchange rates.[8] This mass of money only grew in importance and power following the tumultuous days of the early 1970s. The removal of capital controls limiting the amount of foreign sums that could enter a country, technological advances in communications, and the creation of new financial instruments such as derivatives all converged to create a global financial revolution, whose outcome has been dubbed financial globalization.

Capital controls were dismantled in the United States and Germany in the mid-1970s, the United Kingdom (1979/1986), Japan (the early 1980s), and the bulk of Europe by the end of the 1980s. While only 5 countries out of 19 in the Organization of Economic Cooperation and Development (OECD) were classified by the International Monetary Fund (IMF) as having open capital markets in 1976, the numbers gradually expanded over the ensuing decade. Meanwhile various emerging markets opted to liberalize their capital accounts, allowing more capital to flow in and out of the country. Nations such as South Korea, Mexico, the Philippines, Indonesia, and others were pulled deeper into the global economy on account of rising foreign trade and investment flows. Developing nations allowed greater foreign participation in their domestic banking sector over the late 1980s and 1990s, especially in Latin America and Eastern Europe, extending and deepening the geographic reach of global capital flows. Supporting the rise of financial globalization were technological advances that resulted in falling costs associated with the processing, storing, and transmitting of ever rising volumes of data across far-flung parts of the world. This helped boost daily foreign exchange trading volumes and spur the development of new financial instruments, notably derivatives. Not long after Nixon "closed the gold window," the financial engineers on Wall Street got busy creating new products. Securitization was born, with the launching of currency futures in 1972 and equity futures in 1973. Other derivative products, like Treasury bill futures and futures on mortgage-backed securities, or bonds financed by home mortgage payments, would follow shortly thereafter.

AWASH IN CASH

Leading the charge toward a more globalized world were the financial institutions of the developed world. With barriers removed, money was free to flow where it could find the best deal or highest returns. These investments in turn spurred the growth of financial institutions and stock markets in the developing world, especially in the Pacific Rim, and helped grease the wheels of global commerce.

While in 1973 the total pool of offshore capital available to the international financial markets was roughly $160 billion, by the early 1980s the numbers were exponentially higher. Gross international capital flows totaled $500 billion in 1980 and represented 4 percent of world GDP. Over the balance of the decade, global flows increased until they exploded in the mid-1990s as the global capital markets became more integrated. With computer technology, money could move around the world with a click of a mouse. The appetite among large institutional investors (pension funds, insurance companies, hedge funds, and sovereign wealth funds) for foreign stocks and bonds continued to rise. Financial innovations—namely growth in the derivative markets—also spurred the accelerating pace of financial globalization in the 1990s.

Again, sheer numbers demonstrate the soaring growth of global capital markets. Between 1990 and 2007, the global bond market grew from $18 trillion to $78 trillion. The global equity market surged from $8.3 trillion to $55.5 trillion over the same period. Combined, the size of the world's equity and bond markets was more than double the level of world GDP in 2007, one year before the great financial crisis. In the same year, gross international capital flows totaled nearly $11 trillion, versus $500 billion in 1980, and were equal to 20 percent of world output.

All the above helped create a new world order whereby international funds emerged as a key engine of global growth. Financial globalization—or the unfettered movement of capital across borders—emerged from the breakdown of the Bretton Woods system, enabling money to make the most unexpected links. By the mid-1980s, individual U.S. investors could access foreign bonds and stocks in Bangkok or Buenos Aires. Developing nations could raise capital on Wall Street. Investors outside the United States could easily diversify their portfolios by purchasing U.S. securities, and international banks could gather deposits in Europe or Southeast Asia and make loans locally. All these activities became even more intense in the decade leading up to 2007. Although little understood at the time, the end of the Bretton Woods system was the dawn of financial globalization—a dynamic that would help produce a quarter century of global growth and prosperity, as well as contribute to the great financial crisis of 2008–2009.

THE GLOBALIZATION OF TRADE AND INVESTMENT

The expansion and integration of global capital markets that followed the collapse of the Bretton Woods system not only transformed the world of finance, but the globalization of capital also produced a profound transformation in the "real" global economy—or more specifically on global trade and foreign direct investment, and the standard bearers of globalization—multinationals. As David Smick notes in *The World Is Curved*, "Discussing capital flows may not be as exciting as new computer wizardry developed by specialists living on separate continents, but the financial markets are what got globalization started."[9]

Indeed, money makes the world go round—meaning the more global capital in circulation, the greater the opportunities for cross-border trade and investment, or specifically, the more opportunities for firms to extend their reach beyond their home markets. Global trade volumes had rebounded smartly in the 1950s and 1960s, following the devastation of World War II. Yet as a percentage of global output, exports grew in importance as the pace of financial deregulation accelerated in the 1980s and 1990s. Given the physical distance that separates producers from consumers, and the cost associated with moving goods, global trade constantly requires financing; so the greater the depth and geographic scope of global finance, the greater the opportunities for foreign trade.

This also led to greater opportunities for foreign direct investment (FDI), or the spread of international production by the world's largest companies. Their expansion was aided by a variety of factors. Falling trade barriers transformed such moribund countries as Poland and Hungary, whose adoption of the EU's free trade policies led to rising trade and investment flows with the West. Under Prime Minister P. V. Narasimha Rao, India reduced its average tariffs from 85 to 25 percent in the mid-1990s. Advances in communications technology led to the worldwide explosion in the number of computers in use and the outsourcing of various service activities, of which the most famous is India's growth in back-office support for foreign firms. Industry liberalization occurred across a wide swath of nations, such as Brazil's privatizing government-owned businesses in telecommunications, oil, mining, and electricity. More money flowing between countries and the liberalization of trade and investments also led to the proliferation of regional trading blocs, such as the Asia Pacific Economic Council and Mercosur in South America. Against this backdrop, "going global" was never easier and never as enticing for firms wanting to go abroad than in the last quarter of the twentieth century. The intersection of these trends enabled firms to pursue more sophisticated international production strategies.

From the mid-1980s onward, the strategies of multinationals became more sophisticated. In the words of the foreign direct investment experts at the United Nations, "simple integration strategies" evolved into "complex integration strategies." The latter entailed greater linkages among a corporation's far-flung units and greater interdependence and coordination not only among affiliates and their parents but also among affiliates themselves. A leader in this revolution was the automobile industry, to the point that a new car could no longer be considered "made in America," because its parts could come from Canada, Japan, South Korea, or Mexico. Foreign affiliates, rather than stand-alone units, functioned for the firm as a whole. Again, using automobiles as an example, Toyota USA helped the company become, briefly, the largest carmaker in the world. Specific functions (research and development, marketing, manufacturing, and assembly) were increasingly segmented around the world and carried out by operating units in countries best suited for that particular activity. For instance, in textiles Hong Kong emerged as a dynamic manufacturing sector for many clothing companies based in the United States. Under this process, affiliates maintained multidimensional linkages not only with the parent but also with other affiliates in other nations and with unrelated firms. Using the same example, textile makers in Hong Kong soon were able to contract out piece work to such countries as the Philippines, mainland China, and Malaysia. An international division of labor evolved. Multinationals morphed into transnationals, or true global entities with tentacles in nearly all parts of the world. The shop floors of these companies spanned the globe, with various production and supply chains linked across borders, allowing firms to optimize investment and global inputs by matching production, assembly, and back-office service activities to the locations best suited for those activities.

Putting the above into perspective are figures that chart the explosive growth of foreign direct investment beginning in the mid-1980s. Greased in part by large unfettered flows of global capital, foreign direct investment grew at an annual average rate of 30 percent between 1985 and 1990, roughly three times faster than the growth of world exports and four times faster than the growth in world output. The story was basically the same from 1990 to 2007: foreign direct investment expanded at a 14 percent pace, well above growth in trade (9 percent) and world output (5 percent).[10]

A key metric of globalization, the global amount of inward FDI, was roughly $15 trillion in 2008, equivalent to roughly one quarter of world GDP, and up from just $790 billion in 1982. By 2008, some 82,000 transnationals had sprung up, supported by 810,000 foreign affiliates. Think of the latter as the global foot soldiers of transnationals, or the corporate entities that represent the bridge between the parent company thousands of miles away and the local consumer in Kuala Lumpur or Munich. Underscoring the role these firms play in the global economy, the total output of foreign affiliates topped $6 trillion in 2008, a tenfold increase from 1982 and an amount greater than China's annual output. As a catalyst for trade, the exports of affiliates accounted for roughly one-third of total world exports of both goods and services in 2008. Finally, the number of workers toiling for these affiliates topped 77 million in 2008—more than double the total labor market of Germany, the largest economy in Europe.

In the end, the rise and diffusion of transnationals played a key role in stitching the global economy together beginning in the mid-1980s. The effect was to bring millions of new workers into the global economy and put consumers all over the world within reach of hundreds of low-cost goods and services. Along with financial globalization, the spread of transnationals helped drive the second age of globalization—or the globalization of trade and investment, a process more familiar to people. As David Smick notes:

> When most people picture globalization, they don't immediately picture financial market traders or trillions of dollars moving around the globe. They think of a Kentucky Fried Chicken franchise plopped down in the middle of downtown Beijing, or Dell or Gateway computers being

assembled at rock-bottom prices using parts constructed in Asia, with each separate economy bringing to the table its individual comparative advantage. They think of making a telephone call for technical help on a product bought in Toledo, Ohio, and speaking to a service technician in New Delhi.[11]

As shown, in the post–Bretton Woods era, both financial globalization and the globalization of trade and investment expanded dramatically. Both forms of globalization are interrelated and mutually reinforcing. The globalization of finance helped unlock global savings and deepened the global savings pool, helping to increase the availability of money that could be invested and lowering the cost of credit for many countries and companies, promoting, in the process, growth in various parts of the world. At its most basic level, the globalization of finance has led to greater cross-border lending and borrowing, creating the ideal backdrop for transnationals to expand their global operations. At the same time, the more firms have spread their global wings and extended their production networks, the more demand for global financial services to help facilitate cross-border investment, mergers and acquisitions (M&A), and the intrafirm trade of transnationals.

Conversely, as the aftermath of the financial crisis of 2008 has shown, one form of globalization is highly dependent on the other. In late September 2008, as panic spread around the world after Lehman Brothers collapsed and other Wall Street firms teetered on the verge of financial disaster, the global capital markets seized up—banks were neither lending to each other nor to their best corporate customers. Lending to businesses plunged and trade finance evaporated, precipitating a steep fall in global trade. M&A deals were frozen because of the lack of international credit. The lack of global liquidity caused financing for manufacturers' inventories to dry up. As the global capital markets became paralyzed, the global economy went into a freefall. In the six months following September 2008, global trade, investment, and output virtually collapsed, declining at rapid rates not seen since the Great Depression.

The hinge point of the crisis was New York, and for a very good reason. Finance gurus on Wall Street played the foremost role in expanding the supply of global money, both in recognizable forms and in those that could only be considered exotic. That's because globalized finance, to a significant extent, emerged as one of America's largest exports during the late twentieth century.

AMERICAN DOMINANCE OF GLOBALIZATION

As globalization blossomed over the last 25 years of the twentieth century, so did the economic superpower status of the United States. The two dynamics have largely been synonymous since the end of World War II, with the United States taking the lead in designing, creating, and dominating the multilateral institutions governing the global economy. To the victor goes the spoils—hence, in the aftermath of war, it was the United States, albeit with support from Europe and Japan, that largely set the rules of global economic engagement for the rest of the world in the last half century.

At least up until 2007, it has been largely America's world. American global hegemony has held sway for decades, meaning that during that period the world had been cast in America's mold. As the architect of globalization, the United States programmed world trade to its own likening and interests. The embrace of free-market capitalism, industry deregulation, privatization, and unfettered global capital flows all reflect the underlying economic principles of America. In the quarter century up until 2007, globalization came really in one size—America's.

Buttressing the dominance of the United States was the stunning collapse of the Berlin Wall in 1989 and the disintegration of the Soviet Union a few short years later. For the United States, the script that unfolded in the late 1980s and early 1990s was almost too good to be true. Democracy had triumphed over communism; free-market capitalism had trumped central planning. The world had shifted from a bipolar world to a "unipolar" world, and the United States—the world's lone superpower— unequivocally stood above the rest. "Now is the unipolar moment," intoned political columnist Charles Krauthammer in 1991 in *Foreign Affairs*.[12] Years later, he would write, "On December 26, 1991, the Soviet Union died and something new was born, something utterly new—a unipolar world dominated by a single superpower unchecked by any rival and with decisive reach in every corner of the globe. This is a staggering development in history, not seen since the fall of Rome."[13]

While the Soviet empire was turning to dust, another looming threat to the economic security of the United States at the time, the unrelenting rise of Japan, went into reverse. Around the late 1980s, it was becoming painfully clear that something was dreadfully wrong with Japan's much vaunted economic machine. Evidence was mounting that the nation's staggering real estate boom and bust—and attendant stunning stock market decline—had structurally impaired what once was the world's most feared economy. Almost overnight, Asia's so-called miracle economy and America's most feared economic competitor had been brought to its knees. Concurrently, another economic miracle was in the making—over the "roaring nineties," the U.S. economy reemerged as the envy of the world. The maestro, Federal Reserve chairman Alan Greenspan, emerged as an international rock star thanks to his alleged deft handling of an economy that produced steady growth, low inflation, and booming asset prices. As the United States, the chief architect and underwriter of globalization, reaped the massive rewards of more liberalized global flows of trade, investment, and finance, the rest of the world jumped quickly on the bandwagon. A global consensus emerged around the notion that the best way to promote growth and create prosperity was through the embrace of free-market capitalism and its central tenets. This overriding assumption helped convince many emerging markets to embrace and pursue the "Made in America" brand of globalization.

Over the 1990s, the economic policies of China, Mexico, Russia, Brazil, Poland, and a host of other large developing nations centered largely around how to further integrate their economies with the global economy. Operating under Deng Xiaoping's famous quip, "It doesn't matter whether a cat is black or white so long as it catches mice," China's links with the global economy continued to expand in the 1990s and were capped off with China's entry into the World Trade Organization in 2001. The newly liberated nations of Central and Eastern Europe, meanwhile, rushed to enter the European Union over the 1990s and the early 2000s as the first steps toward greater global linkages. In many emerging markets, policies that at one time favored nationalism and state control gave way to privatization, freer trade, and unfettered capital flows. Closer to home, deeper economic integration was the norm, with the North American Free Trade Agreement (NAFTA) in 1994 marking a historic turning point in fostering greater economic cooperation between the United States and its neighbors, Canada and Mexico.

By the early 1990s, America's military and economic rivals had fallen by the wayside, while the rest of the world queued up to embrace the U.S.-dominated version of globalization. America stood tall against friend and foe alike. While the European Union's move toward the creation of a single market and a single currency over the 1990s bolstered the economic might of the continent, America's share of world economic output (22 percent of the total based on purchasing power parity basis) in 2000 was still larger than Europe's (20 percent). In the military arena, Europe was no threat to the United States, and neither was China, India, or any other developing country, for that matter.

With the end of the Cold War, U.S. military spending gradually declined, although notwithstanding pared-down military expenditures, U.S. military might was second to none. Annual defense spending in the United States was still larger than the next dozen or so big spenders combined over the 1990s. U.S. military dominance was underpinned by America's overwhelming nuclear superiority, in addition to the nation's possession of the world's dominant air force and only true blue-water navy, capabilities that allowed the United States to project its military might to virtually every corner of the globe.

And the United States did not shirk from its role as the world's police officer. It intervened in human rights causes, trying to stop abuses in the Balkans and in Somalia. It answered Iraq's naked aggression in Kuwait by summoning a massive coalition force that humbled the aggressors and placed on them strict sanctions. Yet the victory of George Bush the elder proved to be hard to sustain. After the terrorist attacks of September 11, 2001, America became embroiled in not one war in the Middle East but two, a strategic move that added massively to America's debt and tarnished its brand abroad. The world liked the lone superpower's financial innovations more than its projection of might. Unfortunately for the United States, those same innovations would themselves soon fall into disrepute.

THE GOOD LIFE

Between 1983 and 2007, the U.S. economy grew at a steady pace, suffering only two recessions that were by historical standards short and shallow. Inflation was of little concern thanks in part to greater global competition and low-cost imports, notably from China. Jobs were plentiful—at one point, in 2000, the U.S. unemployment rate dropped below 4 percent. Hence the misery index had been all but forgotten and for good reason—in 1998, the misery index was just over 6 percent. Money was relatively abundant, allowing Americans to purchase homes and all the appliances, furniture, and gadgets that come with buying a house. For anyone who liked to travel overseas, the world was a great deal smaller and accessible.

The pinnacle of all things good was reached in the 1990s and the early part of the last decade. Globalization was in full swing. Technological improvements made the U.S. economy the envy of the world and greatly enhanced the living standards of average Americans. It was a time of prosperity and peace. The peace dividend actually yielded U.S. budget surpluses by the end of the decade. In 2001, then Federal Reserve chairman Alan Greenspan was warning about the dangers associated with federal budget *surpluses*.

While the events of 9/11 shocked the United States and the world, the terrorist attack on U.S. soil had little long-lasting damage on the U.S. economy. The steep decline in interest rates following 9/11 led to an outsized housing boom that fueled rather robust growth at home and overseas. The economic good times climaxed over the five years that stretched from 2003 to 2007. Over this golden period, the global economy enjoyed its strongest period of growth since the late 1960s, with a unique feature of this time being a broader participation in the global boom. Since the former Soviet Union, China, and India participated in the expansion of global trade and investment, a greater share of the world's population was engaged in the global economy. This represented a unique difference from the globalization period of the early twentieth century. Growth rates were not only on the rise in the developed nations but also around the globe. Virtually every region of the world, including Africa, participated in the global economic upswing. Millions of people were lifted out of poverty in the two decades up to 2007.

Against this backdrop, the global stock markets climbed ever higher. On October 7, 2007, the S&P 500 hit an all-time high of 1,565. The Dow Jones Industrial Average climbed to a record 14,166, and the United States was not alone. Around the world, global stock markets were at or near record highs as 2007 came to a close. Rarely had the global mood been as buoyant.

As the first decade of the twenty-first century unfolded, the future looked perfect. Beyond the horizon, however, the storm clouds were gathering. In the search for ever more returns, financiers had been inventing new variations of derivatives at a dizzying pace. These fancy products were supposed to spread risk around to other parties, but instead created more risk for the originators and entire global financial system. As the decade wore on, U.S. households layered yet even more debt and leverage onto their balance sheets, prompting a few brave souls to warn of impending doom. The warnings went unheeded, helping to precipitate one of the worse financial crises in modern financial times.

CHAPTER

2

The Gathering Storm

Debt in modest quantities does enhance the rate of growth of an economy and does create higher standards of living, but in excess, creates serious problems.

—ALAN GREENSPAN, FORMER CHAIRMAN OF THE U.S. FEDERAL RESERVE, 2005

Sometime in the early part of this century a house became more than just a home to average Americans—it became a high-flying, high-yielding, get-rich investment vehicle. Spurred on by record low interest rates, lax credit oversight, and an ever-expanding appetite for risk, U.S. consumers bought homes in droves—residing in some; speculating on others. With credit so cheap and the value of homes appreciating so fast, many U.S. consumers couldn't resist the temptation of real estate. Adding to the allure was the fact that people wanted a safe investment following the dot-com meltdown in 2000/01 and thought they had found one in residential real estate.

On the faulty assumption that housing prices moved in only one direction—skyward—investors bid up homes, condominiums, and apartments all over the country. Commercial real estate enjoyed a similar boom. The median U.S. home prices soared from $153,000 in 2001 to $194,500 in 2004—an annualized return of 8.1 percent, more than double S&P 500 total returns of 3.6 percent over the same period—and the housing mania

27

fed on itself. Building homes became a key plank of the U.S. economy. The share of residential investment in total U.S. output rose to 6.3 percent in the fourth quarter of 2005, the highest level since the post–World War II housing boom. The boom also fueled job growth. Between 1998 and 2006, the number of real estate agents rose from 718,000 to 1.37 million. Demand soared for construction workers, roofers, electricians, landscapers, and anyone that could lay carpet and install a dishwasher. On college campuses, real estate became one of the most popular majors, such was its heady allure. Meanwhile, the number of workers employed by mortgage brokers rose from 240,000 in 2000 to 418,700 in 2006. Real estate, traditionally the bedrock of stability, had become the latest new fad.

For many Americans, the home not only became an investment vehicle but also a way to raise ready cash. Over the 2000s, many U.S. consumers turned their homes into automatic teller machines, extracting ever-rising amounts of equity out of homes as the underlying value rose. As Mark Zandi pointed out in his book *Financial Shock*, "With mortgage rates low and falling, homeowners could increase the size of a loan without increasing the monthly payment. Millions of homeowners jumped on the bandwagon, withdrawing nearly $1 trillion a year in equity from their houses collectively at the peak of the boom."[1]

U.S. consumers had their cake and were eating too. No one needed to save given rising home values, and ever-rising levels of spending continued thanks to the extra cash one could magically extract from one's own home. Savings became a lost virtue among households, with the household savings rate in the United States dropping to roughly zero in the mid-2000s. In contrast, the household savings rate had averaged 8 to 9.5 percent in each decade from the 1950s to 1980s. Not to worry; if consumers needed extra income, they just took it from their homes. Net equity extraction from homes rose from 3 percent of U.S. disposable income in 2001 to nearly 10 percent in 2006. For many Americans debt became a chief means by which to underwrite their consumption. Plus, by leveraging their rapidly overvalued homes, U.S. consumption and the era of cheap credit helped drive growth in various other credit-sensitive sectors like automobiles, furniture, appliances, and other auxiliary industries.

In their seminal work, *This Time Is Different,* Carmen M. Reinhart and Kenneth S. Rogoff succinctly give some historic context to the nature of the U.S. housing boom in the early twenty-first century:

> Since 1891, when the Case-Shiller housing price index began, no housing price boom has been comparable in terms of sheer magnitude and duration to that recorded in the years culminating in the 2007 subprime mortgage fiasco. *Between 1996 and 2006 (the year when prices peaked), the cumulative real price increase was about 92 percent—more than three times the 27 percent cumulative increase from 1890 to 1996!* [Author's italics][2]

Other key housing indicators that should have served as red hot warning signs included the explosion in total residential mortgage debts, which more than doubled from 2000 to 2007, rising from roughly $5 trillion at the start of the decade to $11 trillion in 2007. In parallel with the surge in residential mortgages, mortgage-backed securities rose in value from $3.6 trillion in 2000 to $7.3 trillion in 2007. And key to the ever-expanding housing bubble, the volume of subprime mortgages rose from $120 billion in 2001 (roughly 6 percent of total mortgage origination) to $600 billion in 2006 (over 20 percent of the total). Conversely, conventional conforming mortgages dropped from 61 percent of all mortgages originated in 2001 to roughly 39 percent in 2006.

To help foster the American dream of owning a home, adjustable-rate mortgages (ARMs) become more popular during the course of the decade. The volume of ARMs tripled between 2001 and 2004, from $304 billion to over $985 billion. In this era of lending, many first-time home buyers bought homes by putting no money down and, in some cases, did not provide—because they were not asked for—monthly income statements. According to the National Association of Realtors, 45 percent of first-time home buyers in 2007 did not put any money down. Traditionally, a down payment of 20 percent had been standard, for a very sensible reason. Mortgage holders would lose that money if they defaulted on their loan. Yet in this go-go era, the new consensus held that borrowers with no stake in the game were less of a risk in an environment of soaring home prices.

Besides, many mortgage companies minimized their risk by passing the loans/mortgages on to Wall Street firms, which sliced and diced mortgage-backed securities and sold them all over the world. These packages grew more and more complicated, using risk assessments based on averages that sometimes seemed made up out of thin air. Rating agencies complied by giving triple-A ratings to these securities, even though in many cases they had never seen the type of securitization package they were reviewing. This created a positive feedback loop whereby banks continued to lend with minimal risks to borrowers who wanted to buy their first home or to those who wanted to refinance their existing mortgages. The upshot was more debt piled onto more debt, and rising home prices, which in turn galvanized the lenders and borrowers to do even more business.

In his book *Freefall*, Nobel laureate Joseph E. Stiglitz points out the links in a dangerous loop:

> Securitization had one big advantage, allowing risk to be spread; but it had a big disadvantage, creating new problems of imperfect information, and these swamped the benefits from increased diversification. Those buying a mortgage-backed security are, in effect, lending to the homeowner, about whom they know nothing. They trust the bank that sells them the product to have checked it out, and the bank trusts the mortgage originator. The mortgage originators' incentives were focused on the quantity of mortgages originated, not the quality. They produced massive amounts of truly lousy mortgages.[3]

Since financial shocks in the recent past had come and gone without any real lingering effects, when U.S. residential homes prices peaked in 2006, triggering the subprime crisis, the problems were quickly dismissed on Wall Street and in Washington. The loans were a problem but manageable and confined to the United States, so went the consensus. Shaping this point of view was none other than Alan Greenspan, who judged on October 9, 2006, that, "The worst may be over for housing." In the spring of 2007, Greenspan's successor, Ben Bernanke chimed in with the following: "At this juncture, however, the impact on the broader economy and financial markets of the problems in the subprime market seems likely to be contained. In particular, mortgages to prime borrowers and fixed-rate mortgages to all classes of borrowers continue to perform well, with low rates of delinquency. We will continue to monitor this situation closely."[4]

But as the losses among banks and nonbanking origina-tors of mortgages started to pile up in late 2006 and 2007, the one-time positive feedback loop went into reverse. Very quickly, the housing boom-turned-bust created a vicious cycle of falling home prices, rising delinquencies, and soaring defaults. Sud-denly, thousands of home owners could not afford the homes they occupied, forcing many financial institutions holding mortgage-backed securities to write down the value of these loans on their balance sheet. Profits at many banks cratered. The great unwinding had begun.

The real estate boom of the first decade in the new millen-nium was not just a U.S. phenomenon. McKinsey Global Insti-tute estimates that between 2000 and 2007, the total value of the world's residential real estate more than doubled to over $90 trillion.[5] Relative to other parts of the world, notably Europe, skyrocketing real estate prices in the United States were rela-tively tame. Belgium, Spain, the United Kingdom, the Neth-erlands, Ireland, Australia, Norway, Canada, France, and Italy all saw their home values soar at a faster pace than the United States. In other words, the housing boom was global and one for the ages. So was the mess the housing bust left in its wake.

Gallons of ink have been spilled on the great U.S. hous-ing boom-and-bust, so I will refrain from adding more to the subject. Instead, the focus here is to broaden the lens and docu-ment other warning signals that were ignored or overlooked and whose aftershocks will have a much greater impact on the U.S. and global economy in the future.

GLOBAL FINANCE DISCONNECTS FROM THE GLOBAL ECONOMY

One worrisome signpost was the growing divorce between un-precedented levels of global financial flows on the one hand and

the real global economy on the other. In the 1980s the globalization of finance and trade/investment both accelerated in tan-
dem. In the ensuing decades, however, global finance became a
distinct force unto itself, thanks to the liberalization of capital
controls on overseas investments, the enabling effects of more
advanced technology and falling communications costs, and
the accelerating pace of financial innovation, including such instruments as mortgage-backed securities, credit default swaps,
and the like. While global output and trade also increased over
the past few decades, their rise hardly kept pace with global
financing.

To say that global capital flows dwarfed the value of international trade is a gross understatement. In 1973, well before
financial globalization had gained full sway, the ratio of daily
foreign exchange trading to world trade was 2:1. Less than a
decade later, in 1980, the ratio was 10:1. In 1992, the disparity
between foreign exchange trading and world trade was enormous (50:1). Today, $4 trillion trades daily on global foreign
exchange markets. According to the McKinsey Global Institute, the world's financial assets—including equities, private
and public debt, and bank deposits—nearly quadrupled in size
relative to global gross domestic product (GDP) between 1980
and 2007. At its peak in 2007, the total value of global financial assets reached $194 trillion, 343 percent of world GDP.[6]
The welter of financial products had become divorced from the
products on which their value was based.

Over the past few decades, global capital flows have become
directed less at financing trade and investment and more about
funding a whole host of unrelated activities. Global financial
institutions, not content to perform one or two core functions,
have become financial conglomerates, providing a host of offerings, ranging from corporate finance to commercial lending

to credit cards to wealth management and a bevy of other activities.

Notably, to generate more profits, financial entities have had to invent, design, and champion new financial instruments. Derivatives have become the ultimate growth engine. By the mid-2000s, the average daily turnover in the global derivates market was estimated at $2.4 trillion, and the bulk of the contracts were structured around interest rates, foreign exchange rates, equities, and commodities. The explosion in these highly complex and sophisticated products—dubbed "weapons of mass destruction" by Warren Buffet in 2003—went hand in hand with simpler financial innovations, like "ninja" loans, or loans to subprime home buyers who had no income, no jobs, and no assets.

Adding more fuel to the fire was excessive leverage, a phenomenon encouraged by the regulators like the Securities and Exchange Commission, which allowed the five largest U.S. investment banks to double their ratio of assets to capital to over 30:1 in 2004.

Another critical factor to a global financial sector increasingly divorced from the real economy has been the growth of the "shadow banking sector." As Kevin Phillips notes in his book *Bad Money*:

> A key development within the financial sector over the last decade has been the decline in relative importance of depository institutions. Banks and savings and loan associations had been the big guns through the 1970s, along with insurance companies. Then they lost their old sway before the advance of the new or expanding forces— mutual funds, nonbank lenders, hedge funds, federally related mortgage entities, issuers of asset-backed securities, security brokers and dealers, and others.[7]

Quantifying this statement, Phillips notes that whereas depository institutions and insurance companies accounted for roughly two-thirds of the financial sector's total assets in 1976, by 2006 the combined share was just 30 percent. The upshot: even if regulators had wanted to do their job, they wouldn't have known where to look.

The financial assets of the nonbank financial sector expanded by a 9.4 percent compound average annual rate between 1999 and 2009 versus a 5.8 percent rate of growth among assets of the traditional U.S. banking sector.[8] Due in part to this growth differential, the shadow banks' lending book was bigger than the entire traditional banking sector by 2007. By that point banks supplied only 22 percent of all credit in the United States.[9]

Economist Paul Krugman commented: "As the shadow banking system expanded to rival or even surpass conventional banking in importance, politicians and government officials should have realized that they were re-creating the kind of financial vulnerability that made the Great Depression possible. . . . Influential figures should have proclaimed a simple rule: anything that does what a bank does, anything that has to be rescued in crises the way banks are, should be regulated like a bank."[10]

Outside of Iceland and Ireland perhaps, nowhere has the recent ascent of finance been more prominent than in the United States. Because of the new instruments being invented, the financial service sector overtook manufacturing in the turbocharged 1990s to become the largest sector of the U.S. economy. In 2007, one year before the great financial meltdown, the financial sector accounted for 20 percent of the economy versus less than 12 percent for manufacturing. America's manufacturing base had effectively shifted from the industrial Midwest to the cement canyons of Wall Street.

The value of U.S. manufacturing paled compared to rolling out new credit default swaps and mortgage-backed securities. The financial sector accounted for a staggering 41 percent of all corporate profits in 2007, well above the historic average. With these sorts of numbers, it emerged as the largest sector of the S&P 500 in the first decade of the twenty-first century, accounting for nearly a quarter of the S&P's value in 2006, more than double the share in 1990. All told, the supercharged U.S. financial sector became the growth engine of the United States over the 1990s and 2000s, jumpstarting hyper growth in other credit-sensitive sectors like housing and autos.

The United States was hardly alone in leveraging easy credit to drive growth, however. Europe quickly caught the securitization fever, and in a number of countries, real estate soared beyond anything known before. In Ireland, economic reforms that included a much more free-wheeling financial sector fueled what became known as the Celtic Tiger as the country grew to the fourth richest in Europe. In the housing bubble that accompanied the flood of investments, real estate grew from 5 percent of its economy to 14 percent, a dangerous level that would later help plunge the country into recession. Much the same occurred in the United Kingdom, where financiers would engage in a "race to the bottom" with those on Wall Street—and their banks would have to be rescued on a comparable scale. In 2009 Prime Minister Gordon Brown complained about the international deals of failed banks like the Royal Bank of Scotland: "Almost all of their losses are in the subprime mortgages in America and related to [the Dutch bank] ABN Amro. These are irresponsible risks taken by the bank with people's money in the UK."[11]

The calamity was worst in Iceland, however. The rise of high finance in the tiny island nation of 300,000 people is truly an epic story. Known more for fishing than finance, Iceland was swept up by the free-market mania of the 1990s, and like many other nations, aggressively privatized and liberalized large swaths of industry, including the financial sector. In very short order, as the capital poured in, Iceland transformed itself from one of Europe's poorest to one of its wealthiest nations. At the center of this stunning turnabout was the finance sector.

After opening its capital account, or the amount of capital it would allow to flow into and out of the country, in 1994, and pursuing other market-opening measures in finance, Iceland woke up one day in the early twenty-first century to the mind-numbing fact that the assets of its financial sector were 12 times bigger than the entire economy. Iceland had become the mother of all bubbles. Although the only real endowments of the economy revolved around fish and the potential for thermal energy, Iceland attracted billions of euros, dollars, and Swiss francs, creating a so-called economic miracle in the North Atlantic. However, in the end it was not a miracle but rather a mirage. Over the course of 2008, the bottom fell out of the economy. Credit dried up, the currency collapsed, and the economy came to sudden halt. In October 2008, the nation teetered on the brink of bankruptcy before pulling back from the edge. The damage had been done. In 2008 and 2009, Iceland's economy severely declined, a victim of a financial sector that had grown too fast and too large relative to the real economy.

THE DETERIORATING FINANCIAL HEALTH OF THE UNITED STATES

Another dangerous signpost that many routinely ignored was the carefree attitude in the United States about borrowing and spending other people's money and the attendant deterioration in the country's financial health as a result of this profligacy.

For much of the twentieth century, the United States was a creditor nation—in other words, the nation's foreign assets were greater than its foreign liabilities. However, the tide turned in the late 1980s. In 1988, for the first time since becoming a world power, foreign-owned assets in the United States exceeded U.S.-owned assets in the rest of the world. We as a nation owed foreigners more than they owed us. The United States became a net debtor nation for the first time since World War I, and since then, unfortunately, it has never looked back, burrowing deeper and deeper into debt. In 2009, the total U.S. net international debt stood at $2.7 trillion. That figure represents a massive financial albatross around the country's neck because America's IOU to the rest of the world equals roughly 20 percent of the nation's total annual output.

Any nation that perpetually spends more than it saves, and consumes more than it produces, will eventually find itself in a financial hole. And the faster you dig, of course, the deeper the hole. Americans dug furiously for years up until 2007. The U.S. current account deficits—which represent the nation's savings gap, or the difference between what a nation saves and consumes—surged from just $80 billion in 1990 to over $800 billion in 2006. As a percent of GDP, the current account deficit topped out at 6 percent of GDP in 2006. From 1999 to mid-2007, the cumulative U.S. current account deficit was $4.6 trillion, one of the largest financial holes in America's history.

A few lone voices did express concern about the widening deficit over the 1990s, but in general, the reigning consensus was that the deficits were nothing to worry about. Espousing this view were none other than America's top policy makers.

Speaking in 2005, Alan Greenspan noted that the current account deficit was not a primary risk to the United States. According to then Secretary of the Treasury Paul O'Neil, the current account deficit was a "meaningless concept." And before becoming Federal Reserve chairman, Ben Bernanke opined that America's current account deficit was not America's fault but the fault of excess global savers who had nothing better to do with their money than to send it to the United States. The popular refrain on Wall Street during the 1990s was that the deficit and attendant inflow of capital reflected the underlying attractiveness of the U.S. economy. The advent of the Internet, after all, was "Made in America," and America was at the forefront of the global technology boom, which sparked a great deal of talk about the "new economy." With this sunny view of the future, it was only logical that foreigners would want to send more capital to the world's most dynamic economy, helping to inflate U.S. borrowing and the current account deficit in the process.

These soothing words helped assuage fears about the exploding deficit. So did the fact that as America—the so-called superpower of global borrowing—burrowed deeper into debt and continued to borrow overseas, U.S. interest rates remained remarkably stable. Investors accepted lower and lower yields on U.S. government securities, with the 10-year Treasury yield falling from roughly 9 percent in 1990 to 6 percent in 2000 to roughly 4 percent in 2003. America's widening current account deficit should have in theory, at least, resulted in foreign investors demanding higher yields for taking on more risk. Yet the cheap financing from overseas continued—America's deficit elicited little concern given the premium foreign investors placed on owning government securities backed by Uncle Sam. As a result, leading up to the U.S. housing bust, foreign buying of U.S. assets kept long-term U.S. interest rates at about 1 to 1½ percentage points lower than otherwise, according to abundant academic research.

Thanks to the era of cheap money, borrowing and spending became a favorite American pastime. The rising tide of foreign capital that washed over the United States in the 2000s lowered interest rates and increased the availability of capital, providing the tinder that fueled a consumption binge like no other. The surge in inflows also allowed the U.S. government to enjoy both guns and butter—both waging war in Iraq and Afghanistan and tax cuts. While many nations around the world did not like the U.S.-led war in Iraq, foreign investors did nevertheless help pay for the conflicts by providing low-cost capital to the fighting machine called the United States. To this point, net capital inflows into the United States (foreign purchases of long-term U.S. securities less U.S. purchases of long-term foreign securities) averaged $738 billion annually in the first decade of this century versus an annual average of just $200 billion during the 1990s.

By the time the financial tsunami struck in 2008, never before had the United States been in so much debt. Years of cheap money, reckless borrowing by U.S. households, evaporating savings, and incessant public sector spending left the United States with one massive IOU to the rest of the world.

Reflecting the profligate ways of the United States and the willingness of foreigners to lend money to the United States, the foreign ownership of U.S. securities was at all-time record levels when the financial crisis struck. When the meltdown commenced, foreigners owned 14 percent of U.S. equities versus a share of 5.7 percent in 1982. Over the same period, foreign ownership of U.S. corporate bonds rose from 9.6 percent to 25 percent at the end of 2008. More telling, foreign investors owned roughly half of all marketable U.S. Treasuries at the end of 2008, up from just 15.4 percent in 1982.

Against this backdrop, one question stands out: Who was willing to lend all this capital to the United States?

GLOBAL CAPITAL FLOWS UPHILL

Another critical signpost that something was amiss in the world of finance was the direction that money moved between countries. Historically, global cross-border flows have tended to flow downhill from rich to poor nations, since investors in wealthy, capital-abundant nations are more inclined to invest in capital-scarce yet faster-growing emerging markets. In the first age of globalization, the half century before World War I, worldwide capital flowed from the core countries of Western Europe to the rapidly developing economies of the Americas, Asia, and other places. As the International Monetary Fund notes, "At its peak, the net capital outflow from Britain represented 9 percent of GNP and was almost as high from France, Germany, and the Netherlands."[12] Between 1880 and 1914, nearly half of all international funds flowed to poor countries.

With this historical precedent, as financial globalization gathered steam in the 1980s and as various developing markets jumped on the global financial bandwagon, the common assumption was that global capital flows would flow less among the developed nations and more toward the developing nations. And for a time, the consensus was right.

In the late 1970s and early 1980s, a sizable share of OPEC's excess surplus of "petrodollars" was recycled into the emerging markets of Latin America and, to a lesser degree, Asia. Yet many emerging markets indulged in too much borrowing and began to run large unsustainable deficits. The Latin American debt crisis ensued in the mid-1980s, and the global capital that once flowed freely into the region fled for safer harbors. A painful recession followed across Latin American nations as access to global capital dried up or became increasingly expensive. The lack of credit forced painful economic adjustments in Latin America until the next great wave of foreign capital rolled over the region.

The second wave of financing came in the early 1990s. The euphoria associated with the end of the Cold War, coupled with aggressive market liberalization and deregulation in Central Europe, developing Asia, and Latin America, encouraged foreign investors and banks to yet again pour billions of dollars into the emerging markets. Net flows to the emerging markets soared to $349 billion in 1996, one year before the Asian financial crisis. Net flows to Asia, in particular, rocketed, with flows more than quadrupling between 1991 and 1996, surging from $43 billion to $180 billion in 1996—before plummeting to −$0.2 billion in 1998. Thailand's currency crisis in mid-1997, and the "contagion" that spread far and wide from Southeast Asia, brought the second great wave of capital inflows to the emerging markets to an abrupt and painful end. As foreign investors bolted for the door again, in their haste they left a littered landscape of collapsing currencies, shrinking credit lines, soaring debt levels, and ultimately, imploding economies. The scars from the Asian financial crisis were deep, and they galvanized many policy makers in the developing nations to think "never again."

In the aftermath of the Asian financial crisis, many countries became tired of the financial merry-go-round, in which "hot money" inflows would surge into a particular nation, inflating the currency and prices until the footloose capital decided to bolt, leaving disaster and destruction in its aftermath. After the capital fled, shell-shocked governments were left with massive currency losses, an explosion in foreign-currency-denominated debt, and substantial fiscal losses as governments scrambled to bail out and shore up their impaired banks. Shedding some light on the cost of various crises, the World Bank notes:

> Recent decades have seen a record wave of crises: by millennium-end, there had been 112 episodes of systemic banking crises in 93 countries since the late 1970s—and 51 borderline crises were recorded in 46 countries. These crises both were more numerous and expensive, compared with those earlier in history, and their costs often devastating in developing countries.[13]

In Indonesia, the cost of the nation's financial crisis in 1997 was 55 percent of GDP; Argentine taxpayers anted up a similar percentage after the financial crisis in 1980–1982.[14] These figures are rather large yet do not even begin to capture the human and social costs associated with the financial meltdowns of the past few decades. Thus following the Asian financial crisis and after being buffeted by numerous crises since the 1970s, many developing nations came to equate current account deficits—a consequence of large capital inflows—with financial instability. The two terms were synonymous and to be avoided at all costs.

"Developing countries put aside hundreds of billions of dollars in reserves to protect themselves from the high level of global volatility that has marked the era of deregulation," Joseph E. Stiglitz writes, and quotes one prime minister, "'We were in the class of '97. We learned what happens if you don't have enough reserves.'"[15]

To short-circuit the chance of another destructive cycle, to prevent current account surpluses from shifting to deficits, officials in the emerging markets changed tack in the early 2000s. They became massive savers—shunning consumption (current account deficits) for savings (surpluses). The accumulation of foreign reserves—akin to stuffing money under the mattress—became an overriding objective of many developing nations.

The grand idea behind the accumulation of reserves was twofold. First, the strategy was an insurance policy against the risk of another financial crisis—in essence, the accumulation of reserves was to serve as a war chest for the next crisis. Second, recycling reserves into U.S. assets would help keep currencies in emerging markets cheap and competitive vis-à-vis the U.S. dollar, thereby enhancing their export potential and export-led growth. With these objectives in mind, the savings pendulum in the developing nations swung from a deficit of $17.7 billion in 1999 to a surplus in excess of $400 billion by 2007. Rarely had the world witnessed such a swing in savings in such a short period.

Global savings soared over the first decade of the twenty-first century, rising from 21.1 percent of world GDP in 2001 to 24.5 percent in 2007. Over this period, average savings rates fell among the developed nations but climbed in most emerging markets. Nowhere was the trend as pronounced than in China. Its savings rate soared to 59 percent of GDP in 2007, up from 37.6 percent in 2001.

Bolstered by soaring oil prices, the savings rate in the Middle East jumped from 33.3 percent to 50.8 percent, a staggering jump in savings that gave rise to the growing financial clout of Middle East sovereign wealth funds. Relatively unknown until the turn of this century, the size of these reserves tripled during the 2001–2007 period, according to IMF estimates.[16]

Excess savings also became the norm in Russia, among the nations of Southeast Asia, and even in Latin America, whose savings were boosted by the global boom in commodity prices, a dynamic that helped swell the coffers of many commodity exporters in South America. In the end, the international reserves of the developing nations rose from roughly $885 billion in 1998 to nearly $6 trillion in 2008, a staggering increase, with two-thirds of the total in possession of Asia and the Middle East.

A large share of this excess global savings, in turn, was recycled to the United States, swelling the pool of cheap credit available to the U.S. government and U.S. households. The party was on—U.S. households gorged themselves on easy money and bought larger homes, larger cars, and virtually anything else that suited their fancy. The debt-fueled U.S. consumption boom went hand-in-hand with ever-rising government spending levels. Concurrently, excess U.S. consumer spending and the attendant demand for imports kept the export machines of China and Asia fired up, and bolstered, among many other items, demand for gas-guzzling SUVs in the United States. The price for oil and food soared around the world, stuffing more dollars into the coffers of Middle East oil producers, who in turn recycled some of these dollars back into U.S. securities. The cycle fed on itself—the insatiable appetite of U.S. consumers boosted world exports and the current account surpluses of China and other nations, who in turn funneled their excess savings back into the United States. The recycling of reserves not only reflected the goal of many nations to keep their exchange rates competitive with the dollar, but the outflows to the United

States also reflected the belief among investors that U.S. securities were among the safest and most attractive in the world. With their own investment opportunities limited at home, many foreign investors in the emerging markets jumped at the opportunity to invest more capital in the United States, or in a market that was thought to be transparent, liquid, and among the most sophisticated and developed in the world.

Financiers in the developing nations had sound reasons to invest capital in the United States, not least of which was the less than transparent banking institutions in their own countries. However, as the decade progressed, any first-year economics student could see that the uphill flow of global capital—from poor to rich nations—was unsustainable and inherently risky. Risky for the recipient of this capital—the United States—and for the lenders, notably the largest of them all—China.

CHINA'S TOP EXPORT TO AMERICA—CASH

Ask any American what the country's number one import from China is, and the response is likely to be furniture, toys, clothing, footwear, consumer electronics, and similar consumer-related goods. This response would hardly be surprising since the "Made in China" stamp seems to be ubiquitous in American shopping malls.

Granted, America does import a great deal of goods from China. U.S. imports from the mainland rose from just $ 1 billion in 1980 to over $320 billion in 2007, one year before the crisis. Over the same period, U.S. exports rose from $3.8 billion to $63 billion. This surge in bilateral trade is the most visible manifestation of expanding U.S.-Sino commercial ties. Yet trade is not the largest or most important tie binding the two countries together. It is capital. Unbeknownst to many Americans, including many legislators in Washington, America's top import from China is neither Barbie dolls nor iPods. Rather, it is China's savings or cash. Over the past decade, the mainland has emerged as America's top trading partner and America's chief loan officer.

Capital flows from China to the United States were negligible up until 2001, but they exploded thereafter. Over the 1990s, the capital sent from China to the United States averaged less than $7 billion per year; in 2001, however, capital inflows topped $50 billion and continued to mount as China's own savings soared and as Beijing worked furiously to keep its own exports competitive by buying dollars or bidding up the value of the greenback against its own currency. Thanks to these efforts, China's international reserves totaled $1.2 trillion in 2007 and topped a staggering $2 trillion a year later. In the process, China's reserves overtook Japan's, signaling a new financial order in Asia that would bear directly on the world's top debtor nation, the United States, for some time to come. Japan was the largest holder of U.S. Treasuries up until 2007, holding some $581 billion at the end of the year versus China's total of $478 billion. At the end of 2008, however, China's holdings of U.S. Treasuries were roughly $727 billion.

In 2008, capital flows to the United States from China—or Chinese capital invested in U.S. securities like Treasuries, government agency bonds, corporate bonds, and U.S. equities—soared to a peak of $130 billion, nearly double the level of total cumulative inflows over the entire 1990s. What is more, the amount easily swamped other top U.S. imports from the mainland in the same year, including the import of telecommunications equipment ($53 billion), office machines ($49 billion), apparel and clothing ($29 billion), electrical machinery ($25 billion), and furniture ($18 billion). In the same year, China accounted for nearly one-third of total U.S. capital inflows, underscoring America's rising financial interdependence on a nation whose relationship with the United States swings between sweet and sour. How this relationship evolves over the next decade will affect not only the United States and China, but virtually every other region of the world. Like it or not—and many folks in Washington do not like it—China has become America's financial sugar daddy.

The two nations have never been more joined at the financial hip, an entanglement that has created unease on both sides of the Pacific. This arrangement weakens America's hand when trying to coax China into following America's strategic goals or tactics in such geographic hot spots as Iran, North Korea, and Africa. America's growing financial dependence also inhibits its leverage in negotiations over trade and investment. Increasingly, America has had to speak softly to China since it no longer wields a big stick. The world's largest debtor nation has less clout when dealing with the world's largest creditor nation, hence, despite incessant demands from the United States, China's go-slow approach toward the revaluation of the renminbi. Beijing did yield to global pressure for a more flexible exchange rate in June 2010, although China's currency is not about to be freely convertible any time soon.

At the same time, the stakes for China in America's financial future, after pouring billions into U.S. securities, has never been greater. Not surprisingly, as America's mountain of debt has increased over the past decade, China has become increasingly concerned about massive U.S. deficit spending and its ultimate impact on the U.S. dollar and U.S. securities. Expressing these worries about the financial health of the United States in March 2009, Chinese Premier Wen Jiabao said: "We have lent a huge amount of money to the U.S. Of course we are concerned about the safety of our assets. To be honest, I am definitely a little worried." In November 2009, the Chinese leader reiterated this point: "Most importantly, we hope the U.S. will keep its deficit at an appropriate size so that there will be basic stability in the exchange rate and that is conducive to the stability and recovery of the world economy."[17]

China is so worried about America's fiscal health and its dollar holdings that Beijing has floated the idea of creating an alternative to the U.S. dollar as the world reserve currency. The United States, unsurprisingly, has dismissed the idea. The global economy still pivots around the greenback, according to Washington, meaning large exporters like China are going to be paid in U.S. dollars for a long time to come. For how long remains an open question. It will be decades before the renminbi represents a significant threat to the greenback, but the process has begun, with China's decision to allow Hong Kong to expand the availability of renminbi-denominated products in late July 2010 as one more step in this process.

In the end, both parties need each other. China needs access to the U.S. market in order to keep its export machine humming and its massive workforce busy; and while the United States could probably make do without Chinese-made tennis rackets and running shoes, the world's largest debtor nation would find life a great deal more difficult if it were denied Chinese capital.

The fact that one of the poorest nations in the world, with a per capita GDP a fraction of that of the United States—300 million of its people live on less than a $1 a day—exports its savings to one of the richest nations on earth has to rank as one of the greatest economic anomalies of all time. As we will see in Chapter 8, if an economic cold war does break out between the United States and the developing nations, the excess capital of nations like China will be a key strategic lever over the debt-ridden United States.

THE INCREASING FREQUENCY OF FINANCIAL CRISES

Probably the most surprising aspect of the financial crisis of 2008 was that investors and policy makers around the world were actually "surprised" that such an event occurred. As Martin Wolf of the *Financial Times* notes, "Ours has been an era of financial turmoil."[18] Financial crises are hardly unique, in other words.

As mentioned earlier, according to the World Bank in 2001, some 93 nations experienced 112 systemic banking crises between the late 1970s and the end of the twentieth century. Some nations did not have one crisis but multiple ones. Meanwhile, based on the research of Barry Eichengreen and Michael Bordo, the scholars note that there were 38 financial crises between 1945 and 1971 versus 139 between 1973 and 1997.[19] Roughly two-thirds of these crises since the early 1970s have transpired in the developing nations.

The last point is important to understand. Because the majority of the financial calamities have occurred beyond America's shores over the past few decades, many people in the United States have been lulled into thinking that financial crises are an external phenomenon that typically affects faraway nations. Yet crises at home have not been infrequent. The U.S. stock market crash of 1987 was quickly followed by the savings and loan crisis. The 1998 debacle at Long Term Capital Management was followed by the financial mania associated with the boom and bust of the U.S. technology sector. The U.S. dot-com meltdown that took place at the beginning of the 2000s was followed by a historic boom and bust of the U.S. housing market and subsequent financial crisis.

Why do financial meltdowns occur so frequently? One reason is that, in the era of financial globalization, massive amounts of capital need to be recycled each year. The search for better-than-expected returns typically herds capital into one or two attractive investments, inflating the investment until market conditions change or investors change their minds and bail, deflating the one-time hot investments, whether Brazilian equities, Russian debt, or developing Asian currencies.

Another reason for the increased frequency of crises lies with the fact that in some developing nations, financial liberalization outpaced the nation's domestic financial sector's development. Before the collapse of Argentina's economy in 2001, for instance, the country had become overrun by foreign banks, whose lending favored multinationals, with which they were familiar, and excluded many local businesses whose growth would have stabilized the country.[20] The opening of the capital account, in other words, was premature and therefore a recipe for disaster given the lack of property rights, weak institutions, ineffective clearing mechanisms, lax regulations, illiquid capital markets, outdated technology, and other factors that helped foster more instability than stability.

ON BORROWED MONEY AND TIME

While the quarter century up until 2007 was a blessed period of muted inflation, low unemployment, and infrequent and shallow recessions in the United States, all was not well with the U.S. economy. The good times, with the benefit of hindsight, were basically funded with borrowed money, which meant that the party was on borrowed time. At the beginning of 2008, the midnight alarm was about to strike.

Excess leverage (debt) and excess risk taking were defining features of this period, with early warning signals emanating from both overseas and in the United States. Even while Alan Greenspan warned of "irrational exuberance" in 1998, the debt-fueled party rolled on. Not even the great dot-com boom and bust could dampen the animal spirits of the time. America moved from one bubble (technology) to another (housing).

All the warning signs were flashing, but the party continued, since the great leveraged boom of the early twenty-first century produced robust growth rates in the United States and overseas. Indeed, over the 2003–2007 period the global economy expanded by nearly 5 percent per annum, a rate of growth well above the historic average (3.7 percent). Life was good for many Americans in the mid-2000s, notwithstanding the dramatic events of September 2001 and the fact that the United States was at war. Everything was fine as long as the cost of capital remained cheap, asset prices continued to rise, U.S. borrowers made their payments on time, and the United States continued to attract overseas capital. By the summer of 2006, however, the party was coming to an end. Housing prices began to fall, the cost of capital began to rise, and housing inventories soared. The great U.S. housing boom was about to go bust; the leveraged boom was over. The party was about to turn really ugly.

Financial Armageddon and the Retreat of Globalization

When the music stops, in terms of liquidity, things will be complicated. But as long as the music is playing, you've got to get up and dance. We're still dancing.
—CHUCK PRINCE, *Financial Times*, JULY 9, 2007

Wall Street got drunk.
—PRESIDENT GEORGE W. BUSH

For many who toil on Wall Street, Labor Day weekend is the last gasp of solace before the year-end sprint to the finish. The weekend that heralds the end of summer is typically a time to recharge batteries before heading into the home stretch. The last few months of the year represent the last chance for money managers to beat their benchmarks, for investment bankers to close the deals, for traders to plump up their returns, and for anyone hoping for a decent year-end bonus to shine once more. Adding another layer of angst to the post–Labor Day environment, September and October are notoriously volatile for the financial markets as trading volumes pick up after typically quieter summer months and as money managers of mutual funds begin to close out their books for the end of the year.

Although rested and tanned, many on Wall Street returned to their desks feeling uneasy in early September 2008. The past year, since the global stock markets had scaled new heights back in October 2007, had been long and painful. From these peaks to September 2008, the S&P 500 and Dow Jones Industrial Average had lost 18 percent and 18.5 percent, respectively. Combined, the two indexes lost $3.4 trillion in value. The news was not much better overseas, for the MSCI World Index had dropped nearly 20 percent. The market carnage was universal, as stock markets in Europe, the Middle East, Latin America, and Asia all twisted in a downward spiral. In total, some $13 trillion had been lost in the global stock markets—one of the costliest market swoons in financial history. And that was just losses from global equities—investors had also taken a bath in the imploding global real estate market and in various other asset classes.

In essence, the global financial markets were signaling (correctly) that something was wrong—terribly wrong. In particular, pressure continued to mount in the U.S. housing market, as the bust gained momentum and claimed more victims in its wake. The institutions with the largest exposure to subprime mortgages continued to drop like dominos. New Century Financial filed for bankruptcy in the spring of 2007, while Countrywide Financial, the nation's largest mortgage lender, skirted insolvency by being acquired by Bank of America in early 2008. The collapse and fire sale of Bear Stearns in March 2008, a fate dictated by mortgage-related losses at the investment bank, particularly rattled Wall Street, escalating the Street's level of paranoia. Everyone knew that the financial underpinning of the global capital markets had been dramatically weakened by the housing bust in the United States and Europe. But the extent of the collateral damage was unknown, sowing uncertainty, and it is uncertainty that makes people on Wall Street nervous. The takeover of Bear Stearns was followed by growing losses at other banks and the general deterioration of the U.S. and global economies. By mid-summer 2008, the liquidity problems of many financial institutions had crossed over into concerns about solvency. Highlighting the latter, the FDIC took over control of Indy Mac, a large California-based thrift and mortgage lender, in July 2008.

Against this backdrop, as the world's financial capital cranked back up for business in early September 2008, an eerie calm hung over the Street. The unknowns—"what's next" and "who is next"—weighed heavily on the minds of investors. The fragile global capital markets were also an acute concern of the Federal Reserve, the U.S. Department of the Treasury and other U.S. agencies. Indeed, as recounted in Andrew Ross Sorkin's *Too Big to Fail,* well before Labor Day 2008, key U.S. policy makers and Wall Street chiefs clearly saw and feared the financial train wreck coming down the tracks and worked frantically to avoid such a fate.[1] Their efforts, however, were to no avail.

WHEN THE PLUMBING BLEW UP

As indelicately put by the Bank for International Settlements, "The financial system is the economy's plumbing. And like the plumbing in a house, it is taken for granted when it works, but when it doesn't, watch out."[2]

The financial plumbing of the United States blew up in September 2008. During the month that rocked the global financial markets, the U.S. government put Fannie Mae and Freddie Mac into conservatorship; Lehman Brothers filed for Chapter 11 bankruptcy protection; Bank of America Corporation acquired

Merrill Lynch & Co., Inc.; the Federal Reserve bailed out insurance giant AIG at a cost that would reach over $170 billion; the government also took over Washington Mutual, the largest U.S. thrift institution; Wells Fargo swallowed Wachovia; and Wall Street's most respected investment banks, Goldman Sachs and Morgan Stanley, converted into banks. All these titanic events took place in a matter of weeks. By the end of 2008, none of the Street's largest investment banks existed in its prior form.

Across the Atlantic the situation was not much better. By the end of September 2008, HBOS, Britain's largest mortgage lender, had fallen under the control of Lloyds TSB. U.K. mortgage lender Bradford & Bingley had been nationalized. The Dutch banking and insurance company Fortis required a capital injection from three European governments. To stave off its demise, German commercial property lender Hypo Real Estate had to secure a government credit line. And in Ireland, whose real estate bubble was among the greatest on planet Earth, the Irish government announced a sweeping plan to guarantee all deposits, covered bonds, and senior and subordinated debt of six Irish banks. Not long after Ireland's move many other governments adopted the same extensive safeguards.

The pain spread—to Russian oil companies, German capital goods manufacturers, and Spanish homeowners. Iceland's highly leveraged banks brought the nation to the verge of bankruptcy. The emerging markets also felt the pain, even though many of their banks had avoided taking on the toxic subprime loans exported from the United States. In such a tightly woven global economy, emerging market assets imploded in value on the broad fears that financial crisis in the United States would lead to a global recession, a plunge in commodity prices, and a flight to safer investments than betting on untested companies in faraway lands. The collection of these fears—which all came to fruition in the closing months of 2008—was enough to pummel the financial markets everywhere, the emerging countries included.

Because the financial system is based on trust, the events of September 2008 made everyone extremely cautious and suspicious. Gone was the trust among ordinary citizens who thought the money they deposited with their local bank would be there tomorrow. Borrowers stopped believing that an investment touted as investment grade was just that and not subprime or toxic. Banks simply would not lend to each other on a short-term basis out of the fear that a borrower today could be out of business tomorrow. Securitization—or the process whereby banks and others parceled out risk by slicing up debt into pieces that were bought and sold all over the world—had come back to haunt Wall Street and the global financial markets. Painfully obvious to almost everyone, the elaborate risk-management schemes of banks and many other financial institutions had failed. Reeling from all the turmoil, the global equity markets lost $6 trillion in value over the month of September and continued to crater for the next six months.

In the end, the bursting of the U.S. housing bubble set off a chain reaction of defaults and foreclosures that would ultimately infect one part of the financial sector after another—prime mortgages, commercial paper, bond insurers, auto loans, corporate loans, credit cards, student loans, and the sovereign debt of nations like Iceland and Latvia. Easy credit had triggered the housing boom, and the credit boom itself had been underpinned by the global savings glut, an extended period of very easy monetary policies, lax regulation, and financial innovation—all of which increased risk taking and leveraged bets. When the global credit markets froze in September 2008, global economic activity—consumption, investment, trade—came to a virtual standstill. Both rails of globalization—finance and trade/investment—had become dysfunctional, with problems in one feeding into another. So widespread was the damage from the U.S.-spawned financial train wreck that in late 2008, Paul Krugman, awarded the Nobel Prize in Economics in 2008, ominously warned of the "prospects of a second Great Depression."

Luckily, nothing of the sort happened, but the damage to globalization was severe. After soaring in the prior quarter century, total world financial assets plummeted in 2008, declining a staggering $16 trillion, according to the McKinsey Global Institute.[3] The free fall in assets—roughly four times the size of China's economy—represents the largest annual decline in history, with most of the decline due to the result of swooning global stock market prices. The United States, at the epicenter of the global financial crisis, suffered the largest loss—$5.5 trillion in 2008. Japan and China's losses were also substantial, as both nations suffered a $2.4 trillion drop in total assets. The highly leveraged nations of Central and Eastern Europe were also slammed in 2008, and their financial assets plunged some $2.8 trillion.

Significant losses appeared across the board, with real estate, not surprisingly, the leader among them. McKinsey estimates that global residential real estate values plunged $3.4 trillion in 2008 and by nearly $2 trillion solely in the first quarter of 2009.[4] Cross-border capital flows—including foreign direct investment, bank lending, and purchases and sales of foreign stocks and debt—dropped a staggering 82 percent in 2008. Cross-border flows totaled just $1.9 trillion, down from $10.5 trillion the year before. The largest declines came in cross-border lending, which fell from $4.9 trillion in 2007 to −$1.3 trillion in 2008. This massive swing underscores the global panic of 2008, when many financially impaired institutions frantically withdrew money from overseas, notably among high-risk, highly leveraged emerging markets.

Only massive government intervention arrested the global financial panic of late 2008. In the frantic months after the shocking events of September, the world's central banks slashed interest rates and undertook a number of unconventional measures to inject money into the global capital markets. Concurrently, fiscal policies around the world became hyperexpansionary as governments rushed to stave off economic Armageddon. Albeit reluctantly, the U.S. Congress approved a $700 billion bank bailout package in late 2008, which was followed by a $787 billion stimulus package shortly after President Barack Obama was sworn into office in January 2009. Even before Obama assumed the presidency, amid increasing dire talk of the rising odds of a depression, the U.S. Congress, Department of the Treasury, and the Federal Reserve threw whatever resources available at the badly impaired U.S. economy. Similar frantic moves were pursued and implemented around the world. The European Union, Japan, China, South Korea, Brazil—policy makers in all of these nations went into overdrive to stave off a global depression by boosting public sector spending and increasing the availability of credit. Many central banks cut interest rates to virtually zero. Rarely had the world ever mobilized in such a concerted effort to fight a common cause—the great financial crisis of 2008.

The extraordinary dose of fiscal and monetary medicine worked. Despite being labeled a once-in-a-century event by the International Monetary Fund, the financial crisis of 2008 did not lead to a global depression, as many prominent analysts feared. Yet the ensuing global recession was deep and nasty by almost any measure, revealing just how interlinked the world had become owing to the rise of globalization since the early

1980s. The crisis in global finance had a direct and immediate impact on the real global economy at large.

THE COLLAPSE OF THE REAL GLOBAL ECONOMY

The ripple effects of the financial crisis caught many policy makers off guard, and in some cases, embarrassingly so. When the U.S. subprime monster reared its ugly head in the summer of 2007, many investors and policy makers thought the problem was strictly a U.S. phenomenon. Wise heads spoke of "global decoupling," or the belief that despite a battered U.S. economy and impaired financial sector, the rest of the world was immune to the tremors. Many felt that Europe and the emerging markets could go on their merry way without America.

"It's not logical to talk about a recession in Europe," proclaimed EU Economic and Monetary Affairs commissioner Joaquin Almunia in January 2008.[5] "The U.S. economy . . . has serious problems with fundamentals. We haven't." Meanwhile, Jean-Claude Juncker, head of the Eurogroup of European finance ministers, flatly declared that Europe had no need to resort to fiscal stimulus packages. Remarkably, as the U.S. recession gathered steam in the summer of 2008, the European central bank opted to raise interest rates in early July 2008, oblivious to the impending global train wreck. Across continental Europe, most wise heads felt that the Anglo-Saxon model of finance and capitalism, led by the United States and the United Kingdom, had at long last sparked its own demise. Debt was the rope that finally hung the highly leveraged U.S. economy. Conversely, for those nations that had exhibited modesty and prudence, everything would be fine.

Oblivious to the fact that the German banking sector had become infected by toxic U.S. subprime loans, German finance minister Peer Steinbrück boldly proclaimed that the financial crisis was an "American problem," a by-product of American greed and inadequate regulation that would cost the United States its "superpower status." This bout of Schadenfreude would come back to haunt Steinbrück. Just three days after chastising the United States for financial ineptitude, Germany's finance minister found himself scrambling to orchestrate a multibillion euro package to save German banks and admitting that Europe was "staring into the abyss."[6]

But Germany was not alone in thinking that problems in the United States were confined. Japan initially viewed the U.S. meltdown as "fire on the other side of the Pacific." With better fiscal balance sheets, excess reserves, and rising consumption levels among their emerging middle classes, nations like China, India, Brazil, Poland, and others thought they were sheltered from the economic storm. Until September 2008, the "decouplers" argued that the emerging markets, led by China, were strong enough to stand on their own. Not to worry, went the argument. Flush consumers in Shanghai, Dubai, Delhi, and other parts of developing nations were ready to step in and fill the void left by the highly leveraged U.S. consumer. Any decline in exports to the United States would be countered by rising trade to other nations, notably the high-flying emerging markets. How fallacious that belief was became painfully obvious in the final months of 2008.

The financial maelstrom that engulfed the United States slammed the rest of the global economy like a category five hurricane. Credit is the oxygen of the global economy—the more credit available and the better it circulates around the world, the stronger the world economy. Denied credit in the final quarter of 2008—as one financial institution after another halted lending—the global economy effectively seized up. On a seasonally adjusted annual rate, output declined by nearly 6 percent in the United States and over that level in Europe in the fourth quarter of 2008; the decline in Japan was a staggering 14 percent. The decline in output in Europe and Japan was even deeper in the first quarter of 2009—10 percent and 15 percent, respectively. Meanwhile, global trade measured in U.S. dollars plunged 31 percent between August 2008 and March 2009; the decline in trade volumes was not as severe, although they did crater 22 percent over the same period, one of the steepest declines in global trade on record.

The plunge in exports that befell Europe and Japan was brought on by the severe decline in U.S. consumer spending. Shell-shocked by the financial tsunami that struck Wall Street, American households not only cut back on spending but also increased their level of savings in the latter part of 2008. Savings rose roughly four percentage points of disposable income between the last quarter of 2007 and the first quarter of 2009. That's because U.S. consumers finally found their finances impaired by plunging stock market prices, imploding home prices, and the rising prospects of being thrown out of work. The debt-fueled era of U.S. consumption came to a screeching halt. American households lost around 20 percent of their net worth—a cool $13 trillion—between the second quarter of 2007 and the end of 2008. The Bank for International Settlements stated, "As a percentage of disposable income, this loss was greater than the wealth accumulated over the previous five years."[7] This massive loss in household wealth, not surprisingly, coupled with mounting job losses, led to a sharp drop in U.S. consumption and a stunning collapse of global economic growth. Accounting for roughly 19 percent of total world imports in 2000, the global share of U.S. imports dropped to 13 percent by the end of 2008 and to around 12 percent by the end of 2009.

The fallout was swift and widespread. Trade-dependent developed nations like Germany and Japan were brutally hit by a downturn in export demand, which triggered a downturn in capital investment and new hiring. As the global credit crisis intensified, the high-flying residential and commercial property markets of the United Kingdom, Spain, and Ireland collapsed, taking their respective economies down with them. With their earnings impaired by one of the worst financial crises in history, large and small corporations in the developed nations slashed their payrolls and suspended capital investment projects, adding even more pressure to the staggered global economy. In the end, economic growth among the developed nations imploded in the final months of 2008.

And despite all the chatter about "decoupling," the global fallout did not spare the developing nations. A steep decline in global demand for exports, accompanied by a plunge in commodity prices and capital inflows, left many developing nations battered and bruised. By the end of 2008, many developing nations were staring at depreciating currencies, plunging exports, soaring external financing costs, and swooning equity prices. The debate about global "decoupling" had ended. The inconvenient truth was that a world economy wired together by unfettered global capital flows, which supported ever-rising levels of trade and investment, advanced or declined together. No nation escaped the effects of the global recession that sank the world at the end of the first decade of the twenty-first century.

Not even the high-flying Chinese economy escaped from the wreckage. While China's economy grew by roughly 9 percent in 2009, the annual rate of growth was well below the 13 percent achieved in 2007. India and Indonesia also managed positive growth in 2009, although, collectively, the total output of the developing nations rose by just 1.2 percent for the year, down sharply from 8.1 percent one year before the crisis struck.

Rising risk aversion among banks and investors precipitated a sharp decline in investment in the developing nations. Bank lending swooned, as syndicated loan deals plunged to $123 billion in 2009, roughly half the level of 2008. Banks were not the only institutions pulling back from the emerging markets—so too were large multinationals. Foreign direct investment to the developing nations plunged by 40 percent between the first quarter of 2008 and the third quarter of 2009, and by roughly 24 percent for all of 2009. In all, net private flows to the developing nations fell by roughly 70 percent in 2009 from their peak in 2007.

Beyond the economic costs of the crisis were the mounting human costs. The World Bank estimates that by the end of 2010, 90 million more people are expected to be living in poverty than would have been the case without the crisis. Sadly, others estimate that between 30,000 to 50,000 children may have died of malnutrition in 2009 because of the crisis. The unemployment figures were grim all across the world. People out of work reached double digits across Europe, topping 20 percent in Spain, across the Caribbean and down into South America. In China, with an "official" unemployment rate of 4.2 percent, more than 20 million migrant workers lost their jobs when the global economy seized up in late 2008. The toll, in other words, from the financial crisis extended well beyond the global capital markets and had devastating consequences for rich and poor nations alike.

As 2009 came to a close, however, glimmers of hope appeared on the horizon. The signs of a cyclical economic recovery had become more evident. Policy makers were breathing a sigh of relief. By applying the lessons learned from the Great Depression—in times of crisis, spend and lend like mad—the world's central banks and respective governments had staved off disaster. Sensing that the worse was over, the S&P 500 staged an unprecedented rebound over the course of the year. After plunging to a cyclical low of 676 on March 9, 2009, the index reversed course and subsequently ended the year at 1,115, a 65 percent surge from its March trough. Over the same period, the Dow Jones Industrial Average soared 59 percent. Overseas, the rebound in the global stock markets was even more dramatic. In Germany, the DAX soared 61 percent in 2009, while the main French index, the CAC, gained 56 percent. Outsized equity gains were also scored in the United Kingdom, Spain, and the Netherlands. In the emerging markets like Brazil, India, and China, the gains were even more impressive. Brazil soared 87 percent in 2009, followed by gains of 114 percent and 55 percent in India and China's Shanghai index, respectively.

The year ended on a positive note—yet no one was ready to claim "mission accomplished" in early 2010, and for good reason. While the acute phase of the crisis had passed, the scars remained deep and fresh. The economic destruction of the crisis had caused the suffering of millions of workers in rich and poor nations alike, and this fed the groundswell of political anger directed at banks. With toxic accusations flying, it became very clear in early 2010 that the global economy was not about to return to "business as usual" any time soon. Sensing a shift toward a new era, a grim recognition emerged among the policy elites at the annual World Economic Forum in Davos, Switzerland, in January 2010 that globalization had largely failed, that banks needed more regulation, and that states needed to be more involved in running their respective economies. Ironically, this mood shift was sounded by the longtime champions of globalization, or among the many elites that have benefited enormously from globalization over the previous three decades.

As the second decade of the twenty-first century dawned, globalization was in retreat, and America's global dominance was in decline—both casualties of the U.S.-led financial crisis of 2008 and ensuing global recession. Voices from emerging countries began to proclaim that a historic shift from West to East was taking place. That all sounded noble and prophetic, but what did such a shift really mean? If the leaders of the previous wave of globalization were yanked off to the sidelines, who exactly were the substitutions?

THE RETREAT OF FINANCIAL GLOBALIZATION

The scars from the financial crisis will be deep and long lasting. In particular, the past will not be prologue for unfettered global capital flows. After soaring over the past quarter century, these flows are set to become more constrained and "caged" in the years ahead, a prospect that throws sand in the gears of globalization.[8] Big Western banks, I suspect, will become less global and more tepid in the search for overseas growth and more focused on getting things right at home. Many developing nations, meanwhile, having avoided the worse of the financial meltdown thanks to the heavy hand of the state in regulating banks, are not about to unbound their financial institutions any time soon. In the aftermath of the great financial crisis of 2008, financial conservatism will be the global norm.

Just as the return of globalization in the early 1980s was largely underwritten by ever-rising levels of cross-border capital flows, so the retreat of globalization will be led in large part by more tightly regulated global finance. The exotic global investments of the past are likely to become less exotic and more mundane, in addition to being far more constrained. Since the crisis, global financial reform has become the primary rallying cry of politicians around the world. To what extent the global financial landscape will be recast in the next few years remains to be seen. Proposals vary—French president Nicolas Sarkozy favors the creation of a new Bretton Woods system. China has advocated a new world's reserve currency, one that would dethrone the U.S. dollar as the world's top currency. Germany has opted for a unilateral ban on short selling of all stocks and euro-currency derivatives should the sale be for speculative purposes. "Naked" short selling has also been restricted.

In the United States, the Wall Street Reform and Consumer Protection Act of 2010 (the so-called Dodd-Frank Bill) was signed in law by President Obama on July 21, 2010, representing one of the most sweeping overhauls of the U.S. financial industry in decades. By the time this piece of legislation reached the president's desk, the bill was some 2,300 pages long, although despite its heft, it was lacking in specifics. As a *Wall Street Journal* editorial noted, "Lawyers estimate that the law will require no fewer than 243 new formal rule-makings by 11 different federal agencies. The SEC . . . will write 95 new rules. The new Bureau of Consumer Financial Protection will write 24, and the new Financial Stability Oversight Council will issue 56."[9]

Against this muddled backdrop, the full effects of the legislative behemoth will not be fully known for some time, leaving many parties—on the left, in the center, and on the right—unsatisfied and critical of the legislation. In a *Wall Street Journal* survey, various experts rated the legislation, with former Treasury secretary Hank Paulson doling out a grade of "Incomplete." Harvey Pitt, former chief of the Securities and Exchange

Commission, was less ambivalent, handing out an "F." Bill Gross of Pimco was only slightly less hostile, with a grade of "D+," while Nouriel Roubini of New York University, one of the few economists that warned of the impending housing bust, said the legislation was worthy of only a "C+."[10] In the days after the bill was signed by President Obama, some columnists opined that the banks got off easy and that nothing had really changed— that "the markets are masters again."[11]

Time will only tell. Putting flesh on the legislative skeleton created by Congress will take months, if not years, and involve some of the most intense lobbying efforts in the history of U.S. politics. More certain is this: while many feel the financial overhaul did not go far enough, the general consensus is that massive new layers of regulation will ultimately bite into the future earnings of U.S. banks and financial institutions. The upshot: more constrained earnings among U.S. banks and other financial institutions, coupled with unclear regulations or a muddled road map, will in turn diminish the reach and appetite of banks to venture too far from home. As this trend plays out, financial globalization will stall and could go into retreat.

As part of this outcome, an even greater risk lies in the fact that while preaching unity and cohesion, key G-20 members have crafted financial regulatory reforms in silos—or in an uncoordinated, national, fragmented fashion that will gum up the global capital markets. The United States has struck out on its own. In Europe, Germany stunned the world and its counterparts in Europe by taking the unilateral step toward banning certain kinds of short selling in May 2010. The U.K. government has created its own commission to investigate whether or not some of the largest banks in the country should be broken up. Besides the incoherent and uncoordinated push by various nations to regulate the global capital markets, the Group of

Twenty (G-20) and the Basel Committee on Banking Supervision weighed in with their own rules and regulations in mid-September 2010. Then, the Basel Committee—a group composed of regulators from 27 nations, including the United States—agreed to new global bank capital standards that will require banks to hold much larger capital cushions, among other items. Basel III mandates that banks raise their reserve of common equity to at least 7 percent of their assets, up from roughly 2 percent. The capital-raising standards, however, will not come into effect until 2018 and 2019, leaving plenty of time, according to those who advocated tougher measures, for banks to create mischief. How Basel III ultimately comes into effect remains to be seen; many details were missing from the deal struck in September, layering even more regulatory uncertainty over the global capital markets.

More certain is this: out of the ashes of the current crisis, the global financial architecture of the future is likely to be characterized by tighter rules and regulations regarding capital ratios and liquidity requirements, both measures of a bank's stability, plus their risk-management assessments. The pace of innovation in the financial sector is likely to slow, becoming more heavily monitored. The use of derivatives is likely to be significantly curtailed. In the developing nations, more rules that limit capital inflows are probable, as are measures that encourage the accumulation of international reserves. The World Bank worries that past efforts toward capital account liberalization will either slow or go into reverse: "Authorities in developing countries may take a more skeptical view toward globalization and seek to promote domestic financial intermediation as an alternative to reliance on foreign capital."[12] Since the global financial crisis struck in late 2008, various multilateral institutions like the World Bank, the IMF, and the Asian Development Bank that have long preached against the dangers of capital flows have actually warmed up to the idea of capital controls. The more capital flows become in fashion, the greater the retreat of financial globalization.

The necessity for banks in the developed nations to reduce risk taking and rebuild their impaired capital base implies less cross-border lending, or lending at higher rates. Risk-averse banks, many of them bailed out by their own governments, are expected to focus their future lending at home, at the expense of markets overseas. After expanding abroad, many U.S. and European banks are pulling back, selling their overseas affiliates, denying some developing nations low-cost capital and more sophisticated financial services needed to drive growth, like setting up a new company's initial stock offering. Regarding the latter, as the World Bank notes, American investment banks have participated in 86 percent of the value of developing-country initial public offerings over the past decade, or some 32 percent of the deals done. This has allowed investors in the developed nations to invest in fast-growing companies in the emerging markets, and conversely, provided the needed start-up capital for these firms. At a minimum, foreign bank participation in many developing nations is expected to rise less quickly in the future, helping to reduce the level of global capital flows.

What's more, additional financial regulation is also likely to raise the cost of capital for companies wishing to conduct global mergers and acquisitions and conclude foreign direct-investment deals. Because access to foreign capital is important to global trade and foreign direct investment, the more rules and regulations put in place that inhibits the flow of global capital, the less capital available to financially lubricate the global economy.

In the end, while the design of a new world financial architecture is still in the early phases, the precrisis global financial system now is a thing of the past. Too much damage has been done, and too much government time, effort, and money has been expanded to return to "business as usual." We now confront a world whereby cross-border flows will be more costly and less abundant. Debt is likely to become more expensive, raising the cost of trade financing and the cost of conducting mergers and acquisitions. To nurse their balance sheets back to health, many of the world's largest banks are heading home, selling off assets in foreign markets, thus further contributing to the deglobalization of finance.

In this environment, financial regionalism is likely to gain traction. As the World Bank notes, "The severity of the financial crisis and its transmission through the global capital markets is likely to turn policy makers' interest toward regional cooperation in an effort to buffer shocks originating in high-income countries."[13] The expectation is that many developing nations, while curtailing their financial ties with the developed nations, will broaden their own ties with domestic companies through regional arrangements. The movement toward building regional financial institutions, in turn, could supplant the need for long-standing multilateral institutions like the International Monetary Fund. In Asia, talk of a regional monetary association or union has increased over the past year, an idea that had been debated but ultimately shelved following the 1997 Asian financial crisis. Buffeted yet again by global financial instability, however, various nations in Asia are warming up to the idea of greater regional monetary cooperation. Similar thoughts are surfacing in the Middle East, where Islamic banking is gaining traction.

As a result, global capital markets could become more fragmented and based more along regional lines, a shift that could ultimately lead to more regional trading blocs and a global trading system significantly different from the one in place over the past 50 years. A regulatory tsunami is about to wash over the global capital markets, leaving in its wake a new world global finance.

In time, the consequences of the financial crisis of 2008 will come to be seen as just as powerful and game-changing as President Nixon's decision to close the gold window in 1971. To a very large degree, we are heading back to the future, or to a time when global finance was more restricted and contained. This will promote and contribute to the retreat of globalization.

Pushing the world economy toward the same destination is the rise in trade and investment protectionism. While the global recession of 2008 did not spawn a rash of blatant trade restrictions among nations à la the 1930s, trade and investment protectionism has emerged over the past year under different and nontraditional guises.

SMILING FACES TELL LIES

Global summits rarely yield anything but the summit-ending group photo. Indeed, no high-powered powwow is complete without a mug shot of the world's leaders standing shoulder to shoulder, with big grins pasted on their faces in an attempt to convey unity to the rest of the world. The G-20 London summit in early April 2009—the second such summit among the world's new political elite—was no different.

Despite the fragile state of the world economy, the heads of state of the world's leading economies in London shared plenty of smiles. They also offered plenty of assurances that they understood the lessons of the Great Depression—that nationalist measures to inhibit and restrict cross-border trade would spell economic disaster for the world and undermine an already battered global economy. Not to worry, so the grins seemed to suggest. The world's leaders knew better and were not about to revert to beggar-thy-neighbor trade policies.

Yet, to borrow a phrase from the Motown group the Temptations, "smiling faces tell lies." At least in London they did.

Despite pledges to keep their markets open, the world's leading countries have tilted in the opposite direction since the global financial crisis began. By the middle of 2009, the World Bank had noted 23 new restrictions on trade since the London summit in April and roughly 90 new trade-restricting measures since the first crisis-related G-20 summit of October 2008. In addition, the number of proposed "safeguard" measures, which allow countries to block sharply rising imports without proving unfair pricing, rose from just 2 cases in the first seven months of 2008 to 16 in the first half of 2009.

The proliferation of protectionism has been even more widespread than the World Bank figures suggest, according to the Global Trade Alert (GTA) and its energetic editor Simon J. Evenett, among the most diligent in documenting the rise of global protectionism since the crisis. In mid-September 2009, the GTA noted:

> After taking their no-protectionist pledge, the G-20 members have implemented 121 blatantly discriminatory measures; since the first G-20 crisis summit in November 2008, the world economy has been hit by 192 beggar-thy-neighbor policy measures. Add in another 48 suspicious measures that are likely to have harmed some foreign commercial interests, the total could reach 240; and worldwide, the number of blatantly discriminatory measures outnumbers liberalizing measures five to one.[14]

So much for restraint—and so much for looking out for the global good. Behind the smiles in London and the follow up G-20 meeting in Pittsburgh in November 2009 and Toronto, Canada, in June 2010, it was every country for itself.

The retreat to protectionism has come in various guises, ranging from tariff to nontariff barriers to industry subsidies. The latter stands out since unlike the 1930s, when various governments blatantly raised trade barriers across the board, today many nations have instead decided to resort to state aid to assist troubled industries. Call it protectionism by stealth. Knowing that naked protectionism would be frowned upon by others, many governments have resorted to less traditional ways of protectionism, with state aid and bailouts the most favored policy tools of the past few years. Indeed, since late 2008, G-20 nations have announced twice as many trade-distorting state bailouts as increases in tariffs.

The U.S. automobile industry alone was at the receiving end of $74 billion in government funds in 2009, marking one of the largest state-sponsored bailouts in U.S. industry. Roughly two-thirds of the total ($50 billion) alone went to U.S. auto giant, General Motors, a longtime U.S. corporate icon deemed too big to fail by many U.S. legislators. Never mind the fact that the U.S. auto industry accounts for only 6.5 percent of U.S. manufacturing jobs and that Detroit's downhill path has been largely of its own making. The angst associated with the struggling vehicle maker has been more than enough for U.S. lawmakers to directly subsidize what was once one of the largest companies in the world. The aid has come in the way of direct loans, consumer purchasing programs like the popular "cash for clunkers" program, and investment incentives.

Not unexpectedly, America's trading partners have cried foul over the competitive-distorting effects of such a large government handout. So has Ford Motors, a fierce competitor of GM's who was not on the receiving end of such government largesse. But rather than resist the bailout of the U.S. auto industry, many governments have simply joined in, opting for their own industry- and trade-distorting measures.

As global auto sales plunged in 2009, government incentives ran the gamut. In France, the government doled out billions in preferential loans to automakers and direct, low-interest loans to consumers. Spain also introduced interest-free loans. In the United Kingdom, millions have been spent on worker training. In Germany, like many other nations, financial incentives to scrap older cars for newer, fuel-efficient vehicles provided a one-time boost to auto sales. In Italy, meanwhile, government subsidies have been available for those consumers thinking about purchasing a "green" scooter. Russia has not only granted direct subsidies to consumers and producers, but has also resorted to tariffs on used cars to protect its domestic industry. China, South Korea, and other developing nations have also rushed to protect their automobile industries over the past year, creating, with help from the developed nations, a global automotive industry that beats more to the tune of government subsidies and intervention than signals from the free markets. As the World Trade Organization recently noted, "The longer the subsidies remain in place, the more they will distort market-based production and investment decisions globally, the greater will become the threat of chronic trade distortions developing, and the more difficult it will become to correct those distortions."[15]

And when it comes to state aid, automobiles are just for starters. In the United States, across Europe, and around the world, extending credit and capital to distressed banks and other financial institutions became standard procedure in the aftermath of the crisis. The 2008–2009 financial crisis also unleashed a slew of other trade-distorting or restrictive practices. The latter ran the gamut and included strict local content requirements, public procurement provisions, trade remedy measures, export subsidies, favorable trade finance, migration restrictions, consumption subsidies, and import bans, to name just a few levers at the disposal of states when it comes to protecting their interests and home turf.

Since the crisis erupted, the use of tariffs—the most blatant form of protectionism—has become popular in such key markets as Russia, Turkey, and India. Import tariffs have been raised on a number of products, ranging from iron and steel to cars to soybeans. India has completely banned Chinese toy imports from entering its markets. New Delhi has also taken to protecting its power industry and telecom equipment from Chinese competition by screening Chinese firms out of large contracts in favor of local manufacturers. To protect its domestic producers and prevent massive layoffs, Vietnam has raised tariffs on semifinished steel. China has banned the import of Belgian chocolate and Italian brandy. Paranoid Ecuador, fearing the worst from overseas, has slapped tariffs on some 600 products. Argentina and Brazil have led the way in boosting tariffs on wine, leather, dairy products, and textiles for the entire Mercosur region, South America's largest trading bloc. Meanwhile, the two leaders of Mercosur have taken aim at each other: Brazil is considering erecting trade barriers to industrial imports from Argentina in response to growing barriers to trade in Argentina. In the United States, President Barack Obama imposed a 35 percent tariff on Chinese-made tires in September 2009 as a political favor to American unions. China responded in kind by initiating an antidumping investigation against imports of some U.S. chicken products and auto parts.

While the use of tariffs continues to mount, more ingenious ways of protecting local interests via nontariff barriers have sprouted like weeds. Take Indonesia, for instance. To shield local producers, the giant Southeast Asian state has decided to limit the means of entry of over 500 different goods to just six ports, a move justified on the basis of health concerns, although some of the goods affected include electronics, toys, and clothing.

Many complaints have been made against China's barriers to overseas investment. The *New York Times* reported on May 2010:

> In January, when the Chinese government overhauled procurement rules to encourage more competition, including from foreign companies, Beijing officials exempted all public works projects, which account for half of government procurement. Contracts involving state secrets or business secrets are reserved for Chinese companies, and Chinese bureaucrats have been given broad latitude to exclude companies with foreign owners even if the company has been set up in China and has all of its operations in the country.[16]

Reflecting on the increasing difficulties of doing business in China, General Electric's top executive, Jeff Immelt, candidly summed up China this way in late June 2010: "I am not sure that in the end they want any of us to win or any of us to be successful." From the same article from the *Financial Times*, Joerg Wuttke, former head of the European Chamber of Commerce, is quoted as saying, "After 30 years of progressive market reforms, many foreign businesses in the country feel as though they have run up against an unexpected and impregnable blockade."[17] And adding to the chorus of frustration with China, the European Chamber of Business Confidence survey for 2010 noted that, "The number one issue affecting their operations in China remains the perception that the regulatory environment for foreign enterprises in China has become more difficult—and will worsen further in the coming years."[18]

France, meanwhile, has created its own sovereign wealth fund as a means to shield various domestic corporations from foreign takeovers. No one protects and promotes "national champions" like the French, and perhaps no leader has been as blatant as President Nicolas Sarkozy when it comes to naked protectionism. After offering some $5 billion in subsidies to French automakers, the French leader then promptly called on them to use only French-made parts and relocate their factories from Eastern Europe to France.

Similarly, with millions of Americans searching for work, nobody has a stronger protectionist impulse right now than the U.S. Congress. Buried in the Obama administration's $787 billion fiscal stimulus package are policies that favor domestic goods and services at the expense of imports and foreign suppliers. They are infamously known as "Buy American" provisions and are measures that have infuriated many of America's top trading partners, like Canada, for instance.

According to a report from the *Washington Post*, after the town of Peru, Indiana, had to reject a Canadian supplier of sewage pumps because of "Buy American" provisions and after Canadian pipe fittings in a construction project at Camp Pendleton, California, were ripped out of the ground and replaced with U.S. fittings, a number of towns in Ontario fired back by threatening to bar U.S. companies from their municipal contracts.

More insidious, the *Post* article reported on the case of the Duferco Farrell Corporation, a Swiss-Russian partnership that took control of a bankrupt U.S. steel company near Pittsburgh in the 1990s. The plant employs around 600 people—the bulk of them United Steel Workers—with these union jobs at risk since the company uses imported steel slabs not generally sold in the United States when manufacturing coils.

According to the *Post*, "The partially foreign production process means the company's coils do not fit the current definition of made in the USA—a designation that the stimulus law requires for thousands of public works projects across the nation. In recent weeks, its largest client—a steel pipe maker located one mile down the road—notified Duferco Farrell that it would be canceling orders. Instead, the client is buying from companies with 100 percent U.S. production to meet the new stimulus regulations. Duferco has had to furlough 80 percent of its workforce."[19] Ironically, U.S. unions are supportive of "Buy American" provisions, although these same measures have backfired on organized labor.

With the world's largest economy leading the way, it's no wonder the rest of the world has jumped on the "buy local" bandwagon. State aid and subsidies have become just as popular on the Pacific Rim and across Europe, supported by many of the G-20 leaders who preached openness in London yet practice protectionism at home.

As part of this dynamic, antidumping and safeguard investigations have jumped sharply over the past year. Nearly 90 antidumping investigations were started in the first 7 months of 2009, and they have come in all shapes and sizes: China has undertaken antidumping investigations on imports of polyamide-6 from the European Union, Taiwan, and the United States; the European Union has initiated an antidumping investigation on imports of stainless steel fasteners from India and Malaysia; and India is investigating DVD imports from Thailand and Vietnam. The United States is currently investigating plastic bag imports from Indonesia, Taiwan, and Vietnam. In a burst of candor that was subsequently retracted, the head of Suntech Power Holdings, China's largest producer of solar panels, said that the company was selling its products below marginal cost in the United States, prompting a solar company in Germany to call for a "Buy European" law.

In terms of safeguard initiatives, the number jumped from just 2 in the first seven months of 2008 to 16 in the same period of 2009. Meanwhile, in response to the financial crisis, 11 of the G-20 nations took emergency measures in 2009 that have the potential to restrict or distort global capital and trade flows. More ominously, these measures are not cheap—the World Trade Organization estimates that total public spending associated with these measures (which include firm and sector subsidies) amount to a staggering $3 trillion. The sheer size of these measures are trade- and industry-distorting, since in many cases the emergency measures typically create advantages for domestic sectors and put foreign players at a competitive disadvantage.

All the above make nonsense of the G-20's no-protectionism pledge. Granted, the world has avoided the draconian measures associated with the Smoot-Hawley Tariff Act of 1930—or trade-restricting tariffs that would bring global trade and the global economy to a standstill. Yet the G-20 pledge still rings hollow. The crisis has spawned all sorts of protectionism, including trade protectionism, financial protectionism, labor protectionism, green protectionism, and investment protectionism. Regarding the latter item, as the United Nation's *World Investment Report 2010* noted, out of the 102 new national policy measures affecting foreign investment in 2009, 31 were toward tighter regulations. Just over 30 percent of the new regulations were toward greater investment restrictions, the highest percentage of such measures since the UN started collecting the data in 1992.[20] In other words, when it comes to guarding their own interests, whether the protection is for banks, ailing companies, or workers, governments around the world have never been busier than in the months following the global financial meltdown of 2008.

THE UNMAKING OF AN
ECONOMIC SUPERPOWER

In the end, a new global era is taking shape. The global financial landscape cast by the policies of President Nixon and other
U.S. administrations is being reconfigured. As waves of financial reform wash over the global economy, cross-border capital flows—the glue of the global economy—will become more
bound than unbound in the future. While paying lip service to
open borders and free trade and investment, governments will
continue to lean in the opposite direction, toward myopic and
inward policies that have at their core the principle of let's take
care of our own, the rest of the world be damned. The result:
structurally diminished global trade and investment flows and
the gradual retreat of globalization.

As part of this new era, the developing nations will move
to the forefront as drivers of global growth, a radical departure
from the past. Twenty-five years ago, the notion that China or
India would lead the world out of recession would have been
ridiculed. Then, the prosperity of the United States was joined
by the burgeoning wealth of major European nations—the West
led and everyone else followed. America stood tall as the world's
only economic superpower. Globalization was molded in America's image, an image the rest of the world was all too quick to
embrace.

It was the United States that was responsible for globalization's comeback in the second half of the twentieth century. Yet,
in the end, the same country that led the world to a renewed
appreciation of the virtues of globalization would undo its own
promise. In the early 2000s a new boom in the United States
was fueled by a real estate bubble underpinned by a new class of

house buyer, the subprime mortgage holder. In a dizzying spiral, houses were sold to people without credit by lenders without principle and the mortgages sold in securitization bundles that became so complicated that no one could understand them. The boom in America spread to Europe as well, and everywhere real estate prices rose to unprecedented highs. This artificial bubble was supported by developing countries looking for safe havens for their newly found wealth. In an ironic twist, the poor became the support of the rich.

This inverted pyramid could not last, and in 2007–2008 the edifice of prosperity crumbled and then collapsed in a worldwide crash. As the dust settles, plenty of questions surround the new order taking shape. One thing is for sure, however: the "Made in America" financial crisis has severely damaged America's global brand and undermined American-led globalization. Other countries have awakened to the fact that there are other paths to prosperity and have been emboldened to operate outside the confines and dictates of Western-style capitalism.

The biggest loser of the financial crisis was the United States. Notwithstanding signs of recovery in 2010, America's economy remains bogged down by massive debt, by the burden of waging a two-front war in Afghanistan and Iraq, and by crushing obligations of Social Security, Medicare, and other entitlements. The crisis and its aftermath have been costly to the country's balance sheet, its economic capabilities, global image, and general standing in the global economy. While still among the most powerful nations in the world, the United States, on a relative basis, is no longer the economic superpower it once was. When America speaks, few nations now feel compelled to listen or fall in line. As a new decade begins, adjusting to this new reality represents one of the key challenges before the United States.

Speeding toward a Messy Multipolar World

The crisis has been a transformative moment in global economic history whose ultimate resolution will likely reshape politics and economics for at least a generation.
>   —CARMEN M. REINHART AND KENNETH S. ROGOFF,
>   *This Time Is Different*

On a dark and dreary day in early March 2009, the S&P 500 index fell to an intraday low of 666, a level not seen since September 1996. In 13 years, one of the most closely watched indexes in the world had completely retraced its steps, taking back, excluding dividends, virtually all the gains of investors. After hitting a record high of 1,565 on October 9, 2007, the S&P had shed more than half its value—nearly $8 trillion—by the time the index hit bottom on March 9, 2009.

It was somewhat of a miracle, then, that roughly one year later the S&P 500 index had risen 70 percent from the depths of the prior year. In early April 2010, in fact, the S&P touched and then exceeded 1,192—the exact level the S&P closed on the first Monday after the collapse of Lehman Brothers. The stunning about-face was triggered by growing confidence among investors that the world was not headed for another Great Depression. The nightmare scenario had been avoided thanks to massive capital injections from governments and central banks from around the world. Their all-out fiscal and monetary onslaught on the financial crisis ultimately triggered a cyclical global economic recovery in 2010 and its typical precursor, a rally in global equity markets. A headline in the *New York Times* neatly captured the mood at the moment—"After Jerky Swings, the Economy Begins to Look Nice and Boring."[1]

The U.S. economy had expanded by better than 5 percent on an annualized basis in the fourth quarter of 2009. The U.S. employment picture, to the surprise of nearly everyone, was improving, albeit gradually. Beyond its shores, the global economy was exhibiting signs of strength with each passing week. The article referred to reduced stock market volatility as an indicator that things were returning to "normal." The higher the level of confidence among investors, the lower the volatility of the financial markets. Even the bombed out U.S. housing market was showing faint signs of improvement. Yet beneath the surface the reality was anything but "normal." Indeed, the world financial markets were hammered by rising uncertainty and increased volatility in the second quarter of 2010, with the Dow Jones Industrial Average and S&P 500 falling 9.4 and 11.4 percent, respectively. As the summer of 2010 stretched on, worries began to mount over the durability of the U.S. economic recovery in particular and the global economy in general.

The global structural aftershocks from the financial crisis of 2008 are only now coming into view, and a clear picture will evolve only over the next few years and decades. In one critical sense the financial crisis of 2008 was a circuit breaker—the global financial meltdown broke the supposed inexorable advance of free-market capitalism, throttled the primacy and influence of global finance, and undermined the economic superpower status of the United States. In another sense the crisis accelerated a number of key long-range trends that were already in motion before the crisis struck. The relative economic decline of the developed nations (the West); the rising influence of the emerging markets in general and China in particular (the Rest); the proliferation of regional trading blocs—these seminal trends were fast-forwarded by the crisis and have, in turn, accelerated the move toward a less U.S.-centric, more multipolar world.

This new world will be more complex, fluid, and disruptive, notably for the Western architects and standard bearers of the postwar economic system: the United States, Europe, and, to a lesser extent, Japan. In the years ahead, global power and influence will be more diffused among nations and regions, making it more challenging to coordinate and craft solutions to pressing global problems like climate change, the proliferation of nuclear weapons, the long-running Doha Round of multilateral trade negotiations, and the development challenges of poverty-stricken Africa. The era in which a handful of nations could meet for a weekend and set the global economic agenda for the rest of the world is over. The new era will require far-reaching adjustments for those nations in decline and for those on the ascent. Becoming more acclimated to a new multipolar world will not only challenge nations but also key postwar multilateral institutions like the United Nations Security Council, the International Monetary Fund, the World Bank, and other Western-dominated institutions that have long held sway over global economic governance. Invariably, these institutions will have to yield more to the aspirations of the developing nations and their strategic interests in order to remain relevant.

In the end, there is nothing "normal" or "boring" about the postcrisis world. The financial crisis of 2008 was a tipping point. A messy multipolar world is upon us, one that if improperly handled will further erode the economic superpower status of the United States and result in the further retreat of globalization. As part of a new multipolar world, the following five seismic trends will be instrumental in sculpting the future of the global economy.

THE NEW STEERING COMMITTEE OF THE GLOBAL ECONOMY

Once upon a time, six nations governed the global economy—an elite clique comprising the United States, Japan, Germany, the United Kingdom, Italy, and France. They formally gathered for the first time in Rambouillet, France, in November 1975 to discuss the pressing issues of the day—soaring energy prices and the attendant rise in inflation, unemployment, and stagnant real growth. A year later, a seventh nation—Canada—was invited to join the special club which, dubbed the G-7, considered itself the steward of the global economy. Annual summits among the Group of Seven finance ministers became customary and later expanded to full-blown foreign summits involving heads of state. In 1985, the G-7 was formally organized and became yet another Western-led and dominated organization overseeing the world's economic affairs. Following the Cold War, in 1998, the G-7 became the G-8 when it granted Russia a seat at the exclusive table in hopes of bring the country into the Western fold. Still missing, however, were emerging giants like China and India, whose exclusion called into question the credibility of the G-8 even before the global financial meltdown of 2008.

Any remaining legitimacy of the G-8 was demolished by the financial crisis. The implosion that brought the global economy to its knees emanated from within the G-8 itself. The members of the gang in charge of minding the global shop—led by its chief, the United States— were among the first victims of the financial crisis.

Globally discredited, the G-8 has been supplanted by the G-20, a little-known group that has been around since 1999. The G-20 first emerged from the Asian financial crisis, and it was initially intended to bring various finance ministers from the developed and developing nations together with the goal of promoting global financial stability. For most of the first decade of its existence, the G-20 deferred to the more powerful and influential Group of Eight.

Surveying the wreckage wrought by the financial crisis and recognizing that a broader global venue was needed to arrest the unfolding global recession, the Bush administration played host to the first postcrisis G-20 Leaders Summit in Washington, D.C., in November 2008. Numerous finance ministers were in attendance, but the forum was elevated to include heads of state, signaling how serious the moment was. The Washington gathering represented a stunning shift in global economic power, for the first G-20 summit represented a tactical admission on the part of the United States and Europe that they no longer had the credibility and resources to steer the global economy on their own. On the contrary, they had triggered one of the steepest declines in global output in decades. The committee that had long run the world desperately needed the help of the developing nations, or those countries still solvent and therefore best able to right the crippled global ship.

More chairs were set around the table. In addition to the members of the G-8, the new stewards of the global economy include Argentina, Brazil, Australia, China, India, Indonesia, Mexico, Saudi Arabia, South Korea, South Africa, and Turkey. The 27-member European Union was granted one seat, bringing the total to 20. This group is more diverse and more representative of the global economy. Whereas the G-8 accounted for roughly 56 percent of world gross domestic product and 11 percent of the global population, the combined output of the G-20 represents nearly 88 percent of the world total GDP and 65 percent of the population.

Diversity is nice in principle, but a major question remains: how effective will the G-20 be in steering the global economy? Despite plenty of differences among members, the commitments and the overarching we-must-stand-together rhetoric of the G-20 have brought stability to the world financial markets— at least for now. At the Washington summit, the participants pledged to coordinate regulatory reform initiatives and to use expansionary fiscal and monetary policies to stimulate growth. They also vowed to reform the global capital markets and revamp existing multilateral institutions to better reflect the emergence of new economic powers like China and India. All members disavowed protectionist measures, but as highlighted in Chapter 3, virtually all members have broken this promise in some fashion.

In April 2009, at the London G-20 summit, the global stewards reiterated the commitments made in Washington and established the Financial Stability Board (FSB), a body set up to create and enforce global standards for financial regulation and monitoring. The London summit also pledged to recapitalize the World Bank and IMF as safeguards to mounting financial pressures in the developing nations, and the members vowed to reach an agreement on the Doha Round of trade negotiations. Convening for a third time in September 2009, the G-20 powwow in Pittsburgh again reiterated many of the same pledges and commitments of the prior two summits, while agreeing on a "framework for strong, sustainable, and balanced growth" to coordinate national economic policies and correct global imbalances. The G-20 summit in Pittsburgh also pledged to increase the representation of the emerging markets at the IMF and World Bank by raising their quota by five percentage points to 43 percent of the total.

In making the world look "boring" and "normal" again, the G-20 can claim early success. The fact that the world's most important nations were willing to gather around the same table and hash out policy prescriptions at the height of the financial crisis was instrumental in calming market fears over the rising risks of a global depression. Speaking at the World Economic Forum in Davos, Switzerland, in early 2010, President Nicolas Sarkozy of France correctly noted, "The G-20 is a harbinger of global governance in the twenty-first century. Without the G-20, confidence would not have been re-established."[2]

How the G-20 advances from here remains unclear, however. How will this disparate group function with so many different interests and priorities represented around the table? What is clear so far is that talk is cheap. Despite numerous high-profile pledges, much work needs to be done—the Doha trading round, for instance, continues to flounder, lacking the critical support of both the developed and developing nations. Moreover, much remains to be done to increase the representation of the developing nations in the World Bank and International Monetary Fund. The governance structure of both institutions remains biased toward the developed nations and the United States in particular. The latter—given America's largest single voting share—still enjoys veto power at both the Bank and Fund when actions require a supermajority vote. And while all parties to the G-20 support the idea of establishing a common set of rules for the global capital markets, various governments, the United States included, have been busy crafting their own banking regulations with little coordination with other nations. This is the path to financial deglobalization.

The effectiveness of the G-20 will not be known for some time. As the global recovery gathers pace, the cooperation evident in the early postcrisis days are bound to fade. The threat of global depression had the effect of singularly focusing the minds of the world's top leaders. The solution to the problem was quite simple: throw as much money at the problem as possible. The strategy—akin to a financial "surge" from the world's central banks—worked. In the years ahead, however, more fine-tuning will be needed, and working out the specific details to very knotty problems will test the cohesion of the G-20. Completing the Doha trade round, reconfiguring the share of country quotas at the IMF and World Bank, avoiding various forms of protectionism, refraining from overregulating and strangling the global capital markets—all these issues, and more, could run afoul of domestic politics, regional coalitions, and philosophical differences among various countries. A great many fault lines, in other words, run through the committee that runs the world. "The G-20 is doomed not to address anything that is controversial," Youssef Boutros-Ghali, Egypt's finance minister, commented to the *Wall Street Journal*.[3]

To this point, the G-20 summit in Toronto, Canada, in late June 2010 was long on rhetoric and short on substance. "The best that the G-20 leaders could come up with the other day was polite agreement to disagree," is how *Financial Times* columnist Philip Stephens put it following the meeting.[4] The G-20 meeting in Toronto produced a 25-page closing statement that urged deficit nations like the United States to save more and boost exports, while exhorting surplus nations like China to spend and import more. In general, the G-20 members agreed to cut their deficits by 50 percent by 2013, although deficit reduction measures are to "be tailored to individual country circumstances." This statement was code for nobody is in charge and that nations could pursue policy goals irrespective of what is good for the global common good.

In the end, the new global entity will prove to be noticeably frustrating to the world's last economic superpower, the United States. "The G-20's significance is not in the passing of the baton from the G7/G8 but from the G1, the U.S. Even during the 33 years of the G7 economic forum, the U.S. called the important economic shots," according to well-known economist Jeffrey Sachs.[5] In the future, when it comes to framing and executing global economic policies, Washington will have to cooperate with many more different members of the global steering committee and will have to consider views from such disparate nations as Saudi Arabia and Argentina. The fact that Argentina, bankrupt for most of the past decade, even has a seat at the global policy-making table with the United States speaks volumes about how much the world has changed since September 2008 and how much America's global economic status has diminished.

THE SHIFT (AGAIN) IN THE COMMANDING HEIGHTS

Fashions have a tendency to come and go—wait long enough and what is unfashionable today will be in vogue tomorrow. The same holds true with the public sector's participation in the economy. Over the roaring nineties and the first decade of this century, very few people ever thought that the state would reemerge as the principal driver of economic growth. Governments, however, are now back in the business of business. Around the world, the state is getting bigger, the private sector smaller. Out of the wreckage of the U.S.-led financial crisis has emerged the overriding conviction that deregulated markets cannot be trusted to behave themselves. They need a larger and more "visible" hand of the government.

The global economy configured by the free-market tenets of Lady Thatcher and Ronald Reagan is being overhauled, with the pendulum yet again swinging back toward more state intervention. Speaking to the global revival of industrial policy, *The Economist* noted in mid-2010, "Politicians are reviving the notion that intervening in individual industries and companies can drive growth and create jobs."[6] In the United States, while Washington has pared its ownership of many large U.S. banks, Uncle Sam still owns large chunks of General Motors and Chrysler. In the financial sector, U.S. mortgage giants, Fannie Mae and Freddie Mac, along with insurance behemoth, American Insurance Group (AIG) remain wards of the state.

Washington's participation in the economy extends well beyond the direct control of a handful of companies. It also takes the form of massive government spending, the passage of a historic health-care bill, and the Federal Reserve's easy-money participation in the U.S. housing market. As a telling indicator of the rising economic presence of Washington, America's public sector debt as a percentage of total output rose from roughly 40 percent in 2006 to nearly 60 percent by mid-2010. Nearly three decades after the Reagan revolution, and some 15 years after President Bill Clinton proclaimed the "era of big government is over," the tide has yet again turned. All told, state intervention in what used to be the world's premier free-market economy has rarely been as prominent in the postwar era. "In America, Barack Obama, the effective owner of General Motors and a chunk of Wall Street, has turned his back on the laissez-faire approach of the past: a strategic-industries initiative is under way," according to *The Economist*.[7]

And the economic role of Washington is not expected to be diminished any time soon. The key players—the Federal Reserve, the U.S. Treasury, the White House, and Congress—that rode to the rescue of the economy in 2008 helped to prevent another Great Depression with massive state aid and assistance. It was a bold gamble and one financed grudgingly by U.S. taxpayers. So after spending billions of taxpayers' dollars on bank and automobile bailouts, among other reinforcements, Congress and the executive branch are not likely to hand the keys of the economy back over to the free-market, risk-taking gang that helped precipitate one of the worse financial calamities in history. The primacy of the state is going to be a staple of the U.S. economy for some time to come.

Meanwhile, the relationship between the state and marketplace is also being rethought outside the United States. American-style capitalism has lost its luster in Europe, Japan, and other developed nations where state intervention has always lurked just beneath the surface. Picking industrial winners and losers is back in vogue across Europe, with the French government going so far as to take stakes in a French toy manufacturer threatened by rising Chinese competition. Highlighting this trend, *The Economist* reflected, "From Berlin to Brussels, demand for industrial policy is back. Japan's new government is responding to what it sees as the increasingly aggressive policies of foreign competitors by deepening the links between business and the state."[8] Like the United States, governments across Europe have spent billions of dollars in reviving their economies and are likely to err on the side of staying too involved (even more than they have been in the past) in their respective economies well after the crisis has passed. Promoting national corporate champions remains quite popular in such countries as France and Italy, as has reining in excess risk taking among banks and other financial institutions. Key to the shift in the commanding heights is the movement toward tighter financial regulations in both the developed and developing nations, including broader industry regulation, higher capital requirements, less use of leverage, increased cross-border supervision, and the promotion of domestic banks and institutions as a means to reduce reliance on foreign capital.

Big government has also made a comeback in many developing nations, which believe free-market capitalism has run off the tracks, creating more destruction than prosperity over the decades. Against this backdrop, countries like China, India, and Brazil are increasingly unapologetic about the role the state plays in their respective economies. Around the world, the "Washington consensus," or the unbending belief in free markets, unfettered capital flows, and industry deregulation, is in tatters, one of the first victims of the financial crisis. This ideology is now scoffed at in various capitals of the world and has opened the door for a different credo.

The so-called Beijing consensus has emerged, albeit tentatively, to counter the Washington consensus. Though still ill defined, the Beijing model states that there is nothing wrong with large swathes of the economy remaining under the direct or indirect control of the state, notably the capital markets and domestic banks and financial institutions. Indeed, one of the effects of the U.S.-led financial crisis has been to validate the policies of many developing nations that restrict bank lending at home and abroad and constrain the movement of capital flows. Bank regulations in the developing nations therefore are likely to remain restrictive over the medium term. In Brazil, for instance, credit from state-controlled banks makes up nearly 40 percent of the total credit available for lending; in China, the percentage is closer to 70 percent. India, Egypt, Turkey, and many other key developing nations also maintain tight regulations on their capital markets and are unlikely to untether their banks any time soon. Against this backdrop, investors and multinationals should plan for more financial conservatism in the years ahead.

More broadly speaking, state capitalism has come of age. According to Ian Bremmer, writing in *Foreign Affairs*: "The free-market tide has now receded. In its place has come state capitalism, a system in which the state functions as the leading economic actor and uses markets primarily for political gain."[9] In this world, state governments own major shares in companies in such critical sectors as finance, technology, aviation, cars, telecommunications, power generation, mining, and natural resources. In China, key sectors that have been singled out by Beijing as strategically important and therefore should remain under the control of the government include defense, power generation and distribution, oil and petrochemicals, telecommunications, coal, aerospace, and air freight services. Presently, according to Bremmer, "Governments, not shareholders, already own the world's largest oil companies and control three-quarters of the world's energy reserves." Meanwhile, many large privately owned companies in the developing nations, while not directly controlled by the state, nevertheless enjoy government-favored entitlements as a means to protect and promote national champions. In the end, state-owned enterprises and private national champions in the developing nations have been among the big winners of the financial crisis. As part of the new multipolar world, the role of the state in the private sector will be paramount.

THE RUSH TO REGIONALISM

The speed and severity by which the U.S.-led financial crisis was transmitted around the world, hammering strong and weak economies alike, has shocked many policy leaders into rethinking the costs associated with globalization. Very few nations are ready to opt out completely from the global economy, but support for an unfettered globalized economy and multilateral institutions governing global commerce has declined in the wake of the crisis. Multilateralism looks less enticing to governments today. More appealing are regional arrangements or alliances that encompass not just trade and finance but also defense and energy security. Regionalism was on the rise even before the financial crisis struck, but has become more attractive in the postcrisis world as various governments attempt to hedge against the inherent volatility of being a member of the global economy. In addition, since the U.S. consumer is not expected to drive global growth forward any time soon, many countries have instead turned their attention to their neighbors. Preferential trade agreements between like-minded countries are likely to rise in the future because of many variables.

According to Jennifer Hillman of the German Marshal Fund, nations today favor regional agreements to multilateral ones for multiple reasons:

> First, there are non-institutional alternatives to the multilateral system—ranging from a broad array of private investment tools that supplant the IMF to huge infrastructure projects that are financed by foreign governments or other aid funds, often undermining the role of the World Bank. Second, many developing countries are skeptical about institutions set up by the transatlantic powers in which they don't have a significant voice or any great confidence that the institutions will address their needs. Third, they have found regional agreements easier to reach, either because they don't require solving

some of the hardest problems on the table in multilateral negotiations—for example, agricultural subsidy issues at the WTO—or simply because reaching an agreement on a bilateral or regional basis is easier than trying to reach an agreement among the multitude of parties to any agreement at the multilateral level.[10]

In addition, with each successive financial crisis in the 1990s, constructing regional institutions that could serve as a buffer against the next potential global financial shock has become increasingly urgent among the developing nations. Hence, following the mother of all financial crises in 2008, it was hardly surprising that many parts of the world acted to refortify their defenses against the next crisis. In Asia, for instance, the Chiang Mai Initiative Multilateralism (CMIM) that emerged out of the ashes of the Asian financial crisis was recapitalized—a $90 billion central bank swap arrangement was transformed into a $120 billion arrangement that allows a member to draw on funding to address balance of payment problems and short-term lending difficulties. This program (CMIM) is a larger and more advanced regional financing vehicle designed to strengthen the region's capacity to withstand another financial crisis and to provide assistance to crisis-prone nations. Members include the nations of the Association of Southeast Asian Nations (ASEAN), along with China, Japan, and South Korea. Given their financial clout, China and Japan rank as the largest contributors to the funding facility, each contributing $38.4 billion, or one-third of the total.

Some have speculated that the CMIM is really an "Asian Monetary Fund" in disguise; that claim is a stretch at this juncture, but between the $120 billion at the disposal of members of the CMIM and the agreement by shareholders of the Asian

Development Bank to triple the bank's capital base to $165 billion, Asia has created a regional financial framework that could easily supplant the role of the International Monetary Fund in the future.

Along similar lines, a "Bank of the South" in South America was hatched in late 2007 and formally launched in 2009, although it had a total capitalization of just $7 billion. That figure amounts to peanuts in the face of a crisis, but the financial group consisting of Brazil, Argentina, Ecuador, Bolivia, Paraguay, Uruguay, and Venezuela could grow in strength and numbers in the years ahead. After years of seeking out the IMF, the new coalition indicates a region chafing to be more independent of U.S.-backed multilateral institutions.

Taking a further step, in early 2010, 32 nations of the Caribbean and Latin America agreed to create a new regional organization that excludes the United States and Canada. Provisionally called the Community of Latin American and Caribbean States, the new regional bloc, in time, could pose a direct challenge to the U.S.-influenced Organization of American States, the long-standing and most prominent regional organization. How effective this new organization will be in the future is still uncertain. Yet the very existence of a non-U.S. regional entity right in the western hemisphere highlights the push toward a less U.S.-centric world. As noted by Abraham Lowenthal, "As the self-confidence of Latin American and Caribbean nations has grown, support for Pan-American approaches to the region's problems have waned. The Organization of American States has often been ineffectual, and the Inter-American Democratic Charter, which is intended to strengthen democratic institutions in OAS member countries, has produced few meaningful results. The influence of the Inter-American Bank has also weakened in recent years"[11]

More regional and bilateral deals are in the offing. Between 1948 and the creation of the World Trade Organization in the late 1990s only 124 regional trade agreements were notified or announced. The last 15 years has seen 333 new notifications. As of late 2009, more than 457 regional trade agreements had been notified to the WTO, with 266 of these agreements in effect.[12] One of the largest regional trade pacts in the world came into effect on January 1, 2010. The ASEAN-China Free Trade Agreement launched a trade grouping that is the largest in the world based on population (1.9 billion), with a combined output of $6 trillion. Based on economic value, only the European Union and the North American Free Trade Agreement are larger. The ASEAN-Australia-New Zealand Free Trade Agreement also went into effect at the start of 2010, encompassing some 600 million people and a cumulative GDP of $2.8 trillion.

The shift toward regionalism in Asia is notable, since none of the countries placed much emphasis on regional integration at the beginning of 2000. For many Asian states, regionalism was subservient to maintaining strong commercial ties with the United States, the uber-consumption machine that helped drive Asia's export machines over most of the last few decades. Besides, across Asia, there still lingered a sense of unease about entering into a free trade deal with either Japan or China, because many smaller nations feared that any agreement would place them at a competitive disadvantage against Asia's largest economic players.

Yet with the Doha global trade talks floundering and with the U.S. consumer confronting a frugal future, many in Asia are searching locally for new drivers of growth. As of June 2009, according to the Asian Development Bank, some 109 free trade agreements (FTAs) include one or more Asian states, and over 100 more deals involving at least one Asian country are in the works. Offsetting weak U.S. demand means that more time and effort will be spent promoting regional ties. In addition, the ease with which China has navigated the global economic crisis and the nation's explosive growth has not been lost on many states across Asia, which now are more than ever before amenable to cutting a free trade deal with the mainland. China, meanwhile, regards the spread of regional integration, with Beijing at the forefront of the process, as a way to enhance its economic and diplomatic interests in the region. Even Japan's new government is keen to increase the nation's regional participation, fearing that too much dependence on a weak U.S. economy over the long term will mean bypassing the massive opportunities right next door in China. On a grand scale there is even talk in the region of creating an East Asian Free Trade Agreement (EAFTA) and a Comprehensive Economic Partnership in East Asia within the next 15 years.

Is all of this just talk? "Asian integration—with a common market, free trade and even a single currency as its ultimate goals—is no longer a glimmer in a few madmen's eyes," according to *The Economist*.[13] C. Fred Bergsten of the Peterson Institute of International Economics proclaimed the following: "I think we are headed inexorably and eventually toward an Asian bloc: an Asian bloc in certainly economic terms that will be the biggest part of the world economy, the most dynamic, and most reputably growing part of the world economy."[14] Adding credence to both statements is the fact that a region historically joined by maritime trade is now on the cusp of being linked by thousands of new miles of rail, road, and pipelines. Asia is going continental—or becoming more linked by land than sea.

A twenty-first–century version of the Silk Road could lie on the horizon given all the infrastructure construction spending expected over the next decade. Building roads is one of the strongest activities in Asia right now, with China's push into the country's interior and beyond leading the way. China and Southeast Asia—think Vietnam, Cambodia, and Myanmar— are increasingly linked by highways, which will in time help promote commerce and the movement of virtually everything— goods, people, and ideas. India is building roads in Afghanistan, while India, China, and Russia are keen on linking up with resource-rich Central Asia via pipelines and railways. In June 2009, China loaned Turkmenistan $4 billion to develop its largest gas field, along with a loan to Kazakhstan for $10 billion. In December 2009, a 1,139-mile gas pipeline was started in eastern Turkmenistan, and it will run through Uzbekistan and Kazakhstan into China.[15] A pipeline is under construction between Iran and Pakistan, while Russian Far East oil is being piped across thousands of miles to China.

In terms of rail, the Chinese are set to leapfrog the rest of the world. China dreams of linking Shanghai with London via rail by 2025, with the trip taking just days to complete. That is not to mention the 16,000 miles of high-speed railroads that China plans to build by the same year. Having already laid tracks up the Himalayas to Lhasa, Tibet, China aspires to connect with Nepal, Bangladesh, and even hopes to tie Singapore and Germany, and many points in between, into the Chinese rail network someday.[16]

Greater Asian cohesion in economics could spill over into other areas like security and bolster existing noneconomic regional groupings like the Shanghai Cooperation Organization (SCO), which was formed in 2001 to bring stability to the borders of China and the states of the former Soviet Union. Current members include China, Russia, Kazakhstan, Kyrgyzstan, Tajikistan, and Uzbekistan; Iran has applied for membership. The SCO activities encompass military cooperation, intelligence sharing, and counterterrorism functions, and it has not been shy about contesting the overall geostrategic aims of the United States in Central Asia. In 2005, the SCO formally called on Washington to set a timeline for withdrawing from military bases in Central Asia. Some U.S. experts believe that the SCO is intent on thwarting the energy ambitions of the United States in Central Asia, a hotly contested part of the world for future energy reserves.

Whatever the future shape and ambition of the SCO, the organization and proliferation of others like it represent a larger trend—the rush to regionalism—that will ultimately undermine or neutralize Western multilateral institutions. Regionalism is gaining currency in the Middle East and Africa and among alliances not bound by geography. Representatives of the BRIC nations—Brazil, Russia, India, and China—now meet on a frequent basis, and could, in time, emerge as a powerful global bloc unto itself, challenging the United States and Europe in various parts of the world, such as Africa, and over specific issues like global climate change.

The more these various alliances proliferate without U.S. involvement, the more America looks isolated, its power increasingly diminished by regional blocs and partnerships that possess greater resources than the United States and U.S.-backed multilateral institutions. For instance, the total international reserves of just the BRICs—$3.3 trillion at the end of 2009—were more than ten times larger than the usable reserves of the IMF. The rush to regionalism not only threatens to undermine multilateralism, a key foundation of globalization, but the proliferation of bilateral and regional preferential agreements could also create a global trading system that resembles a "bowl of spaghetti" or "bowl of noodles," in the case of Asia. Popularized by international economist Jagdish Bhagwati, the end result of all the existing and pending trade agreements could be a patchwork of overlapping and competing trade arrangements, involving many different nations and different parts of the world, that looks so unwieldy as to resemble a "spaghetti bowl."[17] The upshot would be a fragmented global trading system that impedes the free flow of goods, services, and capital, and further accelerates the retreat of globalization.

THE FUTURE KNOCKS—AND BRAZIL FINALLY ENTERS

For much of its history, the United States has been the only indigenous economic superpower in the western hemisphere. For the past century, the vast territory that stretches from the Arctic Ocean southward to Antarctica has long been the uncontested domain of the United States, a privilege often taken for granted. The Cuban missile crisis, to be sure, represented a strategic threat, but the threat quickly passed. More recently, the outspoken anti-American president of Venezuela, Hugo Chavez, has been more of a regional annoyance than a geostrategic threat.

The future, however, is bound to be different. As part of the unfolding multipolar world, the United States will need to accommodate an emerging global economic power right in its own backyard. Brazil—no stranger to financial crises and the ultimate perennial country of the future—has arrived, and in a significant way.

No single fact better demonstrates Brazil's different circumstances than the fact that the nation is now lending money to the IMF—in June 2009, the nation agreed to buy $10 billion of its bonds. For years the IMF had doled out capital to Brazil. Or the fact that Brazil has sought to discourage capital inflows over the past year; in December 2009, the country imposed a

2 percent tax on capital inflows in an attempt to slow the torrid pace of foreign capital wanting to buy Brazilian assets. In the past, Brazil has had to periodically travel around the world, cap in hand, begging for capital. In early 2010, the debt of Rio de Janeiro was rated as investment grade by Standard & Poor's, the first Brazilian state to receive such a ranking. Meanwhile, emblematic of the country's new global heft, Brazil took part, along with just a handful of other nations (the United States, China, India, and South Africa) in hammering out the final agreement that emerged from the Copenhagen climate summit in late 2009. Brazil has also recently emerged as one of the world's largest aid donors to poor nations. And finally, while the Brazilian economy was not spared from the global recession of 2008, the economy has bounced back far sooner and stronger than anyone would have imagined.

For one of the first times in history, the United States will have to get used to living in the same neighborhood with an economically vibrant emerging power that has sufficient credibility to contest U.S. regional and global interests. Whether the U.S.-Brazilian bilateral relationship will be one of conflict or cooperation remains to be seen.

Less uncertain is the fact that in less than two decades, the economic reforms of then president Fernando Henrique Cardoso, and continuing with his successor, Luiz Inácio Lula da Silva, have transformed Brazil's debt-laden and hyperinflation-prone economy into one of the most dynamic in the world. Cardoso put Brazil's crisis-prone economy on sounder footing during the 1990s by allowing the currency—the real—to float freely, by granting autonomy to the nation's central bank, and by privatizing a number of state-owned enterprises in such sectors as mining, aviation, telecommunications, and banking. These and other policies, coupled with greater political stability, helped tame inflation, rein in debt, and encouraged rising levels of foreign direct investment.

When Lula assumed the presidency in October 2002, many foreign investors feared that his left-leaning credentials would result in the rolling back of his predecessor's reforms in favor of more antimarket and anti-American policies. Reflecting these worries, some commentators placed Mr. Lula in the same company as Fidel Castro and Hugo Chavez, left-wing, anticapitalist leaders biased toward populist economic policies. Reflecting these fears, in the run up to the general elections in 2002, Brazil's main stock market index, the Bovespa, sagged by 43 percent in local terms.

Lula, however, has proven to be far more adept at running a large economy than many leaders in the developed nations. His economic record speaks for itself. The Bovespa has been among the best-performing stock markets in the world, posting annualized returns of nearly 30 percent from 2003 to early 2010 (based on local currency terms). Based in U.S. dollars, Brazil's stock market has yielded average annual returns in excess of 42 percent during the same period. Under Lula, the market capitalization of the Bovespa increased more than tenfold.

Despite investor concerns about Lula's background, the real has soared against the U.S. dollar over the past few years. Among the world's 16 primary currencies, the real was the best performing currency against the dollar between 2003 and early 2010, appreciating roughly 100 percent against the greenback. Average annual economic growth of 3.4 percent since 2003 has been accompanied by a noticeable decline in inflation, falling from 8.4 percent at the end of 2002 to 4.8 percent at the end of 2009.

Other impressive figures include the following: over the past three years, foreign direct investment inflows have averaged $35 billion versus an annual average of roughly $24 billion over 1995–2002. Exports totaled $60 billion in 2002 but topped

$153 billion last year, a 155 percent cumulative increase. International reserves, meanwhile, soared 546 percent between 2002 ($38 billion) and 2009 ($244 billion). Finally, just before Lula entered office, Brazil's external debt as a percentage of GDP was close to a record high of 48.7 percent. Currently, however, the nation's external debt is just 10 percent. Credit rating agencies have executed a near U-turn. Since Lula assumed power, Moody's has increased its ratings on Brazil's debt five notches, while the S&P has increased its ratings four notches, and Fitch by five. All three credit-rating agencies rank Brazil's debt as investment grade. By way of comparison, only Peru and Mexico in Latin America have achieved the same status.

Supporting the favorable credit backdrop of Brazil is the fact that the nation is currently one of the world's largest exporters of agricultural products, including chicken, orange juice, green coffee, sugar, ethanol, tobacco, soya, maize, and pork. Like the United States, Brazil is an agricultural powerhouse and has emerged, in the past few years, as a global leader in biofuel use. The nation is also self-sufficient in oil and poised to emerge as a significant oil producer with the most recent gigantic offshore oil find described as a "present from God" by President Lula.[18] The Tupi deepwater oil field contains an estimated 5 to 8 billion barrels of light crude, and the discovery could catapult Brazil into the ranks of the world's leading oil exporters later in this decade. Petrobras, Brazil's state-owned oil giant, ranked as the fourth largest oil company in the world at the end of 2009 based on oil reserves. Its 11.2 billion barrels are greater than China's Sinopec and on par with Chevron and Total of France. Other Brazilian global corporate giants include Vale, the world's fourth largest mining company; Embraer, a midrange passenger jet manufacturer whose planes are quite popular in the United States; and AmBev, one of the largest brewers in the world.

In terms of size and scale, Brazil is now the second largest economy in the western hemisphere, and based on some estimates, Brazil's economy could become one of the largest in the world by the middle of this century, trailing only the United States, China, India, and Japan.[19] As icing on the cake, Brazil will play host to the 2014 World Cup Games and will be on full global display in 2016, when it hosts the Summer Olympics.

Ever more confident of itself, Brazilian leadership has not been shy about leveraging its gains on the global stage, to the consternation of the United States. The emergent Latin American powerhouse, for instance, has become increasingly involved with the intricacies of diplomacy in the Middle East, independent of the United States. In a span of a few weeks in late 2009, President Lula welcomed Israel's president Shimon Peres and then Mahmoud Abbas, president of the Palestinian Authority, for talks on the Middle East process. Any Brazilian input that helps bring peace and stability to Israel and the Palestinians would certainly be welcomed by the United States. Yet that potential gain has been undercut, to a degree, by Brazil's hesitation to support tough economic sanctions against Iran. Brazil rankled many in Washington when the Lula administration congratulated Mahmoud Ahmadinejad on his election "victory," and further roiled the waters by inviting the Iranian president to Brazil for talks on energy security. At the time the United States was cobbling together a global coalition to support sanctions against Iran, Mr. Lula welcomed Iran's leader to Brazil with open hugs and smiles for the world cameras. The cuddly moment no doubt infuriated the United States, as did the Turkish-Brazilian deal brokered with Iran in May 2010. That deal nearly undercut U.S. efforts at the United Nations to bring sanctions against Iran and was explicitly criticized by the United States and many other states.

It remains to be seen whether or not Turkey and Brazil can bring Tehran into the international fold. The odds of this happening are slim. Yet Brazil's proactive brokering with Iran does underscore the new willingness of Brazil, and other emerging powers like Turkey, to become involved in high-power global issues that used to be the exclusive domain of the United States and a handful of other power brokers. The new initiatives by the emerging powers, according to Soli Ozel of Istanbul's Bilgi University, were "a sign of the times, that the world is not going to take the diktats of the powers that have run it for the last two to three hundred years."[20] In the end, Washington would do well to come to recognize that Brazil's emergence on the global stage could create serious challenges to U.S. strategic interests.

As part of the new multipolar world, the United States will not only have to become more adept in dealing with China, Russia, India, and key Middle East oil producers, but it will also have to learn to live with a more assertive neighbor, whose global interests extend beyond Iran. For instance, bilateral trade between Brazil and China has soared over the past decade, rising from $2.3 billion in 2000 to roughly $36 billion in 2009, with the bulk of Brazil's ties with China revolving around energy and agriculture. Reflecting the shifting tides of global commerce, China supplanted the United States as Brazil's largest trading partner last year. Financial bilateral ties have also increased lately. For instance, the China Development Bank has extended a $10 billion loan to state-owned oil giant Petrobras as a down payment on future oil shipments. In addition, and the clearest sign yet of deepening Brazilian-Sino commercial relations, China reportedly invested more than $20 billion in Brazil in the first six months of 2010, an amount some 10 times more than all of China's previous investment in the South American giant. Given the surge in FDI in the first half of the year, China is positioned to emerge as Brazil's largest foreign investor in 2010, underscoring the growing ties between the two emerging giants.[21]

Meanwhile, Brazil's own influence in Africa continues to grow. Brazilian investment and foreign aid in Africa have soared as old cultural and linguistic ties between the Portuguese-speaking giant and such nations as Angola and Mozambique have helped grease the wheels of commerce. Two-way trade has soared. In the global race to secure access to Africa's riches, Brazil has joined the fray—underscoring the fact that it is not just Western firms and companies from China and India competing in various markets of the continent.

Closer to home, Brazil is the pivotal member of Mercosur, the large South American free trade group that has often bumped heads with the United States over trade, investment, and a host of other regional issues. Mercosur, for instance, helped kill U.S. ambitions for a Free Trade Agreement of the Americas first proposed by the administration of President George W. Bush. The United States will need Brazil's support if a western hemisphere–wide free trade agreement is going to be forged. Other top challenges—stamping out Latin America's drug trade, boosting regional per capita incomes, promoting a greener regional economy—all will require the active participation of Brazil.

Challenges are already being issued. In April 2010, Brazil threatened up to $830 million in sanctions over U.S. subsidies to cotton growers, following a WTO ruling that U.S. subsidies violated global trade rules. In a novel twist, Brazil threatened to stop charging technology fees for seeds developed by U.S. biotech firms. To the *New York Times*, Robert Z. Lawrence, a professor at the Harvard Kennedy School, remarked, "Traditionally, retaliation in trade has been the preserve of the largest developed countries, which have market power. But this mechanism—suspending intellectual property protection—gives smaller, developing countries a way to enforce their rights under trade rules."[22] The U.S. avoided sanctions with last-minute concessions, but the long-simmering impasse shows Brazil's new might in the hemisphere.

In the end, America's overseas strategic interests have long lain to the east or to the west, leaving the south, or the rest of the western hemisphere, to languish. America's Latin neighbors have long felt neglected by the United States because they lacked the economic importance and global political influence to really matter to Washington. The emergence of Brazil, however, changes the equation. While things are far from perfect in South America's largest country, Brazil is too big to ignore—both economically and politically.

CHINA: COY, CONFLICTED, AND CENTER STAGE

By virtually all accounts, China had a "good crisis." That is, it emerged stronger than any other country in the world from the global recession of 2008. While 2009 was a nightmare worldwide, China achieved a series of milestones. The nation surpassed Germany to become the world's largest exporter of merchandise goods. Thanks to a 50 percent plus jump in automobile sales, China eclipsed the United States as the world's largest car market. PetroChina overtook Exxon Mobil to become the world's largest listed energy group based on market capitalization. Pulling ahead of the United States and a handful of European nations on the clean energy front, China emerged as the world's largest producer of wind turbines and solar panels, and as a sign of the times, eclipsed the United States as the world's number one energy consumer. By early 2010, the Chinese economy was growing at a 12 percent clip, a torrid pace well above the rest of the world and one that unequivocally proclaimed that China was emerging no longer. It had arrived.

The irony is that China is not entirely comfortable sitting at the pinnacle of power. It has not been shy about criticizing the United States for its part in triggering the global recession, going so far as to broach the topic of replacing the U.S. dollar as the world's reserve currency. But in terms of proactive measures of its own, China has been coy about stepping out onto the global stage. It almost feels as if China's moment has arrived too early—for Beijing and the world at large. Beijing, in many cases, would still rather follow than lead.

While China does not want to squander the opportunity to increase its standing in the world, it is reluctant to go against Deng Xiaoping's famous directive: "Observe developments soberly, deal with changes patiently and confidently; maintain our position, meet challenges calmly, hide our capabilities and bide our time, remain free of ambition, and never claim leadership."

Observe, hide, and bide your time—all of that was possible for China a decade ago, when the global economy lived off the profligacy of the U.S. consumer. The world accepted the common refrain from Beijing that China, despite decades of near 10 percent annual growth, was still developing, was poor, and was incapable of leading the world given its own massive internal domestic challenges. Not mincing worlds, China's Premier Wen Jiabao bluntly stated in March 2007, "China's economic growth is unsteady, unbalanced, uncoordinated and unsustainable."

The statement surprised many in the West who even before the financial crisis had dubbed this century the "Chinese century," predicting that the United States is destined to fade into the shadows of the emerging Asian power. Yet notwithstanding the fact that China's economy hardly missed a beat during the crisis, Wen's statement contains a great deal of truth.

Despite its much reported global economic might, China's per capita income—$3,180 in 2008—remains a fraction of that in the United States and Europe. Millions of people (over 200 million in 2005) still live on less than $1.25 a day in China. The mainland's energy and food supplies are woefully insufficient for a population that is rapidly urbanizing. With only 8 percent of the world's cultivated land, China must sustain nearly one-quarter of the world's population. Decades of pell-mell growth has decimated China's environment—"over the last forty years almost half of China's forests have been destroyed, so that it now enjoys one of the sparsest covers in the world," notes Martin Jacques.[23]

China is a large producer of oil, but the country has been a net oil importer since 1993 and now depends on imports for almost half its oil needs. More problematic is China's lack of clean water; this poses a glaring challenge that could ultimately halt or slow the nation's economic rise. According to government figures, roughly two-thirds of China's approximately 660 cities have less water than they need, and 110 of them suffer severe shortages. And what water is available is not fit for human consumption—according to the Chinese government, the aquifers in 90 percent of China's cities are polluted, 30 percent of its river water is unfit for agriculture or industry, and roughly 700 million of its people drink water contaminated with animal and human waste. Though little discussed in the West, the lack of clean water and the deteriorating environment in China is becoming a social and political lightning rod, with the number of pollution-related protests have risen steadily over the past decade.

Demographics represent another herculean challenge. In part due to its longtime one-child policy, China will grow old before it grows rich, placing tremendous pressure on the government to help care for China's elderly. By 2050, estimates project that 10 people of working age will have to support up to seven dependents (young and senior), compared with fewer than four today. Tackling widening income inequalities is another urgent task for its Communist government. According to a recent policy paper for the World Bank, using 2004 data sets, "the urban to rural household per capita income ratio was 3.2 times, and coastal to inland GDP per capita ratio was 2.4 times, which were among the highest in the world."[24]

Making economic sense of China is complicated by the government's pervasive influence in the economy. *The Economist* remarked, "The government and the Communist Party are intimately entwined with the managers of China's financial institutions. Working out who is really in charge is almost impossible. . . . Big credit decisions in China are not advanced by any one bank or any one banker. Credit is infused and withdrawn by central diktat. That process has extraordinary appeal to state planners but is horribly inefficient for individual institutions."[25] An accompanying problem is institutional corruption. In a March 31, 2010, article, *The Economist* sounded another alarm: "The Chinese emphasis on personal connections (guanxi) makes it hard to distinguish between business as usual and corruption. And the weakness of the legal system means that companies operate in a confusing half-light. Transparency International's most recent Corruption Perceptions Index ranks China 79th out of 180 countries."[26]

Above all else, China's growth remains "unbalanced" today, overly dependent on investment and exports versus personal consumption. Consumption levels have soared over the past decade as China's middle class has grown and the nation's higher-income workers have purchased cars, cell phones, computers, and other Western goods largely out of reach to most Chinese consumers just a few years ago. Consumption is taking hold in China, yet is not anywhere near becoming a driver of the economy. Personal consumption expenditures amounted to a mere 35 percent of total output in 2009, one of the lowest percentages in Asia. The comparable figure in the United States is 70 percent. This disparity, along with the other figures just mentioned, does make China a "developing nation," a self-proclaimed label the world finds harder and harder to believe.

All these challenges threaten the underlying strategic goal of China—to create a harmonious society, one economically and politically in unison. This is paramount to Beijing's chief objective—internal stability. Kishore Mahbubani states:

> The Chinese mind has always focused on developing Chinese civilization, not developing global civilization. China today is willing to be a responsible stakeholder in the global order, but it shows little interest in leading the creation of a new global order. The Chinese leaders are acutely aware that it will take China several more decades before it eliminates its rural poverty. Holding China together as a country and as a political entity will be a big enough challenge in this period of rapid change and development. Given these overwhelming domestic concerns, the Chinese leaders have little appetite to lead the world."[27]

In other words, throwing a financial lifeline to the struggling global economy in general or to a near-bankrupt nation like Greece in particular, who approached China early in 2010 for capital, matters less to China than maintaining internal cohesion. Because of its overriding domestic interests, the nation wants to emerge slowly and cautiously on the global stage, remaining more focused on doing what is right for China than what is right for the world.

This paramount factor explains China's resistance, notwithstanding mounting pressure from the United States and G-20, to untether its currency and allow the renminbi to float freely against the U.S. dollar and other currencies, a policy shift that would presumably allow the United States and the world to sell more goods and services to China. Yet even though the government has given in a little on the currency front, Beijing is likely to opt for a closed capital account over the medium term. This will continue to frustrate the United States but unlikely sway Beijing, since the U.S.-instigated global financial crisis only confirmed to China's leadership that a bunkered capital account is the best insurance against the next financial crisis.

Besides the currency, China has been less than cooperative with the United States and Europe in crafting global climate change initiatives, has shown its ambivalence about helping the United States halt the nuclear ambitions of North Korea and Iran, and has done little to champion the Doha trading round, despite the fact that China is one of the largest exporters in the world and a key beneficiary of an open and thriving global trading system. "Beijing has no desire to be the world's deputy sheriff," states *Financial Times* columnist David Pilling, who adds, "Beijing prefers to keep a low profile and get on with the hard slog of building an industrial economy."[28]

Beyond multilateral matters, however, China has not been afraid to raise its profile on the global stage lately. Assisted and financially backed by the government, Chinese energy companies have been very active investors in Africa, Latin America, the Middle East, and even in such hot spots as Iran and Afghanistan. China's primary energy consumption soared by 10 percent a year during 2000–2005, and China's energy consumption is expected to be the equivalent of 87 percent of today's world consumption by 2030. Based on these current consumption patterns, energy security is a top concern of Beijing's.[29] China's bid to secure foreign sources of energy and food is the

most visible manifestation of its becoming more actively engaged in the world economy. But note that this activism is designed to benefit China.

The nation has also concluded currency-swap agreements
with such nations as Indonesia, Argentina, and South Korea,
the first tentative steps toward making the renminbi an alternative to the U.S. dollar. As part of this goal, the renminbi has become the official trading currency between Southeast Asia and
two neighboring Chinese provinces. Meanwhile, Beijing is rac-
ing to set the global standards in such strategic sectors as electric
cars, solar energy, and a host of other green technologies. The
nation also hopes to have a much larger say in creating the next
generation of Internet standards.

In terms of diplomacy, China has also been more active over
the past few years. Beijing's "soft power"—global influence at-
tained through diplomatic, economic, cultural, and other non-
coercive means—has expanded along with China's rising global
preeminence.[30] Having weathered the global crisis better than
most, China's global standing has soared in many parts of the
world. China's massive internal market, large pool of available
capital, and no-strings-attached foreign aid have attracted many
nations to China's diplomatic efforts in the past years. China's
so-called charm offensive or checkbook diplomacy has won Beijing plenty of new allies, opening up new markets for Chinese
companies and providing access to new supplies of raw materials. Aid for trade lies at the core of many diplomatic programs
of China, as Beijing has doled out billions to Venezuela, Angola,
Sudan, Iran, and a host of other nations where U.S. diplomatic
goals are either different or more nuanced than those pursued
by China.

Against this backdrop, some American observers have
warned that China's use of "soft power" represents a grand long-

term strategy to advance China's economic and security interests at the expense of the United States. Feeling triumphant relative to the battle-scared United States, China is poised to throw its weight around and carve out spheres of influence in geostrategic parts of the world long under the control of the United States and Europe; so goes this line of thinking. Others in the United States and Europe are not as worried—at least not yet—about China's grand diplomatic designs. Their argument is that China's "soft power" is limited in scope and designed to gain markets and raw materials to support growth at home, not underpin China's expansion abroad. And besides, according to the less threatening narrative regarding China, some nations in Africa and South America have grown increasingly wary and concerned about the exploding Chinese presence in their home country, creating somewhat of a backlash against China's ever expanding influence in trade and investment.

Friend or foe? Partner or competitor? Rich or poor? Outward or insular? Plenty of contradictions mark the rise of China in the global economy. In a sense, the global financial crisis has spawned an identity crisis in China. While more assertive on the global stage and sensing a historic opportunity to buttress its global standing via the West, Beijing does not want to overplay its hand. It is uncomfortable with the notion that as one of the world's most powerful economies, China must lend a more forceful hand in solving the world's problems. China wants to be a global power but on its own terms and timetable. Hence, China's leaders wish to stay focused on more pressing internal challenges and remain resistant to supporting a global economic system they deem inferior and one they did not have any hand in creating. In the end, the financial crisis accelerated the rise of China and the rush toward a more multipolar world—a dynamic that has made both Beijing and the rest of the world nervous.

China's one foot in, one foot out of the global economy, juxtaposed against the diminished credibility of the United States, leaves the world in a precarious position. As noted by author Martin Jacques, "At the heart of the present global financial crisis lies the inability of the United States to continue to be the backbone of the international financial system; on the other hand, China is not yet neither able nor willing to assume that role. This is what makes the present global crisis so grave and potentially protracted, in a manner analogous to the 1930s when Britain could no longer sustain its premier financial position and the United States was not yet in position to take over from it."[31]

In the end, a multipolar world poses significant challenges for the United States. Working within the G-20, preventing the pendulum from swinging too far toward state capitalism, promoting multilateralism in the face of rising regionalism, dealing with a more assertive Brazil in its backyard, and accommodating a more confident yet conflicted China are new challenges before the country.

The United States will have to grow accustomed to sharing center stage with many other aspiring players. This shift will represent a significant challenge to a nation that has long had outsized influence on the rest of the world. Nor will the transition be easy for the rest of world. History shows that emerging multipolar systems have been more unstable than a bipolar or unipolar one. The rise of new powers is nearly always disruptive to economic harmony.

Making all of the above even more daunting for the United States is the fact that in the messy multipolar world before us, one filled with new challenges and new competitors, America effectively enters this new era broke and financially crippled. The financial health of the United States has never been as precarious as it is today—the topic of the next chapter.

CHAPTER

5

A Handicapped Giant:
Causes and Consequences

We might hope to see the finances of the union as clear and intelligible as a merchant's books, so that every member of Congress and every man of any mind in the union should be able to comprehend them, to investigate abuses, and consequently to control them.

> —PRESIDENT THOMAS JEFFERSON TO TREASURY
> SECRETARY ALBERT GALLATIN, 1802[1]

How long can the world's biggest borrower remain the world's biggest power?

> —LARRY SUMMERS, PRESIDENT OBAMA'S CHIEF
> ECONOMIC ADVISOR[2]

Contrary to Jefferson's hopes, America's finances are not terribly "clear and intelligible" and have become harder to "comprehend" and to "control." The cost of two wars and the tab associated with one of the largest financial crises in U.S. history, juxtaposed against soaring entitlement programs, threaten to turn the United States into a financial cripple. At a minimum, America's deteriorating financial health will handicap its future ability to drive global growth and shape the global economic agenda, as well as compromise its geostrategic influence around the world. America's dependence on foreign capital has never been greater, giving capital-rich nations like China and those in the Middle East more financial leverage over the United States. All the above beg the question posed by Mr. Summers: just how long can the world's largest debtor nation remain the world's top power?

The United States entered the new millennium in respectable financial shape. The country enjoyed a budget surplus in 2000, while the ratio of government debt (held by the public) was quite manageable. Government outlays were below the historic average in 2000. Total revenues were at an all-time high. And Japan, America's longtime ally in Asia, was the largest foreign holder of U.S. Treasuries.

Ten years on, America's financial landscape looks radically different. Before explaining the factors that wrought financial havoc on the United States, let's take a brief look at some of the key trends that portray a nation living dangerously beyond its means.

Taking on debt is nothing new to Washington. Indeed, the federal government's total debt has increased every year since 1956. Over the past decade, however, the level of debt has more than doubled, rising from $5.6 trillion in 2000 to $12.9 trillion in the first quarter of 2010. The latter number includes debt held by the public and debt held in government accounts.[3]

The massive accumulation of debt reflects near constant federal budget deficits—since the 1970s, the United States has posted deficits in every year but four. Thanks to two tax increases over the 1990s, reduced military spending, and strong federal revenues, the United States posted a budget surplus for four straight years, starting in 1998.

In 2000, the debt-to-GDP ratio stood at 34.7 percent. In 2008 (precrisis), the debt-to-GDP ratio was 40.2 percent, above the 40-year average of 36 percent. The ratio is expected to climb to over 61 percent in 2010, which would be the highest level since 1952, in the midst of the Korean War.

In fiscal year 2009, the United States posted its first trillion-dollar deficit, with the fiscal shortfall totaling $1.4 trillion. That was equal to 9.9 percent of GDP, one of the highest ever in peace time. The deficit topped $1 trillion again in the first nine months of fiscal year 2010 and is expected to tally another $1.3 trillion for the fiscal year. Contributing to the soaring deficits have been surging government outlays, which rose to nearly 25 percent of GDP in fiscal year 2009 versus a historic annual average of 20.5 percent. Mandatory programs—including Social Security, Medicare, Medicaid, and other entitlement programs—account for a larger and larger share of the federal budget. Total mandatory spending consumed 38 percent of spending in 1970, but over 60 percent in 2009, when outlays topped $2 trillion for the first time.

Interest owed on America's accumulating debt has become quite burdensome as well, totaling nearly $190 billion in fiscal year 2009. More ominous, the share of public debt owned by foreigners has risen from 7 percent in 1970 to 18 percent in 1990 to nearly 48 percent today. When so much money is held by foreign countries, the debtor becomes more vulnerable to the decisions of other, more autocratic governments. A useful comparison is America's complacent view of importing more and more oil—until OPEC jacked up the price by 70 percent in 1973. That burden has only mounted higher in the 40 years since then.

Regarding America's other deficit, the current account deficit, this gap exceeded 6 percent of GDP in 2006, but narrowed to about 2.6 percent of GDP in 2009. Since 1980, the United States has posted a current account surplus in just three years—the last time was 1991. America's net international investment position is now roughly $2.7 trillion in the red, a figure that is equivalent to roughly 20 percent of the country's total output. The figure represents the difference between foreign-owned assets in the United States versus U.S.-owned assets overseas. As discussed in Chapter 2, that represents a massive financial IOU to the rest of the world.

Because of rising public sector spending and the attendant jump in deficits and debt, the U.S. Congress has had to raise the federal debt ceiling eight times in the first decade of this century. Despite that, Uncle Sam still enjoys a triple-A credit rating—the best there is and one that allows the United States to borrow capital on favorable terms. America's credit rating has remained unchanged since 1917, but its pristine track record is on shakier ground today. In the past, rarely has the subject even been broached; it was a given that the world's sole military and economic superpower would remain one of the best financial bets in the world. But after racking up a massive budget deficit in 2009 and as the fear of sovereign defaults spread across Europe in early 2010, Moody's did offer the following caution: "Unless further measures are taken to reduce the budget deficit further or the economy rebounds more vigorously than expected, the federal financial picture as presented in the projections for the next decade will at some point put pressure on the Aaa government bond rating."[4]

In China, meanwhile, America's credit rating has already been downgraded—a disconcerting fact considering that the mainland is the largest holder of U.S. Treasuries. In mid-2010, Beijing-based Dagong Global Credit Rating Co. rated U.S. sovereign debt as AA with a negative outlook, a move that did not garner much international attention, but one that could be a harbinger of the future if the United States does not get its financial house in order.

The world's largest creditor nation in 1980, the United States is now the world's largest debtor, piling on more debt in the first decade of the twenty-first century than in any other period of the postwar era. "If the federal government was a private corporation," according to David Walker, former U.S. comptroller general, "its stock would plummet and shareholders would bring in new management and directors."[5] The country has certainly seen new management with the Democrats sweeping into power in the 2008 elections. But neither Democrats nor Republicans have had the courage to tackle the urgent and overwhelming financial challenges before the United States.

AMERICA'S "PERFECT FINANCIAL STORM"

How did we get here? What caused America's finances to implode during the first decade of this century?

The United States looks more and more like a financial cripple owing to the untimely convergence of two wars, the financial crisis of 2008, and soaring entitlement liabilities. The bill from each one of these factors, according to various estimates, is at least $1 trillion—and counting. The United States has been engaged in warfare for nearly a decade now, with no end in sight as America's winding down of operations in Iraq have been counterbalanced by its deepening involvement in Afghanistan. The expense of cleaning up the financial crisis is harder to quantify, but one estimate puts the cleanup effort at $2 trillion.[6] Meanwhile, public sector outlays for mandatory entitlements, with Social Security and Medicare at the core, already top $2 trillion a year and are only going to rise as more baby boomers retire and draw on Social Security and health-care benefits.[7]

In short, as the second decade of this century begins, America confronts a "perfect financial storm," one that has saddled massive deficits and debt on the world's last economic superpower.

The larger the deficits, the more the government needs to borrow from the public. Additional borrowing, in turn, increases the total amount of federal debt. Not surprisingly as the deficits have exploded over 2009 and 2010, so has America's IOUs. While the Democrats argue that most of the debt in the past decade was piled up during the untrammeled spending of the second Bush administration, the current Democrat-controlled White House and Congress have not shown much backbone when it comes to reducing the deficit. The best that has been mustered is a bipartisan commission to study ways to cut the deficit, but everyone knows how much power a commission possesses—not much. The two variables—deficits and debt—are toxic and have gradually eroded America's global standing. No superpower has ever persevered for long as the world's largest debtor nation, and the United States will prove to be no exception.

THE COST OF THE WAR

Foreign entanglements are never cheap, and the U.S. military forays into Iraq and Afghanistan are no different. Before delving into the specifics, I want to make clear at the outset that I am not interested in arguing whether or not the wars fought by America in the past decade are right or wrong, justified or unjustified. Rather, the key point here is that wars are expensive and if long lasting and not paid for properly (as in the case of the United States), they can ultimately drain the financial strength of any nation.

As background, U.S. annual defense outlays averaged roughly $90 billion over the 1970s but surged to an annual average of $232 billion in the 1980s thanks largely to the aggressive military build-out under the Reagan administration. When the Cold War ended, the United States reaped a "peace dividend," or a slower pace of military spending relative to the prior decade. Defense outlays averaged $285 billion over the 1990s but subsequently soared in the post 9/11 world.[8]

Operation Iraqi Freedom, the Global War on Terror, and the expanding war in Afghanistan—these foreign endeavors, in addition to other military expenses like monies spent on missile defense systems, research and development, and other programs, helped raise military outlays to an annual average of $463.8 billion in the first decade of this century. During that period the Pentagon's annual budget was larger than the total output of most countries. The cost of waging war in Iraq and Afghanistan rose from roughly $20 billion in 2001 to more than $200 billion by the end of the decade, a surge in spending, according to the National Priorities Project, that puts the cumulative cost of both wars in the neighborhood of $1 trillion.[9] That price tag is in line with numbers from the Congressional Budget Office (CBO).[10] According to the Congressional Research Service, the costs of post-September 11 military operations in Afghanistan, Iraq, and elsewhere totaled roughly $1.1 trillion through fiscal year 2010, making current operations among the most expensive in U.S. history.[11] Currently, the cost of waging war in Iraq and Afghanistan is running at roughly $11 billion a month. As for America's involvement in Afghanistan, putting one U.S. GI in action in Afghanistan costs $1 million a year.[12] With the additional 30,000 troops ordered by President Obama, adding to the force of 68,000, the projected cost of the war is $100 billion per year.

That's a sizable price tag to stabilize a regime widely regarded as corrupt and to wage war in a country that has for centuries successfully repelled foreign powers.

Slice it any way you like, war is costly—even for an economy as large as that of the United States. A $1 trillion price tag is not insignificant, although that figure, based on the research of Joseph E. Stiglitz and Linda J. Bilmes, is not remotely close to the true cost of the wars America has waged this century. Coauthors of *The Three Trillion Dollar War: The True Cost of the Iraq Conflict*, Stiglitz and Bilmes believe that the price of war will ultimately triple the current figures being used by the U.S. government and other independent sources. To arrive at their figures, the authors not only tallied the up-front costs of the wars, reflected in the CBO figures, but also added in other costs like refurbishing the rundown stock of U.S. military equipment and materials, the money spent on the conflict that could have been spent elsewhere, and the future costs of taking care of wounded veterans.

Addressing the first Gulf War in the early 1990s, which was paid for by our allies, and lasted less than two months and cost the lives of 148 soldiers, the authors note, "It seems the Gulf War was almost free. But that fails to take into account the large number of veterans suffering from some form of disability from the war, so that today—more than sixteen years later—the United States still spends over $4.3 billion *each year* paying compensation, pension, and disability benefits to more than 200,000 veterans of the Gulf War.[13] According to Stiglitz and Bilmes, "Overall, in 2005 the United States was paying $34.5 billion in annual disability entitlement pay to veterans from previous wars, including 211,729 from the first Gulf War, 916,220 from Vietnam, 161,512 from Korea, 356,190 from World War II, and 3 from World War I."[14]

Taking care of our veterans, in other words, will continue to be an expense item long after the war's end. "For every U.S. serviceman or woman killed in Iraq, fifteen more have been wounded, injured, or have contracted an illness serious enough to require medical evacuation. More than 350,000 U.S. veterans from the two wars have sought medical treatment . . . The cost of providing medical care and disability benefits may eventually exceed even the cost of combat operations," Stiglitz and Bilmes noted in a provocative article in *Harper's* in early 2009.[15] To this point, mental health disorders were the greatest single cause of hospitalization among U.S. troops in 2009. For the year, there were 17,538 hospitalizations for mental health issues in the military versus 11,156 hospitalizations for injuries related to combat.[16] Against this backdrop, it is hardly surprising that health-care costs in the military have soared over the past decade, with costs expected to top $50 billion in 2011 against a cost of $19 billion in 2001.[17]

Stiglitz and Bilmes also assessed the cost of war to society and the broader economy. Rising divorce rates among military families, the added stress on America's Department of Veterans Affairs health-care system, productivity losses associated with U.S. workers fulfilling their duty as reservists or National Guardsmen—these factors and others like them are additional costs that come with waging war.

Another expense consists of the interest payments on the money the United States borrowed to fight in the Middle East. Rather than raise taxes to pay for military operations, America enjoyed two tax cuts last decade and simply borrowed the funds to wage war. The nation enjoyed guns and butter by eschewing a war-related tax hike—the traditional means of paying for conflict. One of the great ironies of the U.S.-led war in Iraq is that while many nations opposed the U.S. invasion, they still helped pay for it by lending billions of dollars to Uncle Sam.

Finally, the opportunity costs associated with war need to be factored into the equation—the billions spent on war over the past decade could have gone a long way toward upgrading

America's crumbling bridges, fragile rail system, congested highways, and overcrowded and aging airports. After the alarming collapse of a bridge in Minneapolis in 2007, experts said the tab required to repair the nation's bridges could approach $190 billion. As for the railroads, compare the $8 billion the Obama administration allocated as part of its economic stimulus package to the $50 billion China spent on its high-speed rail system in 2009 alone. To keep up, America needs to upgrade a communications network that in many places is 50 years old.

Thus far, America's military engagement in Iraq and Afghanistan has been among the most expensive in U.S. history. Only the cost of World War II—about $5 trillion adjusted in 2007 dollars—has been greater.[18] In the end, very few Americans ever imagined that in the aftermath of 9/11, the United States would embark on one of the costliest military campaigns in history. By the same token, as U.S. financial institutions wobbled during 2007 and 2008, no one had a clue of the pending financial disaster about to slam the United States and the cost of cleaning up the mess.

THE COST OF THE FINANCIAL CRISIS

There is never a good time for a financial crisis, but especially not when a country is waging a two-front war in the Middle East and a sizable chunk of its population is about to retire and begin drawing down on Social Security benefits and other entitlement programs. Yet that is precisely the position the United States found itself in late 2008.

"Shock and awe" was not just a strategy for the U.S. military in Iraq. An equivalent strategy was deployed by the U.S. Federal Reserve and U.S. Treasury, which pumped trillions of dollars into the U.S. economy to prevent the country from plunging into a financial abyss following the collapse of Lehman Brothers in September 2008. Only during times of war has the United States spent so much money so quickly. Billions of dollars were needed to recapitalize U.S. banks and financial institutions, and as part of this salvage exercise, the government spent billions on purchasing toxic assets, billions on direct loans to various banks, and billions in support of the ailing U.S. housing market. Billions of dollars flowed into the U.S. auto industry. Support for Fannie Mae and Freddie Mac, key bulwarks of the U.S. real estate market, also ran into the billions. The same holds true for insurance giant AIG. When all the billion-dollar programs are tallied, the Bs, or billions, turn into Ts, or trillions.[19]

In total, some $4.6 trillion was disbursed in the aftermath of the U.S. financial meltdown, according to the Center for Media and Democracy. A sizable proportion of that total, however, has been repaid to the government or has been reduced through the sale of various assets. Accounting for these variables, the center puts the cost of the crisis at $2 trillion.

Other cost estimates of the financial crisis are not as dire; that said, I suspect the true cost of the crisis will not be known for years and will be just as hotly debated then as now. The U.S. Treasury Department pegs the total cost at a mere $89 billion after all the loans are repaid. Neil Barofsky, the special inspector general of the Troubled Asset Relief Programs (TARP), has estimated the cost at $127 billion. Meanwhile, ProPublica, a Web-based investigative journalism site, estimates a total price tag of $315 billion.[20]

As the various estimates suggest, figuring out the true cost of the great financial crisis of 2008 is not easy. The final number has yet to be determined, although three factors stand out. First, the global postcrisis cleanup effort was not cheap. The IMF estimates that the cost of the global financial crisis was nearly

$12 trillion, and the developed nations racked up the bulk of that spending. While that figure may be reduced in the years ahead, there is little doubt that the cost (directly and indirectly) of the global financial crisis of 2008 will go down as one of the most expensive in history. Second, the crisis struck the United States when the nation was already deep in debt to the rest of the world. Three, bailout costs are only one component of expenses a nation must tally when cleaning up after a financial debacle.

Other costs come in the form of rising public sector spending and diminished revenues triggered by the financial crisis and ensuing economic downturn. Virtually every recession produces a decline in public receipts as personal income and corporate profits decline thanks to shrinking payrolls and falling levels of output and consumption. To plug the gap, government spending usually increases in the short term, resulting in a public sector deficit. Deficits are not uncommon, but as mentioned earlier, the one spawned by the financial crisis of 2008 was extraordinary given the severity of the economic downturn. The greater the decline in output and the larger the decline in receipts, the more government needs to prime the pump and the greater the attendant deficit. Other costs from the crisis include the $9.3 trillion lost in home values, rising interest payments on America's ballooning debt, and the social and human misery felt by millions of laid-off U.S. workers and their families.

In the end, the price associated with cleaning up after one of the largest financial crises in history is likely to run into the hundreds of billions of dollars, if not over a trillion.

THE COST OF FUTURE ENTITLEMENTS

Finally, if the expense of two wars and the cleanup effort following the mother of all financial meltdowns were not enough,

America's finances are also imperiled by what some have called the "silver tsunami," or the rapidly aging U.S. population and the attendant costs that come with caring for retirees, less well off, and the elderly. The federal entitlement programs of Social Security, Medicare, and Medicaid have long represented a clear and present danger to the financial health of the United States. As far back as 1981, Ronald Reagan promised to slash Social Security. When 26 GOP seats were slashed instead in the 1982 midterm election, however, he abruptly changed his tune and agreed to a $165 billion spending package. The same political reluctance to address entitlements has persisted ever since. While many Americans don't want to pay for government entitlement programs, they don't want to live without them either.

Outlays for mandatory spending topped $2 trillion for the first time in 2009, more than double the level at the beginning of the decade. Since mandatory spending on Social Security, Medicare, Medicaid, and other programs like food stamps is just that—"mandatory"—the upshot is that roughly two-thirds of total government spending is on automatic pilot and takes place whether or not the government has the money or not, barring modifications.

More troublesome, net federal spending on Social Security, Medicare, and Medicaid is only expected to continue rising as a percentage of GDP, with the growth in this three-headed monster reflecting the aging of America's population and rising health-care costs. According to the Congressional Budget Office, the share of people age 65 or older is projected to expand from 13 percent in 2008 to 20 percent in 2035. Meanwhile, the share of the population between ages 20 to 64 is expected to drop from 60 percent to 55 percent. Presently, roughly 53 million Americans collect Social Security benefits, although by 2035, the number of recipients is expected to top 90 million. As more Americans opt for retirement, fewer workers pay into the Social Security system. The ratio of workers to retirees today is roughly 3.3:1 versus 16:1 in 1950. At some point in this decade, the Social Security program will start to pay out more than it takes in as the boomers retire in greater and greater numbers, putting even more pressure on the finances of the United States. To this point, thanks to the U.S. recession in 2008–2009 and cyclical decline in revenues, the Congressional Budget Office expects annual Social Security outlays to exceed annual tax revenues in 2010. Starting in 2016, under current law, the program's annual spending will regularly exceed annual revenue, marking another financial turning point for the United States.

Speaking to the looming challenges before the United States, Federal Reserve chairman Ben Bernanke warned in April 2010 that the United States "must begin now to prepare for this coming demographic transition."[21] In unusually blunt language for a central banker, Mr. Bernanke noted that the "the arithmetic is, unfortunately, quite clear."[22]

That was code for: things don't add up—America's finances are on thin ice, which, according to Mr. Bernanke, means that the United States should act now, not later, "To avoid large and unsustainable budget deficits, the nation will ultimately have to choose among higher taxes, modifications to entitlement programs such as Social Security and Medicare, less spending on everything else from education to defense, or some combination of the above. These choices are difficult, and it always seems easier to put them off—until the day they cannot be put off any more."[23]

To avoid America's day of reckoning, the United States must impose fiscal discipline on itself by making politically unpopular but economically sound decisions regarding the U.S. federal budget deficit. Either that, or the global financial markets will do it for us. To the latter point, as Greece went up in flames in early 2010, much of the mainstream commentary in the United States opined that America was not Greece and that any comparison was foolish. In other words, the financial markets would never train its sights on the profligate United States and make the nation pay for its past financial sins since America's economy was too strong and too resilient. Because it is the best of an ugly lot, the United States would remain attractive to foreign investors.

Up to a point, I agree with all of the above—the U.S. economy remains one of the most competitive on planet Earth. What I do disagree with, however, is the it-can't-happen-in-the-U.S. narrative that assumes the financial markets would never turn on the United States the way they have turned on Greece and Europe's other heavily indebted nations. This view is eerily reminiscent of the consensus leading up to the U.S.-led financial calamity of 2008. Then conventional wisdom declaimed that financial crises were the worries of other nations like Mexico, Brazil, and Thailand. This notion was brutally shattered on September 15, 2008. Similarly, the underlying assumption that the United States is immune to the discipline of the financial market could also be decimated. And at some point, many developing nations, in addition to Japan, will begin to consume a larger share of their savings rather than sending it to the United States.

What happens when developing countries like China, Brazil, or Taiwan grow prosperous enough that they decide they would like to spend their hard-earned money on themselves? What happens when more investment vehicles are created in the emerging markets, which will ultimately keep more savings at home? As David M. Smick points out, "Many other economies consume too little and offer too little in the way of safe and credible investment opportunities for global capital. Many of these countries have excess saving because they limit domestic investment opportunities through taxation, regulation, a lack of financial transparency, and the rule of law."[24] Yet this status will not remain frozen. At some point, the emerging markets will begin to consume their own savings, leaving the United States financially high and dry.

THE COST OF SERVICING AMERICA'S DEBT

In addition to the cost of wars, mopping up after the financial crisis, and funding future entitlements, another looming cost needs to be examined: interest payments on America's ever-expanding mountain of debt. When the United States borrows money from lenders, the loan is rarely free. (During the panic of late 2008, however, the demand for U.S. Treasuries was so intense that yields on the three-month bills turned negative at the low point.)

Selling U.S. securities is something America has mastered quite well, and in a stroke of good luck, a large share of America's current debt has been financed at very low interest rates. Indeed, thanks to strong foreign demand for U.S. Treasuries and other securities, the U.S. government paid less interest on its debt in fiscal year 2009 than in the prior year; on new borrowing, America's average interest rate was below 1 percent, prompting Robert Bixby, executive director of the Concord Coalition, to quip, "The government is on teaser rates; we're taking out a huge mortgage right now, but we won't feel the pain until later."[25]

Teaser rates or not, interest payments on America's total debt came to a cool $187 billion in 2009, while for the entire decade America shelled out a staggering $2 trillion to service its debt.[26]

Currently, servicing America's debt represents one of the largest line items of the U.S. federal budget. Gross interest payments easily exceed outlays on such programs as international affairs, agriculture, education/training, veteran benefits, and transportation. Looked at from this perspective, the annual cost associated with servicing America's debt is greater than the annual budgets of most departments of the U.S. government.

In yet another twist in this story, a larger and larger share of net U.S. interest payments is flowing overseas. This reflects America's rising addiction to other people's money. The more the United States borrows overseas, the more it ultimately owes its foreign creditors; America's interest payments on its foreign debt have soared over the past decade. In 2007 and 2008, for instance, interest payments on U.S. government debt held by foreigners totaled $164 billion and $167 billion, respectively, before declining to $144 billion in 2009. Even with this decline, interest paid to foreigners in 2009 was greater than government spending on veterans' benefits and services ($95 billion), education and training ($80 billion), space ($30 billion), and community and regional development ($28 billion).[27] Since 2005, the cost of servicing America's foreign debt has been in excess of $100 billion a year, a sizable chunk of change even for a $14 trillion economy. The primary beneficiary of this trend is China. The mainland, one of the largest holders of U.S. Treasuries, now earns more than $50 billion a year in interest from the United States.[28]

Based on current estimates from the U.S. Congressional Budget Office, the cost of servicing America's debt is expected to top $700 billion a year by 2019. The CBO's projections suggest an additional $500 billion a year in interest expenses by the end of the decade, and based on these estimates, total interest rate payments over 2011–2020 are projected to be a staggering $5.1 trillion, more than double the $2 trillion in interest payments in the first decade of this century.

AMERICA THE VULNERABLE:
THE ODDS OF FINANCIAL WAR

Unbeknownst to many Americans, many dealing with their own personal financial crisis since 2008, the "perfect financial storm" has greatly diminished the financial sovereignty of the United States. Over the past decade, America's financial future has been compromised. No superpower can go about its business when its piggy bank is stuffed with foreign IOUs, when its leaders lack the political will to make difficult decisions, and when its citizens remain oblivious to their dependence on foreign capital. Precisely because America has forfeited its financial independence, it is no longer the economic superpower it once was.

Today, America's indebtedness is a strategic liability that has left the United States vulnerable to the wishes of its primary creditors—China, Middle East oil producers, and other developing nations with excess savings. In this regard, it is important to note the key role foreign governments, working through their central banks and sovereign wealth funds, have played in acquiring U.S. assets. Between 2003 and 2008, foreign governments accounted for roughly two-thirds of average annual net purchases of U.S. securities. In other words, global capital flows are increasingly state-led and directed. Private investors no longer hold the bulk of America's debt—ownership has passed to foreign governments that could, should they want to, decide not to buy U.S. assets in the future or sell their existing holdings, potentially wreaking havoc on the U.S. financial markets.

What is the likelihood of this happening? In August 2007, when the United States threatened to impose trade sanctions on Chinese goods because Beijing refused to revalue the renminbi, China, in turn, threatened to liquidate its $1.3 trillion position in U.S. Treasuries. Such a move would have inflicted just as much damage to the mainland as the United States, if not more. Hence, the threat was quickly dismissed. But the very fact that China would consider the "nuclear option," as dubbed by the media, was a wake-up call to Washington and the financial markets.

OPEC's influence stems from oil, Russia's pivots around natural gas, while China's clout rests on capital. Just as crude oil and natural gas are thought to be "political" commodities, whose prices can be dictated by geopolitics as opposed to economics, so too is the potential for capital to become a political commodity. Since the bulk of the world savings, roughly 80 percent, is now concentrated in the developing nations, led by China, the Rest has considerable leverage over the West in general and the world's largest debtor, the United States, in particular.

Would China ever be so bold as to blatantly use its financial clout? Maybe not against the United States—just yet—but certainly against other states. Just ask Taiwan, whose independence and international recognition have been steadily eroded by China's aggressive use of its checkbook in paying off nations to switch allegiances from Taipei to Beijing when they are recognizing the legitimate representation of the Chinese people. As discussed in more detail in Chapter 7, neither has China been shy in using its newfound financial strength to curry favor in a host of African states, with many deals cut and concluded at the expense of U.S. and European influence.

China's financial influence on the global capital markets was on full display in the last week of May 2010. With the financial markets already on pins and needles over the slumping euro and Europe's rising sovereign debt problems, the global equity markets, including Wall Street, swooned on the news that China was considering reducing its euro exposure. When the story hit the tape that the world's largest creditor nation was considering bailing on the euro, the beleaguered currency and financial assets across the continent sold off, with Beijing's alleged lack of confidence in Europe a good enough reason for the rest of the world to follow suit.

The next day, however, China announced that the rumors were false and that the mainland was not looking to diversify out of euros. In turn, the global capital markets rallied. The world financial markets breathed a collective sigh of relief and went about its business not recognizing the seminal moment—that Communist China, a rather poor nation not that long ago, now had the ability to make or break one of the world's major currencies and could inflict massive losses or gains on the world financial markets with just a few words from its leadership. Substitute the dollar for the euro, and Beijing could have the same direct effect on the U.S. financial markets in the future.

Financial warfare has happened in the past, and it could happen in the future. A noted victim of financial warfare was Great Britain in 1956, and the country meting out punishment was none other than the United States, unhappy with Britain's occupation of the Suez Canal Zone. Then the United States was among the world's largest creditor nations and owned much of England's debt. The United States had leverage over the Brits, in other words, and used the threat of selling a sizable part of its holdings of British pounds to force the British and the French to withdraw their military forces from the Suez region. As Brad Setser noted, "The lesson of the Suez for the United States today is clear: political might is often linked to financial might, and a debtor's capacity to project military power hinges on the support of its creditors."[29]

For a variety of reasons, America's creditors bankrolled the U.S.-led war in Iraq, but whether they will continue to underwrite the next war or ongoing efforts in the Middle East remains uncertain. By lending billions of dollars to the United States, the developing nations have created a false sense of security—both economically and politically—in the United States. America's two-front war has cost the average American virtually nothing. Meanwhile, very few Americans are even remotely aware of the financial umbilical cord that connects America with its creditors in Asia and the Middle East, and this country's rising dependence on other people's money. The world's last economic superpower has mortgaged its future to governments headed by communists or run by authoritarian regimes.

Not to worry, goes the comforting narrative from many quarters. China has no place to park its massive reserves other than in U.S. Treasuries and remains dependent on exports for growth, suggesting ever-rising inflows to the United States from the mainland. Meanwhile, the survival of many Middle East governments is tied to the security umbrella provided by the U.S. military, making investment managers of the Middle East unlikely to decamp en masse from the U.S. financial markets anytime soon. U.S. Treasuries remain the safest investment in the world, so goes the consensus, and consequently foreigners will always be willing to lend money to Uncle Sam.

These are all valid points, suggesting that the financial interdependence of today between the world's largest debtor and its creditors will be maintained tomorrow. Perhaps the current arrangement could go on for quite some time. However, what is missing from this analysis is that America's ability to borrow overseas could be constrained by changes in China or the Middle East. A major change in policy overseas risks leaving the United States financially exposed.

For instance, few Americans realize that a backlash is slowly emerging in China over Beijing's massive accumulation of U.S.

dollar reserves. Commenting on the topic, Chinese Prime Minister Wen Jiabao said bluntly in early 2009, "To be honest, I am definitely a little worried." Luo Ping, a senior official of the China Banking Regulator Commission, was even less diplomatic. He stunned an audience with the following comment in February 2009: "U.S. Treasuries are the safe haven; it is the only option . . . we know the dollar is going to depreciate, so we hate you guys, but there is nothing much we can do."[30]

Mr. Ping's remark did not garner much attention in the United States, but the outburst reflects the fact that domestic criticism is building over China's excess exposure to low-yielding U.S. Treasuries, juxtaposed against America's ever-widening deficit. The Chinese government and many ordinary citizens are increasingly wondering out loud why China continues to send billions of dollars to a country that is engaged in a two-front war, responsible for one of the worst financial debacles in history, deep in debt, and continues to exhibit not one ounce of fiscal restraint. Adding insult to injury, why send billions of dollars to a rich nation like the United States when China remains so poor?

More insulting, the United States continues to demand that the renminbi be allowed to appreciate against the U.S. dollar, which means it is effectively asking China to incur massive exchange rate losses on its dollar holdings, nearly $900 billion in May 2010. The more the renminbi rises against the U.S. dollar, the greater the loss in value of China's dollar reserves. This represents an embarrassing policy bind for Chinese policy makers, and one that could result in a domestic backlash against Beijing's political elite.

In the future, while America's policy actions will influence the nation's ability to attract foreign capital, so too will policies overseas, independent of the United States. Even if the United

States remains "good," the outcome could be "bad" because of events and trends totally outside the control of Washington. Barring a dramatic move to slash the U.S. deficit, reduce current debt levels, and increase the nation's overall savings rate, the United States will remain financially vulnerable. Ben Bernanke warned Congress, "At some point, the markets will make a judgment about, really, not our economic capacity but our political ability, our political will, to achieve longer-term sustainability. At that point interest rates could go up and that would be, of course, a negative for economic growth and recovery."[31]

Harvard professor Harold James makes a telling point about the status of the United States, which can easily borrow money to finance its deficit, and an empire of an earlier age in history, that of Hapsburg Spain:

> The equivalent to the inflow of funds . . . was the story of New World silver, which initially appeared as a source of immense strategic power. It let Spain have something (mostly the services of troops) for apparently nothing; just as in other cases there can appear to be a "free lunch" for the hegemon. The inflow of silver did not immediately lead to Spanish decline, but it did eventually produce a hollowing out of the Spanish economy and in the end also a loss of strategic preeminence.[32]

When Spain's supply of silver dwindled, it could no longer pay for all its wars to protect its far-flung empire. In the meantime, Britain and France built more efficient tax-collecting systems that eventually relegated Spain to a second-rate power. Much like Spain, the longer the United States relies on money it does not earn, the more vulnerable it becomes to global financial patterns that are rapidly evolving beyond its control.

In the shifting tides of world events, favors aren't given for free. Other countries want the good life that Americans have. Nations like Japan, China, and Brazil will ultimately consume more of their own savings, leaving little left over for Uncle Sam. Continuous change represents perhaps the only constant throughout the history of global financial flows. Innovations in other countries will one day make obsolete the current system in which U.S. securities, notably U.S. Treasuries, are the dominant international security to own. Without proper actions and a greater sense of urgency, the economy of the United States will suffer when that day comes. The status quo is unsustainable. The destruction from the "perfect financial storm" has yet to be fully understood by many Americans. Decades from now, however, historians will point to the profligacy of the United States as the beginning of the end for the world's last economic superpower.

The Twilight of Europe and Japan

The West is very absorbed by its own problems and hasn't had the time or energy to look up and see what's happening. That's quite funny because the world is splitting apart, even as we say that we are getting more globalized.

—PARMOD BHASIN, CHIEF EXECUTIVE OF
GENPACT, INDIA'S LARGEST BUSINESS
PROCESSING OUTSOURCER[1]

The deglobalization of finance, the rise of the "Rest," and the crippling debt status of the United States—the convergence of these forces has undermined the global economic dominance of America. But to these powerful trends another must be added: the relative decline of the West, or the fading collective global influence of the United States, Canada, Europe, Japan, Australia, and New Zealand. In particular, the twilight of Europe and Japan and their diminished capacity to affect the global agenda is just as important as the much-told story of the rise of China and India and their attendant ability to shape the world of tomorrow. Their decline coupled with America's increasingly exhausted resources means that the most important forces responsible for the preeminence of globalization have been crippled, leaving the fate of globalization as we know it much in doubt.

Too much attention over the past few years has been paid to America's decline in parallel with China's rise. This analysis misses another potent issue—that America's diminished influence also stems from the fact that its longtime allies and cosponsors of globalization, principally Europe and Japan, are fading fast as influential global players. In the postcrisis world of today, the Western brand does not carry the same sway as it did in the past. America's ability to shape the global agenda in economics, foreign affairs, and other key multilateral issues has been increasingly compromised by politically weak and economically stagnant allies who have in turn lost faith in America's ability to lead. Both Europe and Japan are weighed down by aging populations and hamstrung by massive public sector debt, and increasingly, as a new decade dawns, both parties are considered withering global players.

For example, when the finer points of the global climate-change agreement were hammered out at the eleventh hour in Copenhagen in late 2009, delegates from the European Union were not even present at the table as the United States, China, India, Brazil, and South Africa bargained and haggled over the final accord. Europe's exclusion, not unexpectedly, deeply embarrassed Europe's leaders. After all, they had long championed the agenda to reduce global greenhouse gas emissions and adopt more environmentally friendly policies to save Mother Earth. They had led the first international accord to limit greenhouse gases, the Kyoto Protocol of 1997, which was spurned by the United States in the end. Yet after pushing hard for a meaningful agreement at Copenhagen, Europe was crestfallen by the world's rude treatment. The deal was largely done while Europe was outside looking in. And while the exclusion of Europe and Japan from the final negotiations suited American short-term interests, the legacy of Copenhagen may well come back to haunt the United States.

The devalued global influence of America's allies is hardly a favorable omen for globalization, since the foundation of the world economy for the past 60 years has been solidified largely by Western cooperation and cohesion. Since the end of World War II, the major powers of the West have been the world economy's standard-bearers—the rule makers, regulators, and enforcers, controlling global institutions (including the World Bank, International Monetary Fund, World Trade Organization, and its predecessor, the General Agreement on Trade and Tariffs) that have long shaped and controlled the global economic agenda. Think of it this way: Europe, Japan, Canada, and other Western nations were junior partners with the United States in constructing the edifice and establishing the institutions that would lead to Western domination of the global economy over the second half of the twentieth century.

The demise of communism and the end of the Cold War only strengthened the grip of the West over the global economy. Over the Roaring Nineties, the developed nations, with roughly 12 percent of the global population, accounted for roughly 60 percent of world output on average, based on purchasing power parity rates.[2] The West was responsible for the bulk of world exports and imports, as well as a disproportionate share of foreign direct investment. In terms of personal consumption, again the developed nations led the way, accounting for over three-quarters of global personal consumption over the 1990s. Against this backdrop, Western power and influence reached its postwar pinnacle late in the millennium, and the Western way of life in effect became the desired model for the rest of the world.

Catching up with the rich West was a primary goal of many nations, including China, who grudgingly came to accept the notion that the nation was becoming more "Western." Confirming Beijing's acceptance of U.S.-led rules and regulations governing international commerce, China finally joined the World Trade Organization in 2001. In Europe, meanwhile, the number of EU-wannabes soared after the collapse of communism. Following much preparation and bargaining, 10 new members—the majority from Central and Eastern Europe—joined the European Union in May 2004; in January 2007, two more nations (Bulgaria and Romania) joined, bringing total EU membership to 27 nations. Early in the twenty-first century, Europe appeared more politically united and economically integrated than ever before, a dynamic that lent a great deal of currency to the Western way of managing affairs.

By standing together, by working toward common goals, by boosting global growth and prosperity, and by not allowing specific issues to create deep divisions within, the West—namely, the United States in collaboration with Europe and Japan—succeeded in creating a global economic system that virtually all nations wanted to participate in. For years those nations that played by the Western rules of the game grew and prospered. Hence, over the 1980s and 1990s, and up until the financial crisis of 2008, the world danced to the tune of the West. The West led, the rest followed. All of this changed, however, with the meltdown of the global financial system late in the first decade of the twenty-first century and the ensuing wreckage wrought by the "Made in America" financial crisis.

THE PRIMACY OF THE TRANSATLANTIC ECONOMY

Probably no subject is as unfashionable and uninspiring in economics as the transatlantic economy. It is not discussed on Wall Street, is rarely mentioned in popular media outlets, and appears on the radar screen of a very few in Washington. This negligence is understandable given the universal assumption that the future lies with the emerging markets, notably the uber-developing nations of China, India, Brazil, and others. In contrast, the U.S.-European economic partnership conjures up images of the Cold War period, or a bygone era that has been all but relegated to the dustbin of history.

Many experts in America wrote off Europe as long ago as 1981. That was the year U.S. exports to Asia exceeded U.S. exports to Europe for the first time. This seminal shift in trade was widely reported in the media and deemed irrefutable evidence that future global growth was shifting from West to East—from Europe to Asia. In subsequent years, this view was bolstered by China's unrelenting economic rise, coupled with robust growth across Asia. Concurrently, Europe's underwhelming economic performance, along with its rising public sector debt and declining innovation capabilities lent credence to the notion that while Asia was on the rise, Europe was in decline. America, accordingly, needed to shift its attention and resources toward the Pacific region, while downgrading relations with its Atlantic partner.

Corporate America, though, did the opposite. However unglamorous the transatlantic economy may appear, the economy that spans the Atlantic is the largest and most powerful economic entity in the world. The Atlantic commercial artery—valued at roughly $4.5 trillion in 2009—is massive because no two economic entities in the world have been more melded together than the United States and Europe over the past few decades.[3] Indeed, if globalization means the cross-border economic fusion of two regions of the world, the transatlantic economy is its prime example.

That may surprise many readers for two reasons. First, the common metric by which international commerce is measured is through cross-border trade—or exports and imports. Trade has been the standard benchmark for global commerce for centuries, and if based solely on trade, Asia matters more to the United States than Europe. Total trade between the United States and Asia amounted to $1 trillion in 2008 versus $652 billion between the United States and Europe. U.S. exports of goods to Asia in the same year were nearly 22 percent larger than U.S. exports to the European Union. So case closed—America's commercial interests are unequivocally more dependent on dynamic Asia, not stodgy Europe. Not quite.

Here's the catch: standard trade figures are a wholly incomplete measure of global commerce. A better indicator is foreign direct investment and the sales of foreign affiliates, since companies compete more through foreign direct investment—by establishing a local presence in various foreign markets, by being on the ground—than through arm's-length trade. As *The Economist* stated, "Foreign direct investment is 'globalization' in its most potent form," and represents far more than "capital": "it is a uniquely potent bundle of capital, contacts, and managerial and technological knowledge. It is the cutting edge of globalization."[4]

Foreign direct investment has been at the forefront in stitching the global economy together over the past quarter century. The global figure of inward FDI stock was nearly $18 trillion in 2009, equivalent to roughly 30 percent of world GDP, up from a mere $790 billion in 1982.[5] In the same year, foreign affiliate sales reached nearly $30 trillion versus roughly $16 trillion in global exports of goods and services. Hence, it is investment that binds nations together, not trade. In the case of the United States, U.S. foreign affiliate sales totaled a staggering $5.2 trillion in 2008, the last year of available data, nearly five times greater than the value of U.S. exports.[6] While the United States ranks as the world's largest exporter of goods and services, what

America exports each year pales in comparison to what foreign affiliate sales are year in and year out. U.S. companies, in other words, deliver goods and services to overseas customers more through foreign affiliates than exports. When regarded on this basis, Europe is easily the most important geographic market in the world for corporate America. In 2008, U.S. foreign affiliate sales in Europe totaled $2.7 trillion versus foreign affiliate sales of $1 trillion in all of Asia, a massive divergence that reflects the fact that America's foreign direct investment roots are deepest across the Atlantic, not the Pacific. Of corporate America's 20,000 plus foreign affiliates scattered all over the world, the bulk are embedded in Europe—another fact that may come to the surprise of many readers.

In discussions of globalization's reemergence late in the twentieth century, the narrative typically centers on the opening of new and untapped markets in Central Europe, Latin America, developing Asia, and the Indian subcontinent. The general embrace of Western-style free-market principles in such nations as China, Brazil, India, Poland, and others was supportive of the story of greater global integration, interdependence, and inclusion with and among the developing nations. This narrative is not inaccurate. Yet it does overlook the critical fact that globalization over the past three decades has been dominated by the United States and Europe. Globalization has expanded faster and reached deeper across the Atlantic than between any other two continents or regions in the world.

Contrary to popular opinion, global investment flows have not flowed from the rich, high-wage developed nations to the poor, low-cost developing countries over the past few decades. Rather, despite the many flows from rich to poor, investment has flowed more from one developed nation to another, or to and from the United States and Europe in particular. Over the

1980s, 78 percent of total foreign direct inflows were directed at the developed nations; the United States accounted for 36 percent of the total, the European Union, 31 percent. Over the 1990s, roughly two-thirds of total foreign investment inflows were directed at the developed nations, and the United States and the European Union accounted for 22 percent and 40 percent, respectively, of the global total. Meanwhile, the developing nations attracted just 22 percent of total global inflows in the 1980s and nearly one-third over the 1990–1999 period. When China is excluded from the total, the share to the developing nations is much smaller, dropping to roughly one-quarter in the 1990s. In the first decade of the twenty-first century, the numbers show basically the same trends—the share of foreign direct investment inflows to the developing nations excluding China tallied 29 percent, while the percent to the developed nations was 65 percent of the total.[7]

Leading the charge overseas have been American companies. But the surge in U.S. foreign investment has not been directed at the developing nations, as commonly assumed. Rather, most U.S. overseas investment for the past 50 years has been directed at Europe. In the two decades from 1990 to 2009, U.S. firms invested $2.9 trillion overseas—a sizable sum and a trend many in America believe to be linked to rising U.S. investment to low-cost China. However, the European Union accounted for roughly 55 percent of the total, while China accounted for only 1.3 percent. U.S. firms sank more capital into Ireland and Spain over the same period.

America's preponderance in investment outflows is also true of inflows. While the United States has long been a major source of foreign investment, the country has also been a major recipient of investment—a fact lost on many in the United States who believe that investment flows typically one way—outward. To the contrary, the United States accounted for 16 percent of total global foreign inflows in the last decade and for 22 percent of the total over the 1990s. Interestingly, despite all the talk of Western firms decamping their home markets for low-cost China, for every one dollar China attracted in foreign direct investment over the last decade, the United States attracted roughly three dollars. Who is the primary foreign investor in the United States? Europe. Over the past decade, European firms invested roughly $1.3 trillion in the United States, nearly double the level of the 1990s. As a key source of foreign capital, Europe accounted for roughly three-fourths of total U.S. investment in the 1990s and again during the last decade.

In sum, no two economies have become more integrated than those of the United States and Europe over the quarter century. Today, thanks to large-scale foreign direct investment from both sides of the Atlantic, American affiliates in Europe are increasingly indistinguishable from local European firms, and European firms in the United States are often indistinguishable from local American companies. Affiliates on both sides of the pond are important local sources of jobs and income and critical drivers of economic growth whether in Spartanburg, South Carolina, where German automobile manufacturer BMW turns out 160,000 cars a year, or Grenoble, France, where a number of U.S. pharmaceutical firms conduct world-class research employing local talent. As for the transatlantic capital markets, the ties that link the United States and Europe are also quite thick. U.S. financial institutions are closely linked with their counterparts in the United Kingdom, the Netherlands, Belgium, France, Germany, and other European financial hubs. As a result, although the financial crisis was hatched in the United States, Europe's close financial ties with America helped infect the United Kingdom and the continent with exotic mortgage-backed securities, subprime loans, and other dodgy assets. So when Lehman Brothers went under, the panic and pain immediately struck both sides of the pond.

CRACKS IN THE FOUNDATION OF GLOBALIZATION

If the United States and Europe were married, there is a strong probability that one or both parties would have filed for divorce sometime in the past decade. The last 10 years have been among the rockiest in the modern era for the transatlantic partnership—notwithstanding ever-expanding trade and investment ties between the two parties The problems started early in the decade, after the U.S. dot-com bust and ensuing U.S. economic recession precipitated an economic downturn across Europe. No sooner had the transatlantic economy started to recover when the staggering catastrophe of September 11, 2001, shocked the world.

At first, the United States and Europe stood in solidarity against the terrorist attacks. The French newspaper *Le Monde* famously captured the mood of the time: "In this tragic moment, when words seem so inadequate to express the shock people feel, the first thing that comes to mind is this: We are all Americans! We are all New Yorkers, just as surely as John F. Kennedy declared himself to be a Berliner in 1962 when he visited Berlin. Indeed, just as in the gravest moments of our own history, how can we not feel profound solidarity with those people, that country, the United States, to whom we are so close and to whom we owe our freedom, and therefore our solidarity?"[8]

Meanwhile, for the first time members of the North Atlantic Treaty Organization (NATO) invoked Article 5, confirming that an attack on one member is an attack on all members. The pledge was another show of transatlantic solidarity and sent a clear message to the world that the United States and Europe stood shoulder to shoulder against the war on terrorism. They were bound by history, common values, and shared goals to remain each other's true partners. The weeks following 9/11 represented the high water mark of transatlantic solidarity and cohesion. The goodwill, however, did not last long, with the U.S.-led war in Iraq exposing fundamental fault lines between the United States and Europe.

Entering Iraq in 2003, the United States wanted a strong, politically cohesive, and fully engaged Europe to support American-led efforts in the Middle East in particular and the war on terror in general. Europe, instead, wavered and vacillated and became divided among itself over whether to commit soldiers. France and Germany largely opposed the war, while the United Kingdom, Spain, and Poland, along with a handful of other nations, supported the U.S. war effort. In a fit of frustration with Europe, U.S. defense secretary Donald Rumsfeld made matters worse by referring to "old" Europe and "new" Europe when referring to those nations that opposed or supported the war, a comment that created a tremendous amount of discord within Europe and across the Atlantic.

The transatlantic bickering did not stop there. The U.S. Congress, unfortunately, got into the act in its endlessly helpful way. The three cafeterias in the House of Representatives were ordered to rename French fries "freedom fries." French toast became "freedom toast." The symbolic move aimed at the French lack of support did not end on Capitol Hill. U.S. bar owners were seen on television pouring French wine down drains to applauding and approving patrons. None of this, not surprisingly, did much to engender cooperation between the United States and Europe.

Neither did Robert Kagan's popular and provocative thesis—"Americans Are from Mars and Europeans Are from Venus"—which rattled the transatlantic partnership in the summer of 2002. As boldly proclaimed by Kagan:

> It is time to stop pretending that Europeans and Americans share a common view of the world, or even that they occupy the same world. On the all-important question of power—the efficacy of power, the morality of power, the desirability of power—American and European perspectives are diverging. Europe is turning away from power . . . Meanwhile, the United States remains mired in history, exercising power in an anarchic Hobbesian world where international laws and rules are unreliable, and where true security and the defense and promotion of a liberal order still depend on the possession and use of military might. That is why on major strategic and international questions today, Americans are from Mars and Europeans from Venus.[9]

According to Kagan, the disparity in power between the United States and Europe had grown so great that when it came to "setting national priorities, determining threats, defining challenges, and fashioning and implementing foreign and defense policies, the United States and Europe have parted ways."[10]

In response to Kagan's thesis, my colleague, Daniel Hamilton, director of the Center for Transatlantic Relations at The Johns Hopkins University, and I countered in various publications and multiple forums that instead of drifting apart, in reality the United States and Europe were banding together.[11] Notwithstanding diplomatic tensions over the war in Iraq and the growing unpopularity of the Bush administration across

Europe, transatlantic commercial ties were in fact becoming stronger, not weaker.

Supportive of this view, as the first decade of the twenty-first century unfolded, U.S.-European commercial flows only became deeper. Despite all the hype about the ascent of China and the collective allure of the BRIC nations, U.S. firms continued to plow more capital into Europe than any place else in the world. During the economic boom years of 2003–2007, for instance, Europe remained the favored destination for corporate America, accounting for more than half of U.S. foreign investment over this period. Over the same time frame, the United States accounted for over 70 percent of Europe's foreign direct outward investment. Leading up to the global financial crisis of 2008, America and Europe were each other's favorite foreign investment destination and, by extension, remained the twin anchors of the global economy.

That is still true today. However, the sequence of events starting with the U.S. dot-com bust, followed by the unpopular U.S.-led war in Iraq, and ultimately the "Made in America" financial crisis has left the transatlantic partnership battered and bruised, and in many respects, in disarray.

A HOUSE DIVIDED

Following the recession in 2008, one of the most ruthless comments on Western financial prowess was unleashed by Brazil's president, Luiz Inácio Lula da Silva. Not one to mince words, the Brazilian leader harshly stated: "This is a crisis caused by people, white with blue eyes. And before the crisis they looked as if they knew everything about economics."[12] Rarely had such blunt criticism been leveled at the West's management of the global economy; not surprisingly, Lula's indictment of "white people with blue eyes" resonated among the developing nations. But the searing comment also played well in many developed nations. Indeed, the crisis elicited a number of no-holds-barred comments from America's long-standing economic partners in Europe and Japan. That's because they were the major buyers of Wall Street's financial innovations, and when the entire toxic basket collapsed, they were among the greatest victims.

During the heat of the crisis, Peer Steinbrück, German finance minister, wondered out loud whether Karl Marx was not "all that incorrect" in predicting that unbridled capitalism would ultimately consume itself. Mr. Steinbrück also noted: "One thing seems probable to me, the United States will lose its status as a superpower of the global financial system."[13]

French president Nicolas Sarkozy has also spoken out about the perils of free-market capitalism, even though, ironically, Sarkozy rode to power in 2007 by advocating more industry deregulation and more flexible labor laws. Delivering a keynote address to the World Economic Forum in Davos, Switzerland, in January 2010, the French president slammed bank bonuses, financial speculation, and deregulation, and urged a tax on financial transactions and a tax on imports from countries that do not heed international climate accords. Sarkozy also used the Davos platform to call for a new Bretton Woods system, eliminating the U.S. dollar as the world's reserve currency. The French president received a standing ovation for his passionate anti-American plea to rein in capitalism and dethrone the dollar.

In Asia, Eisuke Sakakibara, former Japanese finance minister, predicted that the world would never return to the consumption patterns that led to the Great Recession. "After this recession is over, things will be different. The American age is over."[14]

Some of the commentary, to be sure, was nothing more than raw populism designed to temper the anger of local electorates suffering from the aftershocks of the financial crisis. However, the anticapitalist barrage and blatant finger pointing at the United States for bringing the global economy to its knees have done little to promote harmony and cohesion between the United States and its Western partners. To the contrary, while the financial crisis of 2008 elicited much rhetoric for the need for coordination and cooperation among the West, words have not been matched by deeds. The two parties have drifted apart in terms of crafting a coordinated policy response to the deepest transatlantic recession since the 1930s. Virtually every nation in the world lowered interest rates and goosed government spending in the wake of the crisis, a widespread Keyesnian response to the crisis, but that is where the policy similarities end. Beyond priming the pump, the policy responses in Washington, Brussels, London, Paris, Tokyo, and other Western capitals were largely ad hoc, uncoordinated, and inward-looking on the whole.

In general, U.S. fiscal and monetary policies have been larger, swifter, and some would say more effective than Europe's policy responses. The United States has also moved much more aggressively in addressing the problems of nonperforming loans on the balance sheets of U.S. banks, with government-led policies forcing many U.S. financial institutions to raise more capital and recapitalize their balance sheets well ahead of their European counterparts. More than a year after the United States required its banks to undergo a financial stress test, Europe got around to the same exercise in July 2010, and by most accounts, Europe's stress tests were not as "stressful" or comprehensive as those conducted in the United States. And despite all the chatter about the need for a globally coordinated response to financial reform, the United States and various European states have been working in silos, with national priorities and interests trumping all others. Presently, a huge regulatory divide yawns between the United States and Europe. And the fiscal and monetary policy gulf is just as wide, with the United States in mid-2010 favoring more fiscal spending despite mounting federal budget deficits versus Europe's desire to cut spending and raise taxes.

In addition to the above, not helping matters was the near financial meltdown of Greece in early 2010, which embarrassingly highlighted the flaws of the European monetary union and internal divisions within the continent. The Greek financial crisis was largely of its own doing, as runaway state spending finally caught up with the nation in late 2009. Once the global financial capital markets grew increasingly nervous over Greece's ability to repay its debt, they demanded higher interest payments on its outstanding debt, a situation that brought Greece to the brink of a sovereign default. This was avoided thanks to a massive financial package cobbled together in April 2010 but only after a protracted and bitter debate within the European Union about whether or not to throw Greece a financial life line. Some countries—notably Germany—opposed a Greek bailout on the grounds that any EU member as profligate and financially irresponsible as Greece should be tossed from the Eurozone. Buttressing this argument was the fact that Greece did cook the financial books in the late 1990s to meet the standards of entering the Eurozone. The Germans were suspicious of the Greek numbers from the beginning, a hunch that was later proven correct when in September 2004 the nation admitted that it had been in breach of the Eurozone's deficit rules for the previous four years. Later, in early 2009, officials in Athens predicted that the nation's deficit for 2009 would be 3.7

percent of GDP, slightly above the 3 percent target. However in late October of the same year, after the socialist government of George Papandreou had replaced its conservative predecessor, Greece informed the EU that the deficit in fact would be an immense 12.7 percent of GDP, an admission that sparked growing credit fears.

Greece, in the end, was granted financial support by other member states, with the controversial help of the International Monetary Fund. Its participation was strongly resisted up to the eleventh hour on the grounds that the IMF was designed to bail out financially strapped developing nations—not a developed economy ensconced in the world's largest economic bloc and sharing the same currency—the euro—with financially frugal Germany. It was Germany, however, that insisted that the IMF take part of the Greek salvage operation, a reflection of Berlin's reluctance to bail out a profligate member of the European Union. A full-blown sovereign debt crisis in the European Union was avoided but not without creating a tremendous amount of ill will between Germany and Greece, as well as stoking tensions between Europe's major economic players, Germany and France.

After several lawmakers in Germany advised that Greece sell a few islands to raise cash, Deputy Prime Minister Theodoros Pangalos suggested that Germany could solve the problems in Greece by making reparations for gold stolen during the Nazi occupation. Not surprisingly, German insistence that any aid to Greece come as a last resort and that Greece pay market-punishing rates to borrow capital infuriated Greek leaders and the general public. Berlin offered no apologies during the crisis, adamant that it would not bail out a nation that had defaulted four times in its modern history; has a retirement age of 61 versus 67 in Germany; and spends 7 percent of GDP on public administration compared to a 3 percent average for the Euro-zone. A high consumption rate, low level of labor force participation, and a chronic penchant to print deficits—all these Greek traits were too much for Germany to underwrite, making Germany the harsh taskmaster during the crisis. Besides, after paying a huge bill to integrate East Germany, the average German was not interested in funding another capital-starved part of Europe.

Commenting on the mood in Germany, Constanze Stelzenmüller, a senior fellow of the German Marshall Fund in Berlin, put it starkly, "Germany is no longer, as a matter of course or principle, the motor, heart and savior of Europe. This isn't the Europe we signed up for. It's much larger, much poorer, and we have to take care of our own."[15]

Germany's unyielding stance incensed not only Greece but also many other EU partners, notably France. While German chancellor Angela Merkel insisted that Greece pay a price for its profligacy and urged other EU states to adopt fiscal discipline in order to avoid the fate of Greece, French president Nicolas Sarkozy favored easier rules on deficit spending, lower interest rates, and other measures to stimulate the economy. The divisions between two of Europe's largest economies became even bigger after French finance minister Christine Lagarde suggested that the German export model had to be reconfigured in the interest of less competitive EU nations, and that Germany, with a large current account surplus, should spend more and save less for the good of member states. The recommendation, needless to say, did not go over well in Berlin. German economy minister Rainer Bruederle fired back: "For countries which have lived in the past off entitlements and neglected their competitiveness to point their finger at others is politically . . . understandable but unfair."[16] Not surprisingly, the French-German split, the plunging value of the euro during the crisis, and Europe's north-south divide epitomized by frugal Germany and free-spending Greece did little to engender U.S. confidence in the European Union.

Indeed, the Greek financial crisis—which pulled back the covers on Europe's public sector indebtedness and which could rear its ugly head again—juxtaposed against robust economic growth emanating from China, India, and the developing nations only served to reaffirm in the minds of many investors and policy makers in the United States that Europe is the past, the emerging markets the future. This realization is likely to spur corporate America to shift its strategic sites away from Europe and toward the more dynamic markets of Asia, Latin America, and others in the years ahead. To many in Washington, rapidly aging, heavily indebted, and increasingly fragmented Europe is more of a withering partner of the United States on the global stage than a forward-looking, dynamic ally.

Lending credence to this view, the same question that Henry Kissinger famously asked back in the 1970s—"If I want to call Europe, who do I call?"—still does not have an answer. While the European Union's Lisbon Treaty, which finally took effect in 2009, was supposed to give the 27-member group a more united, consistent, and weightier voice in global affairs, anyone sitting in Washington today wanting to ring Europe for help or guidance would not know whom to call. The Lisbon Treaty has hardly clarified matters—to the contrary. Europe now boasts separate presidents of the European Council, the European Commission, and the European Parliament. Add to this the six-month-long rotating EU presidency, and Europe's leadership hierarchy has never been more muddled.

Compounding matters, the appointment of Herman Van Rompuy, Belgium's prime minister, as the EU's first full-time president in 2009 was received with a thud. The EU's new foreign policy chief, Britain's Catherine Ashton, received a similarly underwhelming response as well. Both positions—the EU presidency and new foreign policy chief—were created to upgrade Europe's role on the global stage. However, the appointment of two relative unknowns, with little experience in global affairs, has done little to enhance the global might of Europe.

Speaking to Europe's role in the world, *Financial Times* columnist Gideon Rachman noted the following:

> Maybe the Copenhagen and Davos experiences are rather similar, and Europe's role is simply to provide the conference hall and get out, because it is not very central to these debates. But there is a slight European crisis of confidence, first because the kind of theatrics of Copenhagen weren't good for Europe, but also such a mess was made of the appointment of the new president and foreign minister of the EU. The EU is still the largest economy in the world, bigger than the United States and China. But it does not punch its political weight, and a couple of nobodies have been appointed as the president and foreign minister, who people in Europe haven't even heard of, let alone the rest of the world. That's been a blow to confidence. There's a sense that Europe has missed its moment.[17]

If Europe's day has passed—and the signs point in this direction barring significant change—the omens are hardly favorable for the United States and the Western-led multilateral institutions that have long governed the global economy. A cohesive and cooperative Europe has been instrumental in helping the United States mold the world economy in its own image and to its liking. The global economic framework of the past half-century reflects the shared values and goals of the United

States and Europe, and their ability to set aside differences for the good of the global commons. Over the past 60 years, the transatlantic economy has been the anchor of the global economy and the prime example of the mutual benefits of deep cross-border integration, or globalization.

The past, however, is going to be hard to replicate. Even before the financial crisis of 2008 and ensuing transatlantic recession, the United States and Europe were at loggerheads over a number of issues, ranging from the Doha trading round, global climate change, energy security, and a host of industry-specific differences involving genetically modified food, pharmaceuticals, chemicals, air travel, insurance, and many other service-related activities. Different regulatory frameworks, heterogeneous health and safety regulations, fragmented distribution channels—all of these factors across Europe continue to bedevil transatlantic relations and represent key barriers to future economic integration. Agricultural trade remains a notable sticking point between the two parties, as does a highly protected transatlantic service economy.

The myriad responses in Europe to the financial crisis, meanwhile, have only served to highlight how fragmented policy making remains in Europe despite the region's "single market" and "single currency." Notwithstanding these impressive achievements, national interests, in most cases, continue to trump the broader interest and objectives of greater Europe. What could very well emerge from the crisis is a two-tiered Europe, with better positioned and performing economies, like Germany and the tech-savvy Nordic nations, prospering in the years ahead, while the aging and indebted south, or the Club Med members of Greece, Italy, Spain, and Portugal, languish. That is a recipe for more political and economic volatility within Europe and hardly rates as a propitious backdrop for the transatlantic partnership.

The United States has not only been frustrated with Europe's enfeebled response to the global financial crisis, but also discouraged by Europe's measures in other areas, notably in U.S. efforts in Iraq and Afghanistan. Speaking in undiplomatic terms, U.S. defense secretary Robert Gates took Europe to task for its role in Afghanistan: "The demilitarization of Europe—where large swaths of the general public and political class averse to military force and the risks that go with it—has gone from a blessing in the twentieth century to an impediment to achieving real security and lasting peace in the twenty-first."[18] Gates's comments came three days after the government in the Netherlands collapsed in dispute over the role of Dutch troops in Afghanistan.

In the end, if the transatlantic economy was not the foundation on which globalization rests, then the fact that the solidarity and cohesion of the transatlantic partnership are fraying would not be so worrisome. But the ties that bind the transatlantic partnership are weakening and will continue to wither if America increasingly views Europe as weak and divided, and less important in the context of rising China, India, and other strategically important nations, and if Europe, in turn, remains intolerant of muscular U.S. foreign forays in the Middle East and Afghanistan and remains disenchanted with U.S.-led free-market capitalism. Europe too believes in the rise of China, India, and Russia, which has lead key EU states like Germany, France, and the United Kingdom to craft and chart their own course with the world's newly emergent giants. In sum, as existing perceptions solidify and as current trends gain more traction, the risk is that transatlantic partnership is downgraded by one or both parties or allowed to atrophy by benign neglect.

At best, the United States and Europe are in a strained relationship; at worst, the two parties could be headed for divorce court.

JAPAN—THE NEXT SWITZERLAND?

No other region of the world has posted more impressive economic numbers and achieved more commercial success over the past half-century than Asia. Ravaged by the devastation of World War II, Asia was one of the poorest regions of the global economy at the halfway mark of the twentieth century. Japan's per capita income was less than three-fourths its prewar level. In 1950, South Korea's per capita was less than Nigeria's and Egypt's. In the early 1950s, the entire region accounted for less than 10 percent of world output; agriculture was the principal engine of growth at the time, and as the dust settled on Asia following the destruction of war, very few imagined that the region would emerge as a dynamic engine of the global economy a few short decades later.

By the late 1960s and early 1970s, the economic comeback of Asia was plain to see. An economic "miracle" was in the making, with Japan at the forefront. The nation's precursor to China's mix of state and private enterprises, the famed Ministry of International Trade and Industry (MITI), fostered the growth of future international giants such as Toyota, Sony, and Mitsubishi. Japan's innovation of just-in-time inventory controls, forcing companies to sharply raise their quality standards in order to supply new products on demand, swept the world in the 1980s, leaving Detroit carmakers, among other complacent industries, to scramble madly to keep up. Books such as *Japan, Inc.* posited that in a few short years Japan would become number one.

Its rise to the second largest economy in the world compelled other nations in the region to follow suit. Rapidly industrializing right behind Japan were the newly industrialized countries (NICs) of South Korea, Taiwan, Hong Kong, and Singapore. And behind the NICs were other cohorts, the resource-rich members of the Association of Southeast Asian Nations (ASEAN), consisting primarily of Malaysia, Thailand, Indonesia, and the Philippines. The common denominator to the success of these nations—an export orientation that helped create domestic jobs and income, which helped boost per capita incomes and provide the foreign exchange for further investment in a number of industries, ranging from textiles to steel to computers.

Over the postwar era, a V-shaped economic hierarchy developed in Asia. Some spoke of Asia's development resembling a formation of flying geese.[19] Japan, of course, functioned as the apex of the V-shaped configuration and helped pull along the rest of the region. Over time, labor-intensive industries once based in Japan like textiles, toys, apparel, electronics, and furniture shifted first from the NICs, helping these nations to take off, and then to Southeast Asia, kick-starting the industrialization of those countries. In the process, one economic "miracle" after another was hatched within the global economic framework constructed by the West.

For Washington, the orderly and predictable economic rise of Asia helped buttress U.S. economic and security interests in the region and served as a vital bulwark against the spread of communism. By the 1980s, a region once ravaged by war and threatened by communist powers like China and North Korea was securely ensconced in the U.S.-led capital system and shielded under the U.S. security umbrella. The starting point for this scenario was Japan's embrace of the U.S.-built global economic architecture. By looking "west" and by starting an "economic miracle" that was replicated around the region, Japan was instrumental in pulling other Asian states into the U.S.-led global economic system.

Today, however, while Asia remains very much a part of the global economy constructed by the West, the region is dramatically being reconfigured. Japan's miracle economy looks more and more like a mirage. Following a credit-fueled property boom and bust in the late 1980s, Japan's economy has gone nowhere in the past two decades.

In what has become a familiar pattern in the past 20 years, soaring profits led to overexpansion in both the Japanese stock market, the Nikkei, and in real estate. To give one telling example, property in Tokyo's Ginza district reached a high of $139,000 per square foot in 1989. Even after trillions of dollars were wiped out in the subsequent crash, Japanese banks continued to make questionable loans, leading to prolonged stagnation.

The "lost decade" of the 1990s was followed by another lost decade to open the twenty-first century. Crippling deflation, which has deterred spending among Japanese consumers, falling productivity levels, and an overreliance on exports has relegated Japan to the economic slow lane. Since the early 1990s, China has shoved aside Japan to become the region's economic pace-setter. Economic activity in Asia increasingly pivots around the mainland, not Japan. Once considered unstoppable, the land of the rising sun now confronts a future with a shrinking population, fewer workers, more retirees, and a crushing national debt. After years of trying to revive its morbid economy with more state spending, Japan is now saddled with the highest public-sector debt to GDP ratio in the developed world, at around 190 percent. In 2010, state borrowing of ¥44 trillion is for the first time expected to exceed tax revenues of ¥37 trillion, an ugly fiscal imbalance that will only add to Japan's massive debt load.

In an ominous look ahead, state debt is only expected to rise as Japan's population ages and its workforce shrinks. The working age population, according to the government, is expected to decline by 9 percent during the next decade.[20] In terms of demographics, Japan now has as many middle-aged people (age 45 or older) as those under the age of 45. According to figures from the United Nations, Japan's population is expected to fall from 127 million today to just 101.6 million by 2050. By then the nation's working-age population (those workers between the ages of 15 to 64) is expected to total just 49 million workers, down roughly 40 percent from current levels. Meanwhile, the number of people over the age of 65 is expected to rise from roughly 27 million in 2007 to 38 million in 2050, creating a retiree-to-worker ratio that is unsustainable. Given the dire fiscal and financial straits Japan now finds itself in, the nation may be set up for a Greek-style debt crisis. Not that this is a new development. A few years ago a joke made the rounds on Wall Street: What is the difference between Japan and Argentina? Two years.

A financial implosion of Japan is not preordained, yet even if Japan does avoid such a fate, it will not change the fact that the sun is setting on America's longtime economic partner in Asia. Rather than inspire global confidence, Japan instead engenders apathy among many investors and policy makers in Washington. For a country that was once feared by the United States, it is startling how little economic attention America pays to Japan today. In Asia, Washington's focus, of course, is now directed at China. The same holds true for Japan—it too is also focusing more of its attention on Beijing.

Expanding trade is pulling Japan more into the orbit of Asia than the West, with Japan's economy now linked more to Asia than either the United States or Europe; nearly 55 percent of Japan's total exports went to Asia in 2009, the first time Asia has accounted for over half of Japan's total. China is now Japan's largest export market, accounting for 18.9 percent of Japan's total exports in 2009, versus a share of 16.1 percent to the United States and 12.5 percent to the European Union.

On the political front, the landslide victory of the Democratic Party of Japan (DPJ) in August 2009, after nearly 54 years of uninterrupted rule by the Liberal Democratic Party, had raised questions about Japan's future orientation toward the West versus the East. Before he resigned in early June 2010, then Prime Minister Yukio Hatoyama was not considered anti-American, but he did speak in the past about forming an East Asian community that would exclude the United States. "Until now, our connection with the United States has been very strong. Naturally, this will continue to be the case in terms of our national security. But for economic growth, it is necessary to look closely at Asia as a new frontier," Hatoyama told the media in late 2009.[21]

Even in terms of national security and foreign policy, relations between the United States and Japan are poised to change. The DPJ decided not to extend Japan's refueling operations in the Indian Ocean in support of the allied military effort in Afghanistan and wanted to reopen and reconsider an earlier agreement on the relocation of a U.S. air base on the island of Okinawa. It was the latter issue, in fact, that lead to Hatoyama's downfall and abrupt resignation in June 2010. With the United States unwilling to open renegotiations over the American air base in Okinawa, Hatoyama was unable to fulfill a key campaign promise and promptly left office. As of mid-2010, Japan was yet again searching for another prime minister, and found one in Mr. Naoto Kan. The length of Mr. Kan's tenure, however, like many recent prime ministers in Japan remains open to question.

In the end, Japan increasingly looks like Switzerland—comfortable and rich (for now), and increasingly inward-looking, with little influence or care to be a global actor on the world stage. Tokyo does care about the rising military presence of

China, a trend that is expected to lead to greater U.S.-Japanese security ties. That said, Japan's global significance has declined with its sinking economic fortunes. The rise of China, meanwhile, has dramatically reconfigured Asia's economic hierarchy. The flying geese have been scattered. In the region, the mainland now leads while Japan follows; a trend confirmed in 2010, when China's economy surpassed Japan's to become the second largest in the world. As Asia's economic power structure is reordered, the commercial links that have long bound the United States and Japan, or the main links between the West and East, will weaken.

THE TWILIGHT OF THE WEST

Even before the financial crisis struck, the West's monopoly over the global economy was slipping. This shift in economic power, however, from the West to the Rest was subtle and largely non-disruptive and thought by many in the West as a process measured in decades, not years. Yet the financial crisis of 2008 was an accelerator, a fast-forwarding mechanism that has hurtled the global economy down an uncharted path toward global parity between the developed and developing nations. The crisis unmasked the West's credit-driven economic model as destructive and unsustainable, leaving the West increasingly divided among itself and handicapped in shaping the global economic agenda of the future.

Europe's uncoordinated response to the financial meltdown, coupled with the sovereign debt crisis in Greece and lingering risks associated with Europe's sovereign debt, has undermined global confidence in the continent. A two-tiered economy in Europe—with Germany and other successful exporters outstripping growth in the debt-laden south—is likely to create future political and social strains that will do more to divide rather than unite Europe. In Asia, Japan's incompetence in generating growth juxtaposed by the ease by which China sailed through the crisis solidified Asia's new economic order, with the Middle Kingdom firmly on top. These dynamics, coupled with the massive indebtedness of the United States, have left many in the developing nations highly suspicious of the old ways of doing things. The nearly 6 billion who live outside the West no longer feel beholden to Western-dominated institutions and have lost faith in Western ways of economic management. The rest of the world is becoming more detached from the West, forming strands and alliances beyond the traditional global powers of the United States and Europe.

At the same time, the ties that once bound the West so profitably are becoming more frayed. Across the Atlantic, economic ties between the United States and Europe remain thick—for now—although the scars from the U.S.-led war in Iraq, the global financial crisis, and a bevy of industry-specific sticking points continue to weaken and strain the transatlantic partnership. This bears close watching since the transatlantic economy has been the bedrock of globalization and a key pillar supporting America's global dominance. In Asia, Japan's economic linkages are increasingly being redirected toward China and its neighbors. As Europe and Japan struggle to cope with slower growth, large public sector deficits, and deteriorating demographics, the West becomes weaker, and America's underlying dominance wanes.

Set against the aging, indebted, and increasingly divided developed nations are the likes of China, Poland, Brazil, and many other emerging economies, whose confidence and economic vigor seem to grow with each day. The presence of the world's new power brokers continues to rise and is the subject of the next chapter.

Flexing Their Muscle— The New Power Brokers in Action

The West can no longer dominate, given its partial loss of moral authority. For the first time in centuries, the developing East has some say.
> —Ronnie Chan, Chairman of Hang Lung Properties, Hong Kong[1]

Today, the 5.6 billion people who live outside the Western universe will no longer accept decisions made on their behalf in Western capitals.
> —Kishore Mahbubani, Dean, Lee Kuan Yew School of Public Policy at the National University of Singapore[2]

The West is no longer in control of the global economy, and the rest of the world knows it. The new drivers of economic activity are the developing nations. Their collective presence in one market after another is becoming larger and more significant with each passing year. Barbie Dolls, Boeing airplanes, Viagra—name virtually any product, and there is a very good chance that the strongest demand and future sales growth for such items lie in the Middle East, the Indian subcontinent, Africa, Asia, and Latin America. Global food and energy prices increasingly reflect the supply-and-demand equation not of the West, but of the Rest. Similarly, global capital flows are increasingly dictated by actions taken by central bankers and investment managers in Kuwait, Beijing, and São Paulo. The global money centers of New York and London, of course, still matter, but the shift in investment capital—from the West to the Rest—reflects the fact that the world's excess reserves—or savings—are in the vaults of China, Brazil, Russia, and the Middle East.

The Rest is stepping up. The evidence is everywhere and in all fields. Taiwan now has more high-tech researchers than Britain.[3] McDonald's restaurants in Russia are twice as busy as those in the United States.[4] Between March 2002 and November 2009, the number of mobile-phone users in India soared from 6.5 million to over 500 million. The number of credit cards in use in China totaled 175 million in September 2009, a rise of one-third from a year before and a seven-fold jump from 2003.[5] Porsche sold more cars in Russia than in the United States in 2008.[6] Some 316 million people have signed up for cell phone service in Africa in the past decade, a number greater than the total population of the United States. After aggressively scouring the world for oil, the estimated oil reserves of state-owned PetroChina were roughly 21.8 billion barrels in 2008, nearly double the level of Chevron of the United States and Total of France.

These shifts highlight the rapidly changing nature of global business, with the Rest not only responsible for new markets but also new competitors. When the United Arab Emirates put out a $20 billion bid for four nuclear reactors, the winning contract did not go to world-class firms from either France or Japan. Instead, it was awarded to a consortium led by Korea Electric

Power Corporation. Along similar lines, European telecommunication equipment makers were stunned when Belgacom, a Belgium telecommunications company, handed a large contract to China's Huawei Technologies Company. The company won the bid based not only on low-cost pricing but also on the quality of its technology—a deadly combination for industry leaders like Nokia, Siemens, Alcatel-Lucent, and other Western firms.

Welcome to the new world—one neither flat nor curved but messy and multipolar. The last economic superpower—the United States—will face great difficulties adjusting as the tempo of global economic activity beats more to the tune of the developing nations and not American-led globalization. While it is commonplace to speak about a world where the center of gravity is shifting from the West to the Rest, the implications and consequences of this shift have not been fully digested by the developed nations. The emerging markets are not just leading the world out of recession in 2010; they are fortifying their strengths in such key sectors as energy, mining, steel, automobiles, telecommunications, power generation, finance, and alternative energies like solar power. Chinese firms are on the cusp of becoming global leaders in electric cars, solar panels, and more efficient coal-fired plants. Vale of Brazil has emerged as a world-class mining company. South Korea and Taiwan lead the world in flat-screen technologies, among other advanced technologies. Cemex of Mexico is a global leader in cement production. India's software capabilities, quite apart from its back-office dominance, grow stronger by the day. The list of yet-to-be-heard-about companies from the developing nations goes on. New corporate leaders are emerging from the developing nations, and they are set to challenge Western incumbents who are more accustomed to competing against each other (Boeing versus Airbus) than against corporate upstarts (Brazil's Embarer) from the emerging markets. Reflecting this turn in the tide, while 46 companies from the emerging markets were part of the Fortune 500 in 2005, the figure had doubled to 92 in 2009.

At a broader level, control of the world's critical economic inputs—natural resources, capital, and labor—is increasingly shifting to the developing nations, a dynamic that could very well lead to more tension between the well-endowed Rest versus the West. The latter is deep in debt, energy-deficient, and confronting an aging workforce. These debilitating factors leave the United States and many other Western states at the mercy of Middle East sovereign wealth funds, Latin American commodity producers, and Taiwanese contract manufacturers like electronics giant Foxconn, to cite just a few examples.

Confident and emboldened, and sensing that their time has come, the developing nations are poised to flex their newfound muscle. How the United States in particular and the West in general responds to the collective energy and optimism of the developing nations remains to be seen.

KEEPING UP WITH THE SENS AND ZHUS

Richard Freeman first publicized the startling fact that the global labor force had effectively doubled over the course of the 1990s.[7] The Harvard economist dubbed this phenomenon "The Great Doubling," noting that in 1990 only half the world's workforce worked under the umbrella of free-market capitalism. At the time it was concentrated in North America, South America, western Europe, Africa, and parts of Asia. However, following the collapse of the former Soviet Union, India's shift away from self-sufficiency and China's embrace of market capitalism, the global workforce effectively doubled, rising from approximately 1.5 billion workers to roughly 3 billion.

Rarely had so many workers entered the global mainstream at once, spawning, not surprisingly, a great deal of anxiety among politicians and workers in the United States and Europe. Early in the 2000s, the debate over this massive influx of new workers focused on the supply-side effects on the world economy. A billion and a half new workers helped suppress global wages, consumer prices, and in turn interest rates, and helped fatten profits for those international companies able to leverage this massive new labor pool to their cost advantage. Initially, these new global participants were thought of as only workers.

Yet over time these same workers became consumers. The doubling of the global force also unleashed a shocking new surge of demand on the global economy. Hundreds of millions of people have been lifted out of poverty, boosting the living standards and purchasing power of consumers in China, India, Poland, Russia, and a host of other developing nations. China, for instance, has recorded the largest and fastest decline in poverty in history, as the percentage of people living on less than $2 per day fell from 84.6 percent of the total in 1990 to 36.3 percent in 2005. For the developing nations in general, those toiling on less than $2 a day dropped from nearly two-thirds in 1990 to 47 percent in 2005.[8] Further improvement is expected—the World Bank estimates that the percentage of workers earning $2 a day or less will decline to 33.7 percent of the total population by 2015, a far cry from nearly 64 percent in 1990.[9]

Slowly but surely, more money is flowing into the pockets of workers in the developing nations. Their earnings remain minuscule, to be sure, and in many cases what little extra income they have is spent on basic staples, leaving little money for discretionary items. Workers earning $2 a day in the developing markets have their heads barely above the poverty line, hardly in a position to own a car. Yet for those households further up the income scale, the prospect of owning a car is becoming less of a dream and more of a reality.

The actual size of the middle class in the emerging markets remains open to debate. A wage of $2 per day is commonly accepted as denoting the poverty line in the emerging markets, but that limit may be too inclusive. If one defines the middle class as workers earning between $2 and $13 a day, then half the world is now considered middle class. By this definition, the middle class of the emerging markets totaled a staggering 2.6 billion people in 2005.[10] This bar is probably set too low, however. The World Bank defines those in the middle class as people who earn between $12 and $50 per day, and by this measure the middle class of the developing nations is eight times smaller yet nevertheless poised to expand rapidly.

This cohort already numbers some 400 million people, according to the World Bank, a figure roughly one-third larger than the entire U.S. population.[11] More important, the middle class of the developing nations is expected to triple in size over the next two decades, increasing to 1.2 billion by 2030. By then the developing nations will account for 93 percent of the global middle class, up from 56 percent in 2000. This estimate suggests ever-rising levels of consumption in the developing nations. Yet even today, the emerging market consumer outspends the U.S. consumer. In 2010, the United States accounted for roughly 28 percent of global consumption versus a 32 percent share of the emerging markets.[12] Eight years ago, the percentages were roughly reversed—when the U.S. consumer was the most potent spending machine on earth. With a population less than 5 percent of the global total, the United States accounted for nearly one-fifth of global imports in 2000. By 2009, America's share had dropped to below 13 percent.

Times have changed, in other words. The spending power of the U.S. consumer has diminished on both a relative and absolute basis. Purchasing power among developing consumers, in contrast, has accelerated. Whereas in the past factory workers in Asia would trudge off to work on Saturday morning, today they are more likely to head for the local shopping malls for a day of socializing and shopping. Shanghai, Dubai, Mumbai, Ho Chi Minh City, Istanbul, São Paulo—any first-time visitor to these emerging cities is struck by the vitality of the local consumer, out in force and shopping in an air-conditioned mall that might be mistaken, in some cases, for the luxury complex in Short Hills, New Jersey. Granted, those trolling the shopping centers in the emerging markets are the lucky few relative to the rest of the general population. But the numbers and scale of these urban buyers, and their pent-up demand for electronic goods, appliances, automobiles, skin-care products, clothing, and other goods has reached the point that these consumers are increasingly setting global trends, leading in global fashion, and driving global sales in a number of industries.

On the contrary, thrift and austerity are fast becoming the norm in the West—whether the developed world likes it or not. Conspicuous consumption, meanwhile, is rapidly becoming the rage in places like Brazil, India, Turkey, and other emerging markets. Emblematic of this trend, China's automobile market is now larger than America's. While total U.S. vehicle sales imploded in 2009, dropping by over 20 percent from the prior year, vehicle sales in China exploded, surging roughly 45 percent. In other words, what is now good for China is good for General Motors, a market leader in China. GM's automobile sales to China soared to over 1.8 million vehicles in 2009, a 67 percent annual rise that helped offset plunging sales at home and helped stabilize a company that ultimately had to file for bankruptcy.

Ironically, the future earnings of General Motors, now a company 60 percent owned by the U.S. government, increasingly pivot around the Chinese consumer. In the not-too-distant future, this government-owned entity is expected to sell just as many vehicles in China as the United States. Ford Motors, meanwhile, saw its sales in China surge by 44 percent in 2009, also helping to boost the profits of the one U.S. automobile manufacturer that did not receive U.S. government assistance during the financial crisis.

THE INCREASING COMPETITION FOR NATURAL RESOURCES

While booming auto sales in the emerging markets is a blessing for U.S. automobile manufacturers, the same dynamic is a curse for the average American. The more consumers in China, India, Egypt, and other countries take to the road in their shiny new cars and trucks, the more upward pressure on world oil prices and the higher the cost of oil for an energy-dependent America.

Most Americans are oblivious to the rising middle classes of the developing nations and what this new consuming cohort means for the world's already stretched natural resource base. They have yet to recognize that as the new global consuming class adopts and acquires Western life styles—moving from the village to the city, working in air-conditioned offices, driving to work, consuming more protein—the greater the demand and the higher the prices for energy, water, agricultural goods, and other natural resources. The West faces stiff new competition with the Rest for natural resources.

The monopoly the West enjoyed in devouring the world's natural resources has decisively ended. As long as consumers in the developing nations remained poor and lacked the income to purchase a computer or car, or afford a good meal, the West did not have to compete with the developing nations for oil, copper, and soybeans, among other commodities. For much of the post–Cold War era, the equation was rather simple: the developing nations produced commodities, and the West consumed them. Those days are over, however. As *The Economist* notes, "During the past 15 years a new middle class has sprung up in emerging markets, producing a silent revolution in human affairs—a revolution of wealth-creation and new aspirations."[13] As part of this revolution in wealth, the number of millionaires in China is expected to top 1 million very shortly, with the average Chinese millionaire owning three cars.[14]

While the United States can certainly feed itself, the country's energy security remains fraught with risk. One danger lies with the global concentrations of oil supplies. More and more of the world's proven oil reserves are controlled by states and state-owned companies whose interests are not aligned with those of the United States. While Exxon Mobil, Chevron, and ConocoPhillips rank as some of the largest corporations in the United States, these American oil giants, in terms of proven reserves, pale in comparison to Gazprom of Russia, Sinopec and PetroChina of China, and Petronas of Malaysia and the Middle East giants that set atop a huge share of the world's proven oil reserves. "Big oil" has a whole different meaning today.

What matters in the energy field is proven reserves—indeed, an energy company without oil reserves is like a bank without cash deposits. More than 90 percent of the world's proven oil reserves are held by oil companies that are either partially or fully controlled by governments. Energy is too big an industry, too profitable a sector, too strategic a commodity, to be left to the private sector in nations like Saudi Arabia, Mexico, Venezuela, Malaysia, Kuwait, and others, which, over the past few years, have restricted the access of its oil industry to Western oil companies. In a stunning shift in energy power, privately owned multinationals now produce just 10 percent of the world's oil and hold just 3 percent of its reserves.[15]

"In reality," notes Tina Rosenberg, "*nationalized* oil is the trend. And the percentage of oil controlled by state-controlled companies is likely to continue rising, mainly because of the demographics of oil. Deposits are being exhausted in wealthy countries—the ones that exploited their oil first and generally have the most private oil—and are being found largely in developing countries, where oil tends to belong to the state."[16] That spells trouble for a fossil-fuel-driven economy like the United States.

Another risk to America's energy future lies on the demand side of the equation, with the rise in wealth and consumption in Asia of particular importance. The United States should not only be worried about America's dependence on foreign oil, but we should also be petrified (and galvanized) by the stunning gap between Asia's explosive rise in oil consumption on the one hand and the region's paltry oil reserves on the other. The scale of Asia's oil economics is frightening.

The region, home to half of the world's population, accounting for over 30 percent of global output, has become the industrial workhorse of the global economy and is experiencing an urban explosion. Despite all these growth factors, Asia's proven oil reserves are a proverbial drop in the bucket. The region's reserves accounted for just 3.2 percent of the global total at the end of 2009. That is down from 3.7 percent a decade ago, a decline due in large part to falling reserves in China, the region's largest oil producer. The mainland's reserves totaled 14.8 billion barrels at the end of 2009, a 7.5 percent decline from two decades ago.[17] At current production rates, China's oil reserves will be exhausted in less than 11 years. As for all of Asia, the region's reserves-to-production ratio (an indicator of how long proven reserves would last at current production rates) is slightly higher than China's, at 14.4 years.[18]

Asia, in other words, is basically running on empty, even after taking into account efforts at energy conservation and the development of alternative energy sources. The region's share of global oil production has slipped over the past decade, sliding from a share of 10.4 percent in 1999 to 10 percent in 2009. Asia produces plenty of things, but unfortunately oil is not one of them. Barring the discovery of significant new oil fields, the region's contribution to global oil production will continue to decline. That is hardly an encouraging trend for the West, since that decline is juxtaposed against soaring long-term demand. Fed by rapid industrialization and urbanization, along with expanding automobile ownership, Asia's oil consumption soared 25 percent between 1999 and 2009; over the same period, oil production rose by just 5.5 percent in Asia, while proven oil reserves increased by 5.6 percent.[19] That disconnect in oil will ultimately affect U.S. consumers.

Oil consumption in China nearly doubled in the past decade, rising from 4.5 million barrels per day in 1999 to nearly 9 million in 2009. Oil production, however, rose by just 18 percent over the same period. Because the nation's production in 2009 was less than half the nation's total consumption, the gap forced China to step up its overseas search for oil. Beijing has been doing just that over the past decade, emerging as a key investor, donor, and creditor in resource-rich nations like Nigeria, Angola, Argentina, Venezuela, Equatorial Guinea, Gabon, the Republic of Congo, Afghanistan, and a host of other emerging nations. Access to oil lies at the heart of most of these deals, although many projects are bundled around Chinese foreign aid, which typically includes soft loans, trade agreements, arms sales, debt forgiveness, massive construction projects, and massive aid packages.

All the items just mentioned are carrots the West, notably the United States, has long used to curry favor in developing nations deemed geostrategically important to the West. The game, however, is now being played by China and others like India, Brazil, and Russia to the consternation of the United States and Europe. These new players are carving out geostrategic spheres of influence in places like Africa and central Asia as the global race for resources truly gets under way.

One example suggesting that Beijing is up to playing this game occurred when Angola balked at an IMF mandate for transparency in its oil accounting. In swooped the Chinese Export-Import Bank, offering up an interest-free loan instead, with no accounting required. Despite Western protests, China continues to do business with such nations as Myanmar, North Korea, Iran, and Cuba. To the annoyance of the United States, China's energy deals with Venezuela are becoming larger and more frequent. Meanwhile, Beijing has used its seat on the U.N. Security Council to block proposed sanctions against Sudan, which has emerged as a critical source of Chinese oil. China's foreign policy of "noninterference," as opposed to the heavy-handed strictures the IMF has imposed in the past, attracts lesser nations to make deals with the Middle Kingdom.

As a report from the Congressional Research Service noted, China's "assistance often garners appreciation among foreign leaders and citizens disproportionate to its costs: (1) China offers assistance without the conditions that Western donors frequently place on aid (i.e., democratic reform, market opening, and environmental protection). China's policy of 'noninterference in other countries' domestic affairs' often wins international support because it is regarded as respectful of their countries sovereignty; (2) Chinese aid does not require a lengthy process involving setting up and meeting social and environmental safeguards; (3) PRC assistance . . . carries great symbolic value."[20]

"Authoritarian governments," according to *The Economist*, "are using their money to buy influence abroad. Sometimes the money comes as a commercial loan; sometimes, as a grant, frequently, as both. These flows are changing the business of aid, undermining attempts by Western countries to improve their programmes and encouraging recipients to play donors off against each other."[21]

All this, not surprisingly, frustrates and in some cases, infuriates the United States. However, the world's last economic superpower has little leverage over China in Africa, and little leverage over other developing nations out searching for food and energy.

Asia's other giant, India, has embarked on a mission similar to China's—increasingly scouring the world for stable energy supplies. In a country where over two-thirds of the population is under the age of 35, India's oil consumption is just 37 percent of that of China. This gap will likely narrow in the future as more and more Indian consumers embrace cars and as more people migrate from the farms to the cities. Indian energy companies have already been active in such areas as the Caspian Sea, Venezuela, Myanmar, Libya, and Sudan. Like China, its main Asian rival, India refuses to abide by Western dictates in terms of where the oil deal is struck. The end result of the world's other population giant's economic growth puts even more strain on the global oil infrastructure. As a side effect, U.S. oil companies are finding it increasingly difficult to secure their own reserves in the developing nations because of rising competition from Chinese and Indian oil majors.

And the scramble for resources extends far beyond oil. Copper, silver, iron ore, meat, corn, wheat, soybeans—the future price of these commodities will increasingly reflect the rising per capita incomes and attendant jump in consumption among consumers in the developing nations. Between now and 2030, worldwide demand for food is expected to rise by 50 percent, and demand for meat during that time will jump by 85 percent, according to the World Bank.[22] One perverse effect of this shift in diet, as a study published in the August 2008 issue of *Health Affairs* reported, is that 25 percent of adults in China are obese or overweight, mainly those in cities. The study found that the number of obese women in China doubled since 1989, while the number of obese men tripled in the same amount of time.[23]

Across the spectrum, these upheavals will leave U.S. consumers paying even higher prices for commodities, barring an unforeseen jump in supplies. In a seminal shift, prices paid for world resources will increasingly be set by forces outside the United States, leaving American consumers in the unusual position as taking whatever price they can get, subject to the dictates of suppliers and consumers in the emerging markets.

THE NEW FINANCERS

Besides being home to the future consumers of the world and firmly in control of the world's natural resources, another critical input under the domain of the Rest is the world's excess savings or capital. At the end of 2009, nearly 80 percent of the world's total foreign exchange reserves—in effect, the globe's excess savings—were bunkered in the vaults of the developing nations. That equates to a cool $6.6 trillion, a figure that includes China's $2.5 trillion in reserves, accumulated largely by running a massive trade surplus with the United States, and $785 billion among Middle East oil producers, obtained with the help of the long-term run-up in oil prices. These variables, coupled with the surge in debt among the developed nations, have triggered a stunning shift in global financial power. Simply put, the debt is in the West; the savings in the Rest. The poor are "rich," and the rich are "poor."

In this new world, the U.S. Federal Reserve chairman has competition when he attempts to influence global capital markets. Granted, Fed chairman Ben Bernanke ranks as one of the most influential bankers in the world. Yet faceless, barely known central bankers in Delhi, Beijing, and the Middle East now hold tremendous sway over the world money supply—and debtor nations like the United States. In theory, Bernanke has at his disposal the tools to set U.S. interest rates; in practice, however, his ability to do so can be compromised by the moves of other central bankers. If central bankers in China and the Middle East are not comfortable with Bernanke's financial stewardship, they can either sell their U.S. dollar holdings or refuse to buy more U.S. securities at any given time, greatly complicating his life. Because China now owns nearly $900 billion in U.S. Treasuries, it holds considerable financial sway over America.[24] In the end, where the relatively unknown central bankers of the developing nations decide to invest their massive savings, and in what particular assets, directly affects the global credit markets every single day.

The same is true of sovereign wealth funds (SWF)—or government-controlled investment firms. Their numbers have increased over the past decade along with the swollen coffers of the developing nations. To help manage its riches, China created the China Investment Corporation in 2007 and initially capitalized the fund with $200 billion. By the end of 2009, the fund had grown to $290 billion. Russia got into the act in 2004 by creating the Stabilization Fund of the Russian Federation with an initial down payment of $141 billion. At the end of last year, the fund was eighth largest in the world, with some $170 billion under management. Over the last decade, other nations like Chile, New Zealand, Venezuela, South Korea, Kazakhstan, Australia, and Qatar, to name a few, have followed suit, and many nations have more than one fund. At the end of 2009, Abu Dhabi Investment Authority was the largest SWF in the world, with some $630 billion under management. The SWF of Saudi Arabia, at $430 billion, ranked third, behind Norway's. These figures are only estimates since the size of some SWFs are a state secret—in other words, the underlying financial firepower of the developing nations is not completely known and is most likely larger than the $4 trillion estimated in 2008. That handsome sum of capital, not surprisingly, has generated a great deal of angst in the West.

The size of SWFs, their motivations for investing (economic or political), their lack of transparency, and the potential for these funds to seek control of strategic assets in the United States and Europe—all these elements led many in Washington to conclude before the financial crisis that sovereign wealth funds were a clear and present danger to the West. At the height of SWF paranoia in 2005 and 2006, the U.S. Congress kicked around proposals that ranged from establishing a code of conduct for SWFs to formalizing standards that would result in greater transparency, better corporate governance, and clearer accounting rules. Some on Capitol Hill even broached the idea of establishing behavioral guidelines for SWFs.

Then the financial crisis struck in 2008. Almost overnight, SWFs, rather than being thought of as financial Trojan horses suddenly became white knights—the only entities around with the financial wherewithal to rush to the aid of battered Western financial institutions. And rush they did—the sovereign wealth funds of Qatar, Abu Dhabi, Singapore, Kuwait, and Korea pumped billions of dollars into U.S. banks between mid-2007 and late 2008. For their efforts, however, they suffered huge losses and have subsequently redirected their investments elsewhere.

Rather than banks, the 50 or so SWFs in existence are now more interested in investing in more tangible assets like oil and gas fields, agriculture, and commodity-related goods. The funds are also thought to have become more diversified since the financial crisis and more populated with foreign currencies, real estate, foreign bonds, precious metals, and equities. No one really knows the composition of these funds since they are beholden to only one stakeholder: the parent government. However, snippets do emerge every once in a while. In April 2010, for instance, China's giant sovereign wealth fund, the China Investment Corporation, revealed that it owned small equity stakes in such U.S. blue chip firms as Visa, Apple, Goodyear Tire, and Coca-Cola. The revelations did not garner much attention on Capitol Hill since the overriding stakes were rather small and in sectors considered nonstrategic by the U.S. government. SWFs, in other words, are investing below the radar screens of the politicians in Washington. In contrast, however, many emerging market multinationals are poised to make a bigger splash in the U.S. and European markets. In just one recent example, Taiwan's HTC decided that it would no longer be the hidden supplier of cell phones for Sprint. The HTC label, "Quietly Brilliant," is now front and center in all advertising for its full line of models. This change in corporate attitude and strategy speaks to a much broader dynamic—that large companies headquartered in the developing nations are stepping up and out, bent on becoming global players in their own right.

THE TABLES HAVE TURNED: THE HUNTED ARE NOW THE HUNTERS

Shopping is emerging as a favorite pastime for consumers in the developing nations. Yet that passion is not just confined to individuals. For many companies domiciled in the emerging markets, cross-border wheeling and dealing, long an exclusive sport of the West, is rapidly becoming popular in the corporate boardrooms of Mexico City, Moscow, and Mumbai, adding a whole new dimension to global mergers and acquisition.

Since the rough-and-tumble days of Britain's East India Trading Company, global mergers and acquisitions have been the domain of multinationals from the developed nations. Well endowed with capital and possessing superior brands and extensive logistics networks, Western multinationals have long been the global hunters, or the commercial entities with the clout to purchase foreign assets or companies. For decades, global mergers and acquisitions (M&A) were largely a corporate strategy deployed by Western multinationals, and a favorite hunting ground has been resource-rich developing nations and a handful of other emerging markets.

Firms from the developing nations were no match for the hunters since they lacked the sophistication to effectively compete beyond their home market. In some cases, capital controls and other government restrictions kept the companies firmly rooted in local markets. For much of the postwar era, companies in South Korea, Brazil, China, and other locales could only dream of being global players.

Times, however, have changed. Global deal-making is but another lost monopoly of the West. Aspiring multinationals from the developing nations are becoming more aggressive bidders for assets in other emerging markets, crowding out Western multinationals from acquiring oil fields in central Asia, telecommunications companies in Africa, and banks in Argentina, for instance. These same firms have boldly set their strategic sights on assets and popular brands in the United States and Europe, creating, in the process, a whole new competitive landscape for many Western firms.

Whereas cross-border M&A deals initiated by the developing nations have traditionally been directed at other developing nations, the developed nations are increasingly in the crosshairs of corporate entities from South Korea, Mexico, China, and others for a number of reasons. The appeal of the developed markets is manifold—access to global brands, cutting-edge technology, wealthy consumers, and distribution channels are all key variables driving more M&A deals from the Rest to the West.

Some examples from just the past few years: Saudi Basic Industries Corporation bought GE Plastics; Lenovo of China snapped up IBM's personal computer business; Brazilian mining company Vale bought Canadian nickel miner Inco and the Australian mining company AMCI; South African firm Suzlon was part of a deal that acquired Germany's Repower. Meanwhile, Chinese banks have bought large stakes in U.S. and British banks. Russian energy companies have snapped up strategic assets in Europe and Australia, while firms from the Middle East have taken control of companies in the United Kingdom and the United States. Indian companies, among the most acquisition-minded among the developing nations, have also been on a global shopping spree. India's Tata Motors is now the proud owner of Land Rover and Jaguar. Geely Motors of China owns Volvo, the one-time Swedish automobile manufacturer that was once owned by Ford Motors. Even chocolate has caught the fancy of emerging market investors. In 2007, Campbell Soup

Company sold its Godiva Chocolatier unit to the Ulker Group of Turkey. The latter is one of the largest consumer products groups in Turkey, and it paid out a cool $850 million to own one of the premier chocolate brands in the world.

Add up all the deals, and global deal-making has taken a new and interesting twist. Emerging global giants have joined the hunt for global assets, spending nearly $650 billion in foreign mergers and acquisitions in 2007, the peak year of global M&A activity. That compares with a decade-earlier total of just $60 billion, or a 10-fold expansion. Then the developing nations accounted for just less than 5 percent of the global total, although their global share jumped to an average of nearly one-third in the first half of 2010.

In addition to more M&A deals, more emerging market corporations are investing directly in the United States by building out their U.S.-based operations organically or through green field operations. Examples in this emerging field include Suntech Power, one of China's largest solar-panel manufacturers, which plans to open a factory in Arizona in anticipation of rising solar-panel sales in the United States. Chinese battery giant and electric vehicle developer BYD plans to put roots down in Los Angeles as part of its overall strategy to penetrate the nascent electric car market in the United States. Although the initial investment is small—involving the creation of just 150 new jobs in America—BYD made the investment with an eye toward constructing a U.S. assembly plant in the future.

Suntech and BYD are following in the footsteps of their Chinese counterpart Haier, a pioneer in the U.S. market. The Chinese manufacturer started in 1999, sinking $30 million into a refrigeration plant in Camden, South Carolina. In 2006, the company announced a three-year, $100 million expansion plan that should boost employment to roughly 1,000 workers in the future—workers who, by the way, earn roughly 10 times the average Chinese wage. Despite this cost differential, the company finds it more advantageous to "build where you sell," following the strategy of many other multinationals that have sunk stakes into the United States in order to manufacture products closer to their respective consumer base.

Haier has been joined by others from the emerging markets. Russian steel manufacturer Severstal, the fourth largest in the world, snapped up several U.S. steel companies on the cheap during the downturn year of 2008. South Korean automobile manufacturers Hyundai and Kia are now well-known U.S. brands, the former garnering record profits in 2009. Taiwanese electronic manufacturers have become a presence as well, as shown by Acer's 2007 acquisition of Gateway computers. Indian consulting firms such as Infosys have increased their foreign presence in the United States and in Europe, for that matter. Combined, rising foreign direct investment in new plant and equipment, coupled with more cross-border M&A will ultimately increase the in-country presence of many emerging market corporations in the United States.

For many U.S. states and local communities, that new flood of investment means more new jobs, new taxes, and more economic growth. At the national level, however, the rising investment from the developing nations—notably from state-owned companies—risks igniting a backlash on Capitol Hill. An uproar followed when China National Offshore Oil Corporation proposed to buy U.S. oil company Unocal in 2005. The offer was pulled after intense U.S. opposition related to national security concerns. A year later, another deal was torpedoed over U.S. opposition to the Dubai Port deal, a venture that would have granted control of some U.S. ports to a state-owned company from the United Arab Emirates. Both deals served to warn emerging-market corporations to tread carefully in the United States.

Yet even with this shot across the bow, emerging nations will continue to eye U.S. investment opportunities for no other reason than most globally inspired companies from the developing nations are woefully unrepresented in America, still one of the wealthiest markets in the world. Their present U.S. investment presence is nominal—of total foreign direct investment stock of $2.3 trillion in the United States in 2009, the developing nations accounted for just nearly 8 percent. In other words, even after inflows rose more than seven-fold during the first decade of this century, their investment position in the United States remains minuscule. To this point, total investment of the Netherlands in the United States over the last decade—roughly $200 billion—was greater than the total investment of the developing nations. That helps explain the rush among emerging market corporations to catch up in the developed markets of the United States, Europe, and even Japan. They are woefully underrepresented in the West and want to expand their market presence via foreign investment, not just through trade.

At the same time, many U.S. and European firms are similarly rushing to build a local presence in the developing nations. Why? Because contrary to the prevailing consensus, many Western multinationals are also woefully underrepresented in the new growth markets of the developing nations. And unfortunately, where large Western multinationals used to be courted by the developing nations, today the tide has turned—many developing nations are imposing tougher investment restrictions and requirements on the leviathans of the West.

U.S. INVESTMENT IN THE DEVELOPING NATIONS: TOO LITTLE TOO LATE?

It is near gospel in the United States that whenever a U.S. company announces a plan to shutter a U.S. plant and to expand its operations overseas, the preferred foreign destination must be a low-cost, low-wage country like Mexico or China. Or in the case of white-collar service jobs departing the United States, the destination must be high-tech India, the outsourcing capital of the world. This perception—that America's overseas investment bias tends toward the developing nations—does not square with reality, however.

One of the best-kept secrets in the United States is this: rather than too much U.S. investment in the developing nations, there's too little. If the developing nations represent the future of global economic activity, and, as we've seen, they most likely do, then many U.S. and European companies are not ready for the future. Presently, too much of America's global infrastructure—physical stock, workforce, R&D expenditures, foreign affiliate sales, and profits—is sunk in the slow-growth, high-wage, mature markets of Europe, Japan, and the developed nations in general. Conversely, too little of America's global assets are employed in the robust, demographically favorable markets of the developing nations. As a result, at a time when global demand is shifting from rich to poor nations, many key developing nations have become less receptive to accepting Western investment, leaving corporate America dangerously embedded in countries whose growth will be painfully halting in the near future.

That will come to the surprise of many who cling to the notion that U.S. firms have all but abandoned the United States for cheaper locales in Asia, Latin America, and central Europe. While America's foreign investment in the developing nations has increased on an absolute basis over the past decade, it was slightly less than one-third of the total over 2000–2009. That ratio essentially remained steady from the prior decade, when it was around 30 percent of the global total.

Similarly, looking at America's overseas stock of foreign direct investment—a cumulative total of $3.5 trillion in 2009— the developing nations accounted for less than a quarter of the total.[25] That is a rather minor share, considering the mega attention and fears that come with each new announcement of U.S. firms investing in a high-flying emerging market. At the level of individual countries, the figures are quite revealing: for instance, corporate America's foreign investment stock in China ($49.4 billion) and Brazil ($56.7 billion) is on par with Spain ($50.6 billion). While India has captured the attention of many Americans, U.S. investment stock in India—$18.6 billion in 2009—is less than its share in Italy ($31.5 billion). U.S. investment in Norway is nearly four-fold the amount in Turkey, a key emerging market straddling Europe and the Middle East. Finally, America's investment stake in Ireland in 2009 was nearly four times all of corporate America's total investment in Africa— notwithstanding the latter's treasure trove of natural resources.[26]

One caveat to the above numbers: the figures, from the U.S. Department of Commerce's Bureau of Economic Analysis (BEA), are not complete—they don't capture all the investment, such as joint ventures and third-party agreements, the United States is making in the developing nations. And the figures do not account for the fact that in many cases U.S. multinationals will use certain nations as an export springboard to other nations in the region. For instance, a great deal of product (technology and pharmaceutical products) is exported by U.S. affiliates in Ireland to central Europe and northern Africa. In Southeast Asia, Singapore serves as a production springboard or distribution hub for U.S. multinationals selling goods in Thailand, Indonesia, Vietnam, and other neighboring nations. Still, with these caveats aside, the fact remains that the bulk of America's global infrastructure—foreign capital stock, overseas workforce, and foreign affiliates—is sunk in Europe, Canada, and Japan.

Not surprisingly then, highly skilled activities of U.S. affiliates remain concentrated in the developed nations. To this point, according to figures from the BEA, more than 80 percent of the research and development (R&D) conducted by U.S. foreign affiliates takes place in the developed nations. This is despite the fact that millions of science and engineering graduates are being pumped out by Chinese and Indian universities each year.

Even on the employment front, the bias remains toward wealthy, high-wage nations. In 2008, the last year of available data, U.S. affiliates employed just over 10 million foreign workers worldwide, and 57 percent of this workforce toiled in the developed nations. Many in America blame China for declining U.S. manufacturing employment, although the combined number of workers employed by U.S. manufacturing affiliates in Germany, France, and the United Kingdom is more than double those employed in China. Most tellingly, the developed nations still yield the greatest share of corporate earnings to U.S. multinationals, accounting for 70 percent of U.S. foreign affiliate income this decade.

All the above suggests that corporate America's global infrastructure is presently configured for a bygone era wherein the developed nations, notably countries in Europe, drove the global economy. Since the late 1950s, U.S. multinationals have principally focused on the developed nations, a strategy that has served them well given the wealthy consumer markets and availability of skilled labor in these locations. Many other developed nations face the same dilemma—such as France, Germany, Japan, and the United Kingdom. Although Japanese firms have recently enlarged their presence in China, its investment in the developing nations as a percentage of the global total was less than 30 percent in 2008. France and Germany are far behind that: their share of foreign investment in the developing nations was 12 percent and 14 percent, respectively, in 2008. Roughly a quarter of Britain's overseas investment was pumped into the developing nations. That is not surprising given that corporate Europe's external focus has long been on the greater European Union and the United States.

MEMO TO THE WEST: THANKS BUT NO THANKS

Rather than too much U.S. or European investment in the developing nations, there is far too little. Yet at precisely the moment when Western firms—confronting saturated markets and a rapidly aging workforce at home—need to expand their presence in the most dynamic parts of the global economy, the reception from key nations has been anything but warm and fuzzy. Cracking any foreign market is never easy, but the task is becoming harder in the developing nations thanks to stronger local competition and rising investment barriers. The latter run the gamut from promoting and protecting domestic national champions, to limiting how much of a firm a foreign company can own, to mandatory technology-transfer clauses. In addition, many developing nations have kept Western multinationals at bay by imposing specific product standards and testing requirements, by discriminatory taxes, and by requiring that foreign firms use local suppliers.

Notably out in the cold are U.S. oil companies. They increasingly confront resource nationalism in a number of petro-states, as well as less attractive incentives when allowed to partake in large oil projects. In general, Western oil companies are increasingly assuming secondary roles to state-controlled oil giants like Brazil's Petrobras. That state firm will take the lead in developing Brazil's newly discovered massive offshore oil field, leaving Western firms as financial partners and limiting "their ability to help set the pace for the oil fields' development, while giving Petrobras significantly more power to generate jobs and award lucrative contracts," according to a dispatch from the *New York Times*.[27] In Mexico, the nation's oil and gas industry remains largely closed to foreign investors, while other nations in Latin America—Venezuela, Bolivia, and Ecuador—continue to favor policies that limit and reduce the presence of foreign energy companies. Bolivia's President Evo Morales has gone further than most, nationalizing the nation's oil and gas reserves in 2006, the telephone company in 2008, and the country's power sector in 2010.

The energy investment restrictions in Indonesia are not much better. The government enacted new regulations in December 2008 that require foreign bidders for energy service contracts to use a minimum of 35 percent domestic content in their operations. Foreign mining companies must also give preference to local subcontractors and service companies. In 2009, Indonesia enacted rules that give preferences to local and domestic companies in the telecommunications sector as well.

China in particular has become a much tougher market for Western firms to plant roots in. After aggressively courting multinationals for over two decades, Beijing has turned cool toward many types of investment, forbidding foreign participation in some sectors while limiting foreign activity in others. Foreign banks, for instance, are not allowed to own more than 25 percent of a Chinese bank; credit card offerings can be done only via a joint venture with a Chinese firm. Owning more than 50 percent of a Chinese motor vehicle manufacturing company is forbidden.[28] The telecommunications sector is off limits to foreigners, and as Internet giant Google found out, Beijing is quite serious about controlling Internet access and content in China. Rather than live by China's strict censorship rules and regulations, Google closed shop in China in 2010, leaving one of the largest markets for the Internet in the world for nearby Hong Kong. Google is not alone; prior to the company's high-profile battle with Beijing, other U.S. Internet firms like eBay, Yahoo!, Facebook, and MySpace foundered in China in the face of stiff government control of the Internet.

Even in sectors long thought to be open to foreign direct investment, like food and beverages, the whims of government regulation can change quickly and halt deals. For example, Coca-Cola's planned purchase of China's biggest juice maker, Huiyuan Juice, was scotched after the bid ran afoul of China's new antimonopoly law. Multinationals "are seeing the golden China opportunity become a mirage" according to one Chinese government relations chief of a major technology supplier.[29]

Western technology leaders have been alarmed by China's new program of "indigenous innovation," which aims to boost China's local technology capabilities at the expense, according to Western firms, of U.S. and European technology leaders. As part of this trend, new technology rules governing sales to the Chinese government would force U.S. and European multinationals to hand over proprietary information like data-encryption keys and software codes if they wish to be certified to sell technology to the Chinese government. Since this information could end up in the hands of their Chinese competitors, Western technology firms are reluctant to play along, yet risk being boxed out of one of the largest and fastest-growing markets in the world.

Similar barriers have been erected in other fields. New patent rules could affect the ability of foreign drug companies to operate in China. The market access of foreign insurance companies remains restricted. Foreign wind and solar producers have complained of being shut out of big renewable energy deals. Promoting and protecting "new renewable" industries like wind, solar, and biomass power has become more blatant over the past few years. China's 2008 stimulus package, which allocated large sums to large wind power projects, requires that preference be accorded to Chinese companies. Since 2005, no foreign firm has sold equipment to a wind farm being established under the auspices of the NDRC Concession Project. The foreign share of China's annual new purchases of wind power equipment fell from 75 percent in 2004 to 24 percent in 2008. Some analysts have estimated that the foreign share will fall to 15 percent in 2009 and to 5 percent in 2010.[30]

"Every year," according to *BusinessWeek*, "China issues more than 10,000 new standards governing industries from mobile phones to autos. That's more than the rest of the world combined. . . ."[31] The unstated goal of many of these regulations is to give an advantage to local Chinese firms so that they can carve out large market shares in key industries at the expense of Western firms. This is done by promoting Chinese standards, by enforcing local content regulations, by mandating equipment procurement preferences for Chinese-owned companies, and by providing domestic subsidies such as tax breaks and other incentives to local companies.

After leveraging foreign direct investment to kick-start its reentry into the global economy over the past 30 years, China is rethinking the domestic role of FDI. So are other countries like India, which continues to keep many foreign investors at arm's length. India's banking and insurance markets, for instance, remain difficult to crack, with foreign equity participation in the Indian insurance sector limited to 26 percent. In the banking sector, foreign banks may not own more than 5 percent of an Indian private bank without approval of the government. Foreign law firms are not authorized to open offices in India. Minority ownership is largely the rule in the telecommunications sector, while India's retail sector remains largely closed to foreign investment.

The upshot from all of the above: at precisely the moment when corporate America needs to build out its presence in the developing nations, the developing nations have become pickier and less welcoming to foreign investment. Foreign investment is still courted in the emerging markets, but today deals are being done more on the terms of the host nation as opposed to we-know-best Western multinationals. Many developing governments are more confident of their home-grown capabilities and believe that with the appropriate spending on infrastructure and education, they can spawn their own indigenous innovation, create their own national champions, and nurture their own global brands.

This new muscular stance, in turn, will make life harder for those Western multinationals with long histories in the emerging markets, like leading Western food and beverage companies and energy companies. Think Coca-Cola, Procter & Gamble, Nestlé, and Avon, in addition to Exxon Mobil, Royal Dutch Shell, and Total. These companies at least have some footprint in the emerging markets. But that is not true of Western pharmaceuticals, which are woefully underrepresented in the emerging markets and could confront a bleak future if they do not successfully increase their market presence outside of the West. That is going to be a tall order. According to research from IMS Health, the top 15 pharmaceutical companies in the world derive less than 10 percent of their sales from the emerging markets. In China, whose pharmaceutical market surged 26 percent in 2008 and is expected to double in size by 2013, the world's top 15 drug firms derived just 0.9 percent of their combined sales in 2009. In the high-growth markets of Brazil, India, and Russia, the figure was just 2.9 percent for the top drug companies in 2009.[32] Moves are afoot to penetrate these markets, but local competition is intense, and many state-owned pharmaceutical firms have first mover advantage. Playing catch-up in these markets will not be easy.

Western banks confront similar challenges. The world's savings may be in the developing nations, but most large American and European banks are not, except for a handful of companies like HSBC, Citigroup, Santander, and Standard Chartered, whose emerging market roots were planted decades ago. Even for these veterans, the competition in many key developing nations is intense notably because of the near-monopoly position of state banks. In China, for instance, state banks control more than 90 percent of the sector's total assets. In India, nearly 80 percent of the loans were originated by state banks in 2009, and the state-controlled State Bank of India controls one-quarter of the market. In Russia up to 54 percent of the banking sector's assets are under state control; in Brazil, the figure is around 41 percent. Reflecting the size of indigenous financial companies in Brazil, Citibank's bank assets in the nation were just a fraction of the industry in 2009, with the bank ranked tenth overall.[33] Citibank and other foreign banks not only confront a handful of well-capitalized state banks in Brazil but also a number of powerful privately owned banks like Itau Unibanco and Bradesco.

The list of challenges goes on. In many emerging nations, Western banks must overcome indigenous restrictions that favor local banks over foreign institutions. A dearth of investment opportunities is yet another impediment to gaining a foothold in the emerging markets, since many governments distrust Western banking institutions and do not allow local firms to fall under the control of foreign banks. Taken together, some of the largest financial institutions in the world now reside in the developing nations, protected and under the control of the state, leaving many Western banks on the outside looking in.

THE COMING WAR FOR TALENT

Another area of competition between the United States and developing nations lies with skilled labor, or the lack thereof. A war for global talent is under way, as the likes of China, India, Brazil, and others increasingly draw from a dwindling pool of globally skilled labor at the expense of the United States and the West. America no longer enjoys the advantage in attracting the world's best and brightest. Even though Silicon Valley and America's world-class university system continue to attract the world's most talented scientists and engineers, the draw of America is not as powerful as it was before. The rise of the Rest is making home look a lot more attractive these days.

More highly skilled workers that would have done virtually anything in the past to reach the shores of the United States are staying home. Meanwhile, talented immigrants in the United States are returning to their home countries, prompting some to warn of "reverse brain drain" in the United States, the United Kingdom, and other Western nations. Behind both of these trends are a number of factors, notably the global diffusion of research and development. More and more of the world's top-notch research is now conducted in the hypergrowth markets of China and India. Today, a bright young engineer or scientist in India does not have to travel to Silicon Valley to fulfill his career aspirations. He instead can choose from 200 research and development centers belonging to Western multinationals right in India, notably in Bangalore, nicknamed India's Silicon Valley. Microsoft, Intel, Google, IBM, and General Electric are just a few high-tech leaders that have opened R&D centers in India over the past decade, employing local talent, while luring overseas workers back home.

Those workers returning to India are known as RNRI— or returning nonresident Indians. Exact numbers of returning workers are hard to come by, but one study estimates that 40,000 RNRIs now work in India's information technology industry.[34] In China, those returning from overseas are known as *hai gui* or "sea turtles," drawn home by government incentives, the rapid growth of high-tech research in China, better pay, and the prospects of working in one of the fastest-growing economies in the world. "In China," according to Changyou Chen, a former scientist at a Southern Californian biotech company, "I have better career opportunities and do what I love to do because I am respected for what I have learned in the United States and what I can bring to China. Also, China is willing to provide you with a lot of initial resources, such as grant money, starting funding, lab space and equipment, so you can hire people and pick your projects."[35]

Both India and China are actively courting their fellow countrymen and women to return home, doling out grants, cash awards, lab equipment, apartments, and other goodies. Whether they succeed or not directly affects the United States, since skilled immigrants have been key players in America's high-tech industry for decades. According to research by Vivek Wadhwa, immigrant-founded tech companies generated $52 billion in revenue and employed 450,000 workers in 2005.[36] In terms of creating new companies, immigrants have founded 35 percent of the start-ups in the semiconductor industry. In computers/communications and software, the figures were 31.7 percent and 27.9 percent, respectively, underscoring the phenomenal success of immigrants in driving U.S. technological innovation.

Today, however, the United States can no longer take these skilled workers for granted. Multiple opportunities abound for the world's best and brightest, and the United States is increasingly just one among other nations vying for the world's most talented workers. What's more, the looming war for talent comes at an unpropitious time for the United States given the country's aging workforce, deteriorating quality of public education, and dearth of U.S-born students taking advanced degrees in science and engineering. Regarding the last point, during the 2004–2005 academic year, roughly 60 percent of engineering doctoral students and 40 percent of master's degree students were foreign nationals; in addition, non-U.S. citizens comprised the bulk of the U.S. graduate student population in science, technology, engineering, and medicine. According to Vivek Wadhwa, recent foreign students earning advanced degrees in the United States are less inclined to stay permanently in the United States as opposed to previous graduates.[37] Compounding matters, the annual quota for H-1b visas that allow U.S. firms to bring foreign skilled labor to the United States remains stuck at 65,000; in 2008, the entire H-1b quota was reached or filled in just one week.

All the above is hardly encouraging for the U.S. technology sector in particular, or for the U.S. manufacturing base, which is fast running out of skilled manufacturing workers. That sounds counterintuitive given the steep job losses in the U.S. manufacturing sector over the past decade. But according to a report by Deloitte, Oracle, and the Manufacturing Institute, and reported in the *Financial Times*, the problem lies with too few manufacturing workers in the United States, not too many.[38]

The crux of the problem is that many U.S. manufacturing workers are on the verge of retiring while young workers to replace them are nowhere to be found. According to the report, nearly 20 percent of U.S. manufacturing workers are age 54 or older, while only 7 percent of manufacturing workers are under the age of 25.[39] In other words, the world's largest manufacturer—yes, the United States—will face a labor crunch in manufacturing in the not-too-distant future. In some cases, the crunch has already arrived. In early 2010, Siemens, the German engineering group, posted some 600 vacancies for engineers in the United States, up from 500 the prior year. The Illinois Manufacturers' Association, meanwhile, expects the state to need 30,000 new workers a year to replace the retiring baby boomers. Roughly 40 percent of Boeing workers are eligible for retirement in five years. If the financial crisis of 2008 had any silver lining, it is the fact that many elderly manufacturing workers have delayed their retirement due to the financial debacle's impact on their savings. Those workers staying on a few extra years, however, will not resolve the upcoming skills shortage emerging in the U.S. manufacturing sector.

Making this shortage worse is the unskilled composition of the U.S. labor force. Of America's total workforce of 133 million in April 2010, as counted by the U.S. Bureau of Labor Statistics, 12.2 million workers, or 9.2 percent of the total, lacked even a high school education. Another 39 million workers had only acquired a high school degree—a degree that is valued less and less today given the deteriorating quality of America's public school system. In total, over 50 million American workers had a high school education or less in early 2010, accounting for nearly 40 percent of the total.[40] These workers are the most exposed to the expanding skilled work base of China, India, South Korea, and other emerging nations. The larger the number of unskilled workers in the United States, the greater the need for American companies to tap into the emerging markets for talent. Germany, France, and the United Kingdom face a similar shortage of skilled workers.

Looking further down the road, the war for talent could very well reshape the global landscape for business innovation. The nation with the most talent has a leg up on others in driving innovation and creating new industry standards. These advances, for decades, were fostered by the developed nations. The past, however, will not be a prologue. Mobile money—money transfers via cell phones—is taking off in Kenya. India's Tata Motors has introduced a no-frills $3,000 car for the masses. These are but two examples whereby "the rich world is losing its leadership in the sort of breakthrough ideas that transform industries," according to *The Economist*.[41]

In the end, the war for talent between the developed and developing nations will be instrumental in determining the winners and losers of the future. The last economic superpower no longer has a monopoly on global talent, or the world's best and brightest. That said, it is incredible that at a time when skilled labor has never been more important to the nation's future, across the United States, public schools are slashing their education budgets in response to the financial crisis. Meanwhile, America is rapidly losing its lead in producing college-educated talent. To this point, according to the latest from the College Board, the United States now ranks twelfth among developed nations in the percentage of 25- to 34-year-olds with college degrees.[42] Finally, as it pertains to attracting and retaining the world's best and brightest, any serious discussion about rethinking and overhauling America's immigration policies remains hostage to bipartisan political bickering. In the war for talent, America is one of her own worst enemies.

A NEW WORLD AND NEW FAULTLINES

Consumers, natural resources, capital, talent—most of the critical inputs to economic growth now lie outside the control of the United States, an unfavorable turn that has helped undermine America's economic superpower status. There is nothing "super" about an economy that is overly dependent on other people's oil and natural resources, deep in debt to the rest of the world, and increasingly reliant on emerging market consumers in the face of stagnant and mature markets at home. Compounding matters, America is woefully unprepared to replace the very workers that have vaulted the U.S. economy to the top of the heap. The United States is failing to produce home-grown talent, making the nation more dependent on foreign skilled labor.

For decades, the world has been largely accommodating to the outsized needs of the United States and its ever growing appetite for other people's resources. In the U.S.-centric world leading up to the financial crisis of 2008, America was at the center of the global economy and enjoyed near-uncontested access to the world's oil supply, excess savings, and skilled labor pool, rarely ever contemplating, let alone preparing for, the day when the rest of the world would begin to demand and contest these same resources.

But that day has arrived. The United States must adjust to this new reality—a reality in which new power brokers are at work, competing against the United States in virtually all spheres of influence and virtually all areas of economics and commerce. How the United States responds to this environment will go a long way in shaping the future of globalization.

For the developing nations, there is no turning back. As Kishore Mahbubani has pointed out, "The past twenty years have probably seen some of the greatest changes in human history. The biggest shift is that the 88 percent of the world's population who live outside the West have stopped being objects of world history and have become subjects. They have decided to take control of their own destinies and not have their destinies determined by Western-dominated global processes and institutions. They believe that the time has come for the West to cease its continuing domination of the globe."[43] The battle has been joined.

If America fails to adjust to the messy multipolar world before us and resists the winds of change, the entire global economy will suffer. No nation will be spared the setback to globalization and a world increasingly fragmented and inward looking. The course of globalization will be decided by how the mature and stable (the West) react to the young and restless (the Rest).

We are at a transformational moment for the global economy. We stand on the cusp of a world that confronts two paths of the future: one is a path of disintegration and fragmentation of the global economy as the developed and developing nations turn against each other, hoarding resources, restricting market access to outsiders, and curtailing cross-border capital flows and workers. An economic cold war emerges from this path and is the primary subject of Chapter 8.

The other path is much more benign—that of globalization reincarnated. That from the ashes of one of the worse financial crises in history, the world comes together and uses the prevailing seminal trends of today to reconfigure a world economy more open, more integrated, and more cohesive than ever before. This possibility is discussed in Chapter 9.

The Coming
Economic Cold War

*The next 20 years of transition toward a new international
system are fraught with risk.*
—GLOBAL TRENDS 2025,
NATIONAL INTELLIGENCE COUNCIL

The United States confronts a different world from the one
it faced just a decade ago. At the beginning of the twenty-
first century, few questioned the global primacy of the U.S.
economy and the benefits of free-market capitalism. U.S.-led
globalization—greater openness, industry deregulation, and the
unfettered cross-border movement of capital, goods, and people—
was the overarching mantra of many countries, a megatrend so
powerful and ubiquitous that it was universally deemed to be
irreversible. It was a unipolar moment for the world's "indispensible" nation, possessor of the world's most potent military, most
competitive economy, and most sought-after culture.

But as a new decade dawns, the global landscape looks
radically different. America is exhausted by most accounts; its
economic superpower status diminished by costly wars, the
financial crisis, and massive liabilities associated with future
entitlement programs. Japan and Europe are increasingly

impotent—too demographically stagnant, too much in debt, too resistant to change, too distracted by their own problems to be anything but passive players on the global scene. After living well beyond their means for years and following massive bank bailouts and recession-fighting policies, the developed nations are deep in debt and condemned to a prolonged period of slow growth, a burden that will sap their global clout for years, if not decades. The Anglo-Saxon economic model has been devalued by one of the worst financial meltdowns in history. Once a given, the virtues of global interdependence are now open to debate.

Meanwhile, backed by one of the fastest growing economies in the world, China's swagger on the global stage—best illustrated by Beijing's suggestion for the end of the U.S. dollar's world reserve-currency status—speaks volumes about the reemergence of the Middle Kingdom. Leveraging its checkbook, China is carving out spheres of influence in Africa, the Middle East, central Asia, and Latin America at the expense of traditional Western interests. The Beijing consensus is increasingly viewed in many developing nations as an alternative to the much disliked Washington consensus. Likewise, having deftly navigated the financial crisis, the global standing and self-confidence of India, Turkey, and Brazil have soared. As part of a new multipolar world, new alliances among nations and regions are taking shape as countries search for new markets, economic resources, and alternative sources of growth now that the U.S. economy is too structurally impaired to carry the global economy. Flush with cash and backed by their governments, state-owned companies from resource-rich locales like Russia and the Middle East are on the prowl for Western assets. These firms, along with emerging corporate giants from Brazil, India, and Mexico are encroaching on the traditional turf of Western multinationals. The rise of new corporate challengers from the developing nations signals the end of Western dominance of global commerce and is emblematic of a new world order.

This order represents a discernible break from the past—namely, the rich nations no longer control the global economy, and the poor countries know it. Having long monopolized the world's resources, the West now finds itself in competition with the Rest for control of the world's critical inputs—natural resources, capital, and labor. While this trend has been subtly evident for the past decade, the global financial crisis of 2008 accentuated and accelerated the process. The demise of existing global orders and the emergence of new powers often spawn times of turbulence and uncertainty, and the current environment is no different. Pervasive insecurity in the developed nations juxtaposed against rising confidence in a handful of powerful emerging markets will make for a very tense global backdrop over the next decade.

We stand at a pivotal point in world economic history—a point in which the choices and decisions we make will influence and define geopolitics and global economic affairs for decades to come. Given the dramatic changes that have overcome the economies of the West and the Rest, we face two potential scenarios: the first scenario, which we discuss in this chapter, is an economic cold war between rich, developed nations and poor, developing nations. The second scenario, covered in Chapter 9, is the reincarnation of globalization.

ECONOMIC COLD WAR

In this first scenario, the United States and the developed nations, rather than adjust to a new global landscape and accept their diminished relative role in the world economy, deny reality and cling to the old order in which the developed nations dictated the global economic agenda, dominated multilateral institutions, and enjoyed first dibs on the world's resources. In other words, the West continues to lead, and the Rest is expected to follow. The policies and structures of the past, however, are unacceptable to the developing nations who feel that the time has long passed where the United States and Europe control the global economic agenda. To paraphrase China's president Hu Jintao, the students are no longer willing to take orders from the teachers. As a result, tensions rise between a U.S.-led developed nations bloc and a China-led developing nations cohort. Growing worker discontent and rising nationalism and xenophobia in both the developed and developing nations help create this global economic chill. Various forms of protectionism ensue, entangling the global economy in a web of regulations and cross-border barriers that inhibit the unfettered flow of people, goods, and capital.

Economic nationalism becomes rampant around the world. Banks are legislated to be home-bound, their cross-border activities greatly restricted resulting in financial deglobalization. Tired of fickled and footloose capital inflows, the developing nations, flush with their own savings, opt for more stringent capital controls while imposing more restrictions on outward flows. An us-versus-them mentality takes hold between the developed and developing nations. Both parties become unyielding in their positions, with spreading economic nationalism at home making it all but impossible for key policy makers to find multilateral solutions. Defending globalization becomes the best way to lose political legitimacy and power at home. Tensions reach a breaking point, and an economic cold war breaks out, fragmenting the global economy and all but ending the current phase of globalization and its attendant growth.

In this world, global reregulation replaces deregulation. The private sector takes its cue from the public sector—politicians—rather than the market. State-led industrial policies become fashionable again. Banks effectively become utilities, or risk-averse institutions whose principal mandate is to support the local and national economy. Cross-border capital flows are restricted; capital is again "caged," hindering growth in world trade and investment. Multinationals are politically browbeaten to become more local, less global at home, while simultaneously given the cold shoulder overseas, impairing their global reach and their global earnings. This, along with a rise in tit-for-tat trade and investment protectionism leads to a reduction in global trade and a decline in global mergers and acquisitions, further pushing globalization into retreat. Xenophobic fears over immigration spike, leading to a mass exodus of guest workers from the United States, Europe, and other parts of the world. Worker remittances to Honduras, Morocco, Sri Lanka, and other developing nations plunge, creating even more global recessionary pressures. Consumers are big losers, with rising trade barriers and the hoarding of resources resulting in higher prices for food, energy, and other staples. Global capital markets swoon as investors take cover. All told, the global economy sputters to a halt and enters a prolonged period of slow or no growth.

Sound fanciful or far-fetched? Not if the credit-fueled boom of the past two decades in the West is followed by a prolonged period of sluggish economic activity, lackluster employment growth, and mounting frustration and anger among the shriveling middle classes of the developed nations. Such a backdrop would spawn even more government intervention in the United States, Europe, and elsewhere, and encourage policies that put domestic interests first over international and global interests. In a world of economic stagnation, rising protectionism would beget more protectionism, leading the world down a dangerous path toward an economic cold war.

Speaking to the risks associated with a prolonged period of stagnation in the United States, Nobel Prize–winning economist Michael Spence told the *Financial Times*, "I have this gnawing feeling about the future of America. When people lose the sense of optimism, things tend to get more volatile."[1] Indeed, things will get volatile if the global economy loses steam and goes into reverse, a prospect raised by the global economic slowdown at mid-2010.

THE 3 A.M. CALL

During the 2008 Democratic presidential primary pitting Senator Hillary Clinton against her Senate colleague Barack Obama, the Clinton campaign ran a provocative ad that raised the specter of an international crisis and asked voters who they wanted in the White House if such an event—or a 3 a.m. call—occurred. The suggested crisis was of the traditional sort—a terrorist attack against a U.S. embassy overseas or another 9/11-like event that threatened to harm millions of Americans. The ad played on fears related to foreign security and defense, not economics and finance. However, it's possible that economics and finance will prompt a 3 a.m. call in the not-too-distant future.

There are various paths to an economic cold war, with the scramble for the finite resources of Mother Earth juxtaposed against the soaring new demand in the developing nations chief among them. As part of an economic cold war, the hoarding of resources (resource protectionism) threatens to become a favorite weapon of the developing nations, putting at risk the resource-deficit, debt-laden United States. Oil is and always will be a political commodity—or a political weapon—of the developing nations. Combined with skyrocketing demand from the likes of China, India, and other developing nations, the increasing concentration of oil among a handful of state-owned companies domiciled in the Rest makes oil an even more potent political commodity. Natural gas could serve the same purpose. An existing framework already exists for such a cartel, with the Gas Exporting Countries Forum serving as a gas equivalent to OPEC's oil cartel. At the head of this table sits Russia, joined by other gas exporters like Qatar, Iran, Egypt, Libya, Algeria, Bolivia, Venezuela, Trinidad and Tobago, and Equatorial Guinea. This is a disparate group, to be sure, yet with strong-armed leadership from Russia, a natural gas cartel could emerge virtually overnight.

And speaking of Russia, the country has not been shy about using its natural resources to its geostrategic advantage. Unhappy with Ukraine, Moscow shut off all natural gas supplies to the country and other eastern European nations in January 2009, sending a chill across Europe since the region is substantially dependent on Russia for natural gas and other resources. Closer to home, in February 2008, Venezuela threatened to cut off oil supplies to the United States because of a favorable ruling for Exxon Mobil to seize Venezuelan assets to compensate for nationalization of two Exxon Mobil–owned development projects within the country. In late April 2010, Bolivia nationalized four power companies, including two with 50 percent stakes by Britain and France, in order to tighten state control over this sector.

Other commodities could be subject to the same restrictions and political whims of those in charge. Protecting and husbanding one's resources have become all too prevalent over the past decade. Take iron ore. India, one of the world's largest suppliers, controls how much is sold on the world markets, and in 2009 its mining giant National Mineral Development Corporation imposed a 10 percent royalty on the "selling price" of mined iron ore. In 2008, Japanese and South Korean steel mills agreed to a 65 percent increase in iron ore prices from Brazil, the sixth annual increase in a row. In the same year, China announced a 100 percent export tax on yellow phosphorus, a crucial mineral for many phosphorus-based products. The decision was altered after outcries from around the world, but the decision left executives in many of the related industries shaken.

China also has moved to limit exports of rare earth minerals, making sure the needs of its industry are met before any rare earth production is allowed for export. In August 2009 it announced that it would curtail all exports of dysprosium and terbium, two minerals vital to manufacturing an array of high-tech products such as hybrid cars and cell phones. Although it rescinded this total ban, the restriction remains severe and in June 2010, the *China Daily* reported that the government was considering a proposal to put all private and unauthorized mines that produce rare earth minerals under the control of the state.[2] All of this leaves the United States notably exposed.

Unbeknownst to many Americans, rare earth materials are critical to the U.S. defense industry, yet despite this importance, it is China that has a virtual monopoly on this critical resource. The mainland produces about 97 percent of rare earth oxides.[3] In other words, China could easily disrupt the U.S. defense supply chain by hoarding or preventing the sale of rare earth materials. These are key inputs in the production of precision-guided munitions, lasers, radar systems, avionics, satellites, and other critical components of the U.S. military. Rare earth elements are also used in a number of other high-end products like hybrid cars, wind power turbines, fiber optics, and computers. The United States, incidentally, has significant rare earth reserves although the production of such materials has been allowed to atrophy over the past few decades, and according to estimates from the Government Accountability Office, it could take up to 15 years for the United States to build out a reliable rare earth supply chain.[4]

Yet another commodity that could trigger conflict in the future is water, the world's most precious commodity, notwithstanding the fact that the earth is covered with it. However, 97 percent of Mother Earth's water supply is salty and therefore not fit for daily use. Of the remaining 3 percent, 2 percent, while considered fresh water, is locked in snow and ice. That leaves around 1 percent for human use—for a global population of 6.5 billion heading for at least 8 billion in the next two decades. Without any doubt, two atoms of hydrogen joined to one of oxygen—water—may be mundane to most people, but is critical to the future growth of the global economy.

Nearly one in four human beings lives in areas of water scarcity resulting from inclement weather, water waste, and subpar agricultural practices. Currently one in eight people in the world lack access to clean water, while in 15 years, some 1.8 billion people will live in regions of water scarcity. The water infrastructure in the United States and overseas is crumbling while demand is rising. In many developing nations, rapid urbanization has caught policy makers off guard—the growing thirst of booming cities has emerged as a key catalyst for the unfolding global water shortage. In June 2008, the Asian Development Bank called for major rethinking of how countries in the region develop and build cities in the face of tightening water constraints.

Right now, Asia's cities are expanding by close to 100,000 people per day, one of the fastest levels of urbanization the world has ever experienced. It took 130 years for London's population to grow from 1 million to 8 million residents. Dhaka, the capital of Bangladesh, is expected to grow from 10 million people to 22 million people in just the next 10 years. Meanwhile, the Asian Development Bank projects 1.1 billion people will move to cities in Asia during the next 20 years—in their words, the migration is of a "magnitude never before attempted by humanity."[5]

The situation in the Middle East is not much better. The Jordan River has been largely reduced to a trickle, the surface of the Dead Sea has shrunk by one-third, the Sea of Galilee is at its lowest point ever, and in Iraq, the Euphrates River is drying up, imposing a host of economic problems on the war-weary nation. According to the *New York Times*, "In Northern Syria, more than 160 villages in the past two years have run dry and been deserted by residents. In Gaza, 150,000 Palestinians have no access to tap water. In Israel, the pumps at the Sea of Galilee (Lake Kinneret), its largest reservoir, were exposed above the water level, rendering pumping impossible. In Lebanon, 70 percent of wastewater is dumped into groundwater-polluting cesspools, and Jordan is struggling with just 10 percent of its average rainfall."[6] Water scarcity, in other words, represents a massive economic and geopolitical challenge to the Middle East and could easily spark conflict in the region, as well as conflict in other parts of the world.

Water, for instance, remains a key source of tension between two of Asia's largest economies, China and India. In play is the water that flows from the icy plateaus of Tibet and China's grand design to build a dam at a strategic point—the "Great Bend" of the Yalong Tsangpo River—that would divert water to the mainland, leaving northern India parched. Underscoring the strategic importance of water to China, Chinese Prime Minister Wen Jiabao is on record of saying that water scarcity threatens the "very survival of the Chinese nation."[7] In the midst of the global water shortage stands the United States, the world's most profligate consumer of water. While Americans use about 100 gallons of water at home each day, around 46 percent of the people in the world do not even have water piped into their homes. But global demand for water is soaring, and a commodity that most Americans take for granted each day is about to get a great deal more expensive in the future. Envisioning future conflicts among states—developed and developing nations alike—is not that hard. In the not-too-distant future, the world could confront a major resource war over water, pitting various nations and aligned interests against each other.

THE BATTLE OVER NONTRADITIONAL ENERGY SOURCES

In addition to all the above, cold war–like tensions are also likely to develop over the emerging marketplace of alternative energy. Tapping the abundant resources of wind and solar energy means gigantic investments in both manufacturing and infrastructure. Yet in the search for cures to ailing economies and creating jobs, this imminent boom shows plenty of potential of being restricted for nationalist advantage.

China, which is investing heavily in the clean energy sector, has already raised barriers to protect its fledgling efforts. When it authorized its first solar power plant in the spring of 2009, it required that at least 80 percent of the equipment be made in China. At the same time, the government took bids for 25 large contracts to supply wind turbines, and every contract was won by one of seven domestic companies. In September 2009, the European Union Chamber of Commerce in China complained that none of the world's five largest wind energy operators have a single national development project in China. Yet Europe seems like a glass house on this issue. For instance, in March 2009, European governments backed a plan to impose tariffs on American biofuels. Although both subsidize this industry, Europe claimed that the United States subsidized its industry more.

Government support for alternative energy in Europe has been important to the growth of solar power because of its expensive installation costs. In 2007, German solar panels accounted for half of all the world's production, but this was made possible only because of heavy government subsidies. The situation is similar in Spain, where solar technology took a 40 percent dip in 2009 that corresponds to the cutbacks made by the Spanish government, which was heavily affected by the financial crisis. Given its unpromising start, the scramble for alternative energy can be expected to develop in a similar fashion, highly vulnerable to desires for protectionism.

Such efforts can be found already in the nascent market of the United States. In June 2009, Canadian suppliers of alternative energy protested being shut out of alternative energy contracts related to the U.S. $787 billion stimulus bill. In September 2009, Governor Arnold Schwarzenegger had to oppose a plan by the California state legislature that would limit how much energy could be imported from out of state, a measure designed to protect local interests in the country's largest market for alternative energy. Numerous venture capitalist firms have bet billions that the United States can become the leader in the alternative energy industry. The approval of a controversial wind farm off Cape Cod in Massachusetts in April 2010 promises to usher in a wave of similar farms off the East Coast. The firm Bluewater Wind alone has wind parks planned in five states: Delaware, New York, New Jersey, Maryland, and Rhode Island. While the turbines for the Cape Cod venture will be supplied by Siemens of Germany, America's firms are fast catching up in the offshore wind field, projected to supply 18 percent of the country's energy needs by 2030.

While many areas of technology help support cross-border fertilization, the growth in energy alternatives could well promise the opposite. All the way down the chain of manufacture are precisely the sorts of well-paying blue-collar jobs that Americans have been losing over the past two decades: factory production, transportation, construction, and maintenance. The same cycle holds for solar energy as well, particularly once the price of solar receptors for roofs on individual homes is driven down. Politicians all over the globe have realized the advantage of protecting this source of labor for its own, and the U.S. 2009 stimulus plan promises to be only an opening salvo in this burgeoning new field.

In the meantime, green protectionism has gained prominence in the halls of the U.S. Congress and is gaining traction in Europe and even China. To this point, on June 8, 2009, the *New York Times* ran an eye-catching headline that will come to define the future of the United States and the developing nations under a cold war scenario. The headline: "China and the U.S. in Cold War–like Negotiations for a Greenhouse Gas Truce." Responsible for more than 40 percent of the world's greenhouse gas emissions, the United States and China are locked in negotiations over gigatons of greenhouse emissions, reminiscent of the megatons of nuclear might that used to pit the United States against the Soviet Union. Whether the two parties can narrow their differences will decide the fate of global climate-change talks. Not surprisingly, India has closed ranks with China.

Both nations fear that any cap-and-trade program agreed upon by the United States will come with provisions that domestic or national action on climate change be conditional upon similar regulations in competing nations. The upshot: those nations not willing to cap or restrict greenhouse gas emissions could confront U.S.-import barriers and other retaliatory measures.

Returning to the prospect of a late night call to the president of the United States, such a call might come from Moscow some day. The voice at the other end is speaking on behalf of the world's 13 largest state-owned oil companies, in possession of more than 75 percent of global crude reserves. The demand is simple: allow the hostile takeover of Exxon Mobil, one of America's premier energy companies, by one of its own, Gazprom, the Russian energy giant. Let the deal proceed, the voice says, or the world's major oil producers will withdraw crude oil from the global markets and sell it among themselves, cancel numerous exploration contracts with U.S. oil companies, and halt the purchase of U.S. securities. Backing up the threats, other state-owned resource companies in Africa, South America, and central Asia have agreed to follow the same steps if the United States does not allow the deal to go through.

The president, in turn, pleads his case with the distant caller—it is Congress, he says, that opposes the sale of Exxon Mobil, along with the general U.S. public, fearful of a U.S. corporate icon like Exxon Mobil falling into the hands of a foreign company. The hostile bid has only inflamed anti-Russian sentiment in the United States, which, in turn, has stoked anti-Americanism in Russia and throughout the developing nations. The caller is not listening and abruptly ends the conversation, leaving the president in stunned silence and wishing that the United States had done more—much more—to reduce its dependence on foreign oil over the past few decades.

This is only one scenario—a number of triggers could prove ominous in the near future. Whereas the United States and the former Soviet Union vied for influence in various theaters of the world in the first Cold War, in the future the United States and a handful of powerful emerging nations like China will vie for economic influence in such commodity-rich regions like central Asia and Africa. Tensions over tapping the last frontiers—minerals below the Arctic Ocean and outer space— are also likely to intensify in the future.

"BUDDY, CAN YOU SPARE A JOB?"

Finding work for millions of workers in both the developed and developing nations represents another divisive variable that could trigger an economic cold war between the West and Rest. Lost on many in the West is this: rising unemployment is not just a problem inflicting pain on the developed nations. It is a global challenge.

"College students, laid-off workers, and migrant workers waiting for jobs are my biggest concern," Chinese premier Wen Jiabao stated in a recent interview. The Chinese leader is hardly alone. Whereas the threat of intercontinental missiles kept world leaders awake at night during the first Cold War, the swelling ranks of disillusioned workers and the attendant effect on social stability are what haunt leaders today. This fear prompted Vice President Joseph Biden—famous for speaking first, thinking later—to proclaim in July 2009 that the U.S. economic recession was "worse than expected." The second-in-command was referring to the sharp rise in the U.S. unemployment rate, which climbed faster than anyone in the administration or Wall Street expected. President Obama's best and brightest expected the U.S. jobless rate to peak at around 8 percent when they peddled the massive fiscal stimulus package to the country in early 2009. Yet a few months later, the U.S. jobless rate stood at 9.7 percent and would peak at just over 10 percent; by July 2010, the nation's unemployment rate had dipped to 9.5 percent. That is the official rate—add in discouraged workers not looking for jobs, and part-time help, and America's unemployment rate at mid-year 2010 was closer to 16 percent. Worse still, the jobless rate for workers between the ages of 16 to 24 reached nearly 20 percent over the first half of 2010.

The U.S. recession of 2008 obliterated jobs across the landscape. By some estimates, the downturn wiped clean some 7 million jobs, leaving millions of workers without work and income. The loss of jobs since December 2007 was equal to net job gains over the previous nine years, making this the only recession since the Great Depression to wipe out all the job growth from the previous expansion. What's more, as of June 2010, nearly half the workers (46 percent) unemployed in the United States had been out of work for six months or more, a level of long-term joblessness not seen since the Labor Department started keeping track in 1948. In mid-2010, 4.7 million workers had been without work for a year or more.

The picture outside the United States is not much better. Many other global leaders are haunted by Biden's words—that the global recession was "worse than expected" and took an unprecedented toll on jobs at home. According to the International Labor Organization (ILO), 2009 represented the worst global performance on record in terms of employment creation. And even as the global economy showed signs of life in 2010, near double-digit unemployment rates were the norm in the United States and most of Europe. In spring 2010, the jobless rate in Spain was approaching a whopping 20 percent, while the unemployment rate in Belgium stood at 11.6 percent. In spring 2010, the jobless rate in the Euro area was 10 percent, yet higher in such nations as Belgium (11.6 percent), France (10.1 percent), and Greece (12.1 percent). Poland's jobless rate was

12.3 percent in April 2010 and is expected to go higher. Turkey's level of jobless was close to 15 percent. In that unemployment afflicts rich and poor nations alike, many developing nations are staring at double-digit unemployment rates as well. In South Africa, one of Africa's more advanced economies, nearly one in four workers is out of work. Despite being one of the fastest-growing economies in the world, India's jobless rate was above 10 percent in early 2010.

Nowhere in the developing nations, however, is the pressure to create jobs as great as it is in China. That will come as a shock to many U.S. lawmakers and the popular media who wrongly assume that China's stellar economic growth record has been more than sufficient to keep workers employed and generally happy at the expense of workers in the West. Even before the financial crisis of 2008, China's mounting ranks of jobless workers were becoming an acute problem for the Communist Party.

Over the past decade, for instance, millions of Chinese workers have been cashiered from state-owned enterprises. Between 1999 and 2005 alone, more than 21 million workers were fired in this fashion, leaving many workers and their families without incomes and without the health-care, housing, and educational benefits that came with a job in the public sector. Meanwhile, the financial crisis resulted in massive layoffs among China's army of workers. A staggering 41 million Chinese workers lost their jobs on account of the global financial crisis, with the largest declines coming among China's migrant workers, numbering some 20 million, by official estimates. Many of these same workers have gone back to work with the cyclical rebound in China's economy, although many Chinese workers now harbor the same fears that long haunted workers in the United States and Europe—that their job will ultimately be sent offshore to lower-cost locations in Southeast Asia. More and more Chinese companies are not only outsourcing low-end production to Vietnam and Cambodia, but they are also embracing productivity-enhancing technologies that will result in layoffs; substituting machines for labor will only exacerbate the loss of manufacturing jobs in China for some time to come. That is a familiar refrain in the United States but one not yet understood in China.

Among the unemployed are Chinese workers with college degrees—newly minted graduates expecting suitable jobs with impressive salaries. In the class of 2008, more than 30 percent of the 5.6 million university graduates had yet to find employment as of the middle of 2009. That is hardly a propitious omen for the 6.1 million students who graduated in 2009 and 2010. Times have become tough in China. When the city of Suzhou needed maintenance workers for 58 public restrooms, 870 people applied, including 40 college graduates.

In total, some 10 million new workers enter China's labor force annually, although the economy has been capable of creating only 6 to 8 million new jobs a year. Meanwhile, many Chinese workers with jobs are increasingly dissatisfied with working conditions and other related issues. Hence, the number of worker protests in China has soared, rising from 87,000 in 2005 to 127,000 in 2009. In May 2010, workers staged a walkout at the plant of Honda, a Japanese car manufacturer, unhappy with the 24 percent wage increase the company had agreed to. A host of other Western multinationals (U.S. food giant KFC, for instance) have had to ante up more pay to pacify a Chinese workforce that is less docile and less tolerant of current wages in China and prevailing working conditions. In the end, the Middle Kingdom may have the most dynamic economy in the world, but it confronts the same policy dilemmas of other governments around the world: how to keep workers engaged and gainfully employed, thereby maintaining peace and stability at home. Failing this challenge, the greater the level of worker unrest in the developed and developing nations, the greater the risks of protectionist measures that ultimately unwind global trade and investment and push the world toward an economic cold war.

MIGRANT WORKERS—HELP NOT WANTED

If governments around the world fail to keep their respective working classes happy, one result could be the erosion of one key pillar of globalization: the cross-border movement of workers. In the not-too-distant past, migrant workers were welcomed by many developed nations confronting acute labor shortages and a marked decline in working-age populations as a result of aging. Ireland and the United Kingdom competed for workers from Central and Eastern Europe. Spain and Italy became more receptive to migrant workers from the Middle East, North Africa, and Latin America. Germany and Austria tapped into the low-cost labor pool of Turkey and Hungary. The surge in oil prices and the attendant construction boom in the Middle East triggered a global scramble for overseas workers, with millions of workers decamping from Bangladesh, Sri Lanka, and India for the Gulf states. The United States and Canada pulled migrant workers from all directions—from Eastern Europe, Central and South America, and Asia, a dynamic that helped deepen the economic bonds between the United States and numerous less fortunate nations.

Thanks to the rising cross-border tide of migrant workers, over 200 million people resided outside their country of birth when the financial crisis of 2008 struck. This "diaspora nation" outranks all but four other nations by the size of its population and represents a key component of globalization. The benefits from migrant workers cut both ways—in the developed nations, the benefits from migrant workers have come via lower-priced goods and services. In such key labor-intensive sectors as agriculture and construction, migrant workers in the United States and other rich nations have been instrumental in lowering costs for food and housing. Migrant workers are also consumers, helping to boost demand and growth for basic services in the host nation.

In addition, the economic benefits to the migrant's country of origin have been immense. Indeed, remittances to the developing nations totaled a record $328 billion in 2008, which represents a key source of in-country financing for education, health care, housing, and other related activities. Migrants typically triple their real earnings by working abroad, a pay differential that benefits both the host and home country.

The financial crisis and global recession of 2009, however, have put a brake on recent trends. Employment growth in the developed nations has come to a sudden stop—jobs are not being created but rather are being destroyed, triggering a backlash against migrant workers. In Spain, former construction workers are returning home to their villages hoping to find work in agriculture, yet few jobs exist since the folks out in the fields picking strawberries, artichokes, and asparagus are from Morocco, Poland, and Romania and are willing to work at a fraction of Spanish average wages. Not surprisingly, as the level of unemployment has climbed around the world, both rich and poor nations have adopted more anti-immigrant policies. Among these, employment restrictions are being applied more diligently now; the number of migrant workers allowed in host nations is being reduced; and programs to encourage workers to return home are proliferating. Meanwhile, the rate of new immigration has slowed dramatically, given the unavailability of jobs in nations once begging for foreign labor.

As the world struggles to regain its footing following the financial crisis of 2008, a key risk lies with more governments looking inward instead of outward, further promoting protectionist policies. Economic nationalism thrives in this environment and rests on the assumption that prosperity begins and ends at home. The last time economic nationalism of this sort reared its ugly head was during the Great Depression of the 1930s, which was sparked by a collapse in global output and trade and the end of globalization.

This inward-looking sentiment has characterized many countries' reaction to the social unrest created by the recession of 2008. The recent passage of an anti-immigration law in Arizona is only the most prominent manifestation of suspicion of foreigners found far and wide. Italy recently passed tough new legislation against illegal immigrants, with a fine of up to 10,000 euros and six months in detention before being repatriated. As part of a growing backlash against immigrants, Belgium has banned the wearing of the *burqa*, or Islamic face veil, in public, and France may soon follow. All these signs are troubling, because one key variable that will precipitate a coming economic cold war will be the rising premium on creating jobs for millions of workers in the developed and developing nations alike. And adding more stress to the above is growing income inequality within nations, yet another challenge for various governments that could result in less cross-border movement of people and workers.

THE END OF THE DOLLAR'S REIGN

Hoarding one's natural resources and protecting one's workers are two catalysts for an economic cold war and the retreat of globalization. Another likely trigger: a capital boycott among the world's largest savers, a prospect that would doom the last economic superpower and the world's largest debtor nation— the United States.

Let's return once again to the idea of a 3 a.m. call to the sleepy-headed resident in the White House. Under this scenario, the voice on the other end of the line could be the U.S. ambassador to China informing the president that China, fed up with America's spiraling budget deficits, threats of trade protectionism, and overbearing military presence in and around the Korean peninsula, plans on dumping billions of dollars of U.S. Treasuries when the U.S. credit markets open in a few hours. Beijing also plans to announce that henceforth China will accept only renminbi, not dollars, from its trading partners, a direct assault on the dollar's world reserve-currency status.

The stunning move by one of America's largest creditor nations threatens to leave the debt-laden United States financially high and dry, and wreak havoc on the world financial markets. It also threatens the dollar since any move by China to dump dollars would trigger a stampede for the exits among other foreign investors. As the president listens, he knows that the move by China will create economic chaos in the United States and around the world. He also knows that Congress will move quickly to curtail U.S. imports from China and impose other measures that restrict and inhibit bilateral contacts between the two parties. The battle lines will be drawn very quickly. Various parties around the world will be forced to line up behind the two protagonists. The last vestiges of globalization are set to vanish.

Hard to imagine? Not really. It does not take much of an imagination to envision a desperate U.S. government, confronting stubbornly high unemployment at home, pressing China so hard to revalue its currency that the blatant pressure from Washington evokes and triggers a violent anti-American backlash across China. Beijing, in turn, is forced to resist or retaliate against the United States. So great are the demands on China to revalue the currency that any adjustment would leave the Communist Party leadership looking weak and humiliated in the eyes of its population, circumstances unacceptable to any and all Chinese. A skirmish over the currency triggers tit-for-tat protectionism that ultimately leads the United States to greatly restrict market access to Chinese goods, prompting China to dump its massive holding of U.S. Treasuries or halt buying any new U.S. securities. Either action would severely penalize the United States. The actions plunge both economies into recession, dragging the rest of the world with them. The rest of the world takes sides, with many developing nations falling into the camp of Beijing, enticed by promises of more aid and trade with China. The global economy fragments, and globalization collapses.

Financial mercantilism is yet another path that could lead to an economic cold war and the end of globalization. Under this scenario, unhappy with the United States and Europe, the capital-rich surplus nations continue to build large excessive reserves, but rather than invest their excessive savings in the debt-laden developed nations, they create institutions and financial arrangements that keep the capital within the developing nations themselves.

Under this scenario, China continues to openly campaign for another reserve currency to replace the U.S. dollar. The mainland accelerates and promotes the renminbi's use in international transactions. Having signed currency-swap agreements with Argentina, Belarus, Hong Kong, Indonesia, Malaysia, and South Korea in the past, the central bank of China gathers more willing participants in Latin America, Africa, and central Europe. To bolster the global appeal of its currency, Beijing accelerates the move to develop a more liquid securities market at home—a prerequisite if the renminbi is to become a challenger to the U.S. dollar. To this end, Beijing pushes up its timeline for turning Shanghai into an international financial center; instead of 2020, the deadline is now 2015 or sooner. Concurrently, Beijing promotes and constructs the infrastructure for the creation of a single monetary unit for Asia, with the Chinese currency, of course, at its core.

As part of all the above, cross-border activities of financial institutions are severely curtailed, reversing the decade's long trend toward financial deregulation and the internationalization of the world's capital markets which have been instrumental in facilitating global trade and investment, promoting global mergers and acquisitions, and opening new geographic markets to the world at large. Accordingly, the globalization of capital withers, and global interdependence goes into reverse.

THE RISE OF INVESTMENT PROTECTIONISM

Despite assurances from the leaders of the G-20, trade protectionism is not very far from the surface in many parts of the world and could become an acute problem against a global backdrop of stubbornly high unemployment, rising worker unrest, and the hoarding of resources. In addition, as more trade takes place among the developing nations themselves, many developing nations that had previously bowed to the trade demands of the developed nations may be less inclined to do so in the future.

But it is not just trade protectionism that is likely to spark an economic cold war. A more likely catalyst will be investment protectionism—or the resistance on the part of both the developed and developing nations to allow their home-based corporate leaders to invest and own assets in each other's markets. Companies in the developing nations now want to go beyond trade, and increasingly prefer to do business locally or in-country via joint ventures, mergers and acquisitions, or green field investments. Rather than provide products via arm's-length trade, the emerging giants in the developing nations want direct access to markets in the United States and Europe at precisely the moment when xenophobic politicians in the United States and across Europe are increasingly concerned about the rising in-country presence of foreign firms from such nations as Brazil, Turkey, Russia, and others. The fact that many of these companies are state-owned or partially owned by the state only adds to the paranoia. Concurrently, many governments in the developing nations are less receptive of large Western multinationals entering their markets and crowding out or decimating local firms.

What many in the West fail to realize is that when it comes to investment, or carving out an in-country presence via foreign direct investment, multinationals from the developed nations enjoy a huge advantage over their counterparts in the developing nations. Firms from the United States, Europe, and Japan have lead the way in extending their global reach through foreign investment and affiliates sales, operating on the ground, around the world wherever possible. Today, however, many large corporations from the developing nations want to follow in their footsteps and are adopting the same strategies. They want direct access to the large and wealthy markets of the United States and Europe, although many governments in the West are becoming increasingly uncomfortable with this prospect.

In the end, it is investment protectionism that remains the key risk to the global economy in the years ahead and a likely spark for an economic cold war. Global commerce and competition is rapidly shifting from trade to investment, a trend that will increasingly pit state-owned companies in the Rest against private sector firms in the West. The former are likely to become a lightning rod for politicians in the United States and Europe given the massive state resources and privileges that back and support these firms.

As Ian Bremmer notes in *The End of the Free Market*, "In recent years, a growing number of domestic Chinese companies, many of them state-owned, have lifted their game to a level at which they can compete with foreign rivals within the Chinese marketplace. As state-owned companies become ever more important to their country's political and economic development strategy, they build more leverage within the state bureaucracy, gaining influence they can use to persuade political officials to create new rules and regulations that advantage Chinese companies at the expense of their foreign competitors."[8]

EACH TO HIS OWN

All the factors discussed above could lead to a more fragmented and Balkanized global economy, in which regionalism and various alliances take shape that pit one part of the world against another. Under this scenario, Asia, led by China, would strike out on its own, with Beijing creating its own regional sphere of influence at the expense of U.S. and European strategic interests. South America would increasingly coalesce around a Brazilian-led regional trading bloc. Europe would become the fortress it always threatened to be, turning its back on Turkey, the Middle East, and Africa. In an economic cold war scenario, the United States, China, and other major global players like the European Union, Turkey, Brazil, and Russia would compete ferociously for influence in various parts of the world. The race for influence and control in the energy-laden countries of central Asia would intensify between the United States, Russia, and China. Turkey would continue its push to become a regional Middle East power broker. Various nations in Africa would be courted and cajoled by the world's major powers given the continent's abundant natural resources.

In this environment, the United States would increasingly find itself at odds with rising economic powers-cum-authoritarian regimes like China and Russia, as well as Iran and, potentially, Venezuela. These regimes would become even less shy about contesting the United States in key strategic areas of the world, leveraging their soft powers and economic resources to advance their own interests. China would continue to generously lend capital to various African nations with no strings attached or on very generous terms, thus undercutting the longtime influence of U.S.-backed multilateral organizations like the World Bank and the United Nations. Similarly, Russia, Iran, and Venezuela would use their oil wealth to build foreign alliances and allegiances with various state and nonstate actors. Many of these regimes would actively attempt to undercut or neuter Western-based organizations that used to hold significant sway in the developing nations, like the United Nations, the Organization for Security and Cooperation in Europe (OSCE), and the Organization of American States (OAS). In an economic cold war, the Western-led multilateral institutions of the past would largely become ineffective.

THE AFTERSHOCKS OF AN
ECONOMIC COLD WAR

The costs associated with a cold war will be substantial. Consumers around the world will face rising prices for basic staples and consumer goods. An economic cold war entails a world economy laden with trade restrictions, with import tariffs and nontariffs layered on top of the global economy as nations seek to protect domestic producers and shift toward self-sufficiency rather than interdependence. Global multinationals, after spending decades and millions of dollars building global production networks, would have no choice but to revamp and rethink their nearly destroyed global supply chains. Disrupted and short-circuited by an economic cold war, production would be increasingly brought "home." Global supply chains would be shortened and become more regional rather than global. Capital flows would be curtailed and become more biased toward the home market. As part of this environment, U.S. firms would be denied access to foreign markets, foreign capital, natural resources, and the best and brightest of the world, as stricter immigration laws and visa requirements inhibit the flow of skilled and semiskilled labor.

Against this gloomy portrait, it is important to recognize that globalization's permanence is hardly guaranteed—particularly now that America's wherewithal to lead the global economy has been impaired by the financial crisis, juxtaposed against China's resistance to shoulder the burden of the global commons at the expense of more inward challenges. A rudderless, economically stagnate multipolar world, devoid of leadership yet full of competing interests and spheres of influence, is a recipe for economic disaster—a path toward an economic cold war.

But this is precisely the world we confront today given China's one foot in, one foot out position in the global economy, set against the diminished credibility of the United States. It is worth repeating Martin Jacques, author of *When China Rules the World*, "At the heart of the present global financial crisis lies the inability of the United States to continue to be the backbone of the international financial system; on the other hand, China is not yet neither able nor willing to assume that role. This is what makes the present global crisis so grave and potentially protracted, in a manner analogous to the 1930s when Britain could no longer sustain its premier financial position and the United States was not yet in position to take over from it."[9]

Under a scenario of an economic cold war, the liberal order of the past few decades would be dismantled by the aftershocks of the great financial panic of 2008 and the attendant global recession, and by the tectonic shift in economic power, with the gravity of world economic growth moving from the United States and developed nations to China and the emerging countries.

Explicit in the coming economic cold war is a world economy taking on many of the characteristics of the dismal period between 1913 and 1950—a period marked by conflict, stagnant levels of trade, capital controls, little international migration, and the fragmentation of the existing global economic order. Today, as a new decade dawns, a similar fate awaits the world economy if the developed nations, led by the United States, and the developing nations continue on the path of nonreconciliation and noncooperation. The decline of globalization and the end of U.S. dominance are central to this scenario.

We have a choice to make. Do we raise the protectionist walls and make the decisions that will lead us to the fractured and bleak world of an economic cold war, or do we confront our challenges and work to overcome geostrategic and economic differences in a way that benefits all nations—both developed and developing, the West and the Rest? The second scenario, discussed in the following chapter, foresees this more optimistic outcome and is dubbed "globalization reincarnated." Under this scenario, greater cooperation and coordination between the developed and developing nations deepens the expanse and ties of globalization. Both parties come to recognize that their fates are unequivocally bound together and therefore find the wherewithal to work jointly on such key global issues as climate change, sustainable energy security, and the proliferation of nuclear weapons. Under this scenario, the integration of the global economy broadens substantially and becomes more binding, a dynamic that helps promote global growth and reduces the risks of wars and cross-border conflicts.

Impossible? No. Likely? The outcome will largely depend on how the United States, the last reigning economic superpower, adjusts to the new world order taking shape.

Globalization Reincarnated

Just as the world accommodated the rejuvenation of Europe in the post-War world, it must now accommodate the rise of new Asian economies in the years that lie ahead.
—MANMOHAN SINGH, PRIME MINISTER OF INDIA

We must recognize that no nation—no matter how powerful— can meet global challenges alone.
—U.S. PRESIDENT BARACK OBAMA, FROM THE
NATIONAL SECURITY STRATEGY, MAY 2010

If the scenarios discussed in the previous chapter come to fruition—if an economic cold war does erupt and ultimately leads to a fragmented global economy and the demise of globalization—historians will look back on the early twenty-first century and marvel at how things might have been. How, with a little more awareness, tolerance, and courage, the global community could have embarked on a different path to prosperity in the postcrisis world.

Our current situation does not have to end badly. While the financial crisis of 2008 has thrown parts of globalization into reverse and undermined the economic superpower status of the United States, a more robust and inclusive global economy could still emerge in the years ahead. We have reached the end of globalization as determined and designed by the United States but not the end of globalization if America and the West can embrace a new configuration with different characteristics— Chinese, Indian, Brazilian, Egyptian, and many others. This represents a significant challenge to a country that likes to think of itself as "indispensible," and one that is long accustomed to sitting at the head of the table, giving orders—not taking them.

The challenges in front of China, India, Russia, and other key developing nations are no less daunting. Having arrived on the global stage, are these nations ready to assume the mantle of global leadership? Will they be able and willing to subordinate national self-interests for the good of the global commons when it comes to tackling weighty global issues like climate change, the proliferation of nuclear weapons, resource shortages, and aid and development for the world's poorest nations? The answers to these questions are unclear. What is clear is that the aftershocks of the global financial crisis present a golden opportunity for the world's leaders to recast, reinvent, and reenergize globalization.

As highlighted in previous chapters, the globalization of the late twentieth century was largely driven and dictated by the West. Under this framework, globalization was not really "global" given that cross-border flows of trade, capital, and people pivoted on the United States and the developed nations, namely developed Europe. In the precrisis world, the bulk of foreign direct investment flowed to and from the developed nations, with a few outliers like China. Global mergers and acquisitions were the exclusive preserve of the rich nations. Trade and investment ties between the developing nations were shallow and underdeveloped, leaving many countries like Brazil, Turkey, Poland, and Mexico reliant on the United States and Europe for export growth. Companies from the developing nations were mainly traders—dependent on delivering goods to foreign customers through exports. Multinationals from the West were largely investors, relying on in-country foreign affiliates to deliver goods and services to overseas markets. Meanwhile, the cross-border flow of people was largely one way—from poor to rich nations.

In the postcrisis world, though, the potential exists for globalization to become deeper, more inclusive, and better balanced. In the multipolar world that is unfolding, cross-border trade and investment among the developing nations is accelerating. Traditional foreign direct investment flows are being altered, with more investment emanating from the developing nations and flowing to developed and developing nations alike. Global M&A increasingly bear the hallmark of the developing nations as new emerging corporate giants from Brazil, Mexico, India, and other nations increase their global footprint via mergers and acquisitions. While the developed nations, notably the United States, remain a beacon of hope and a primary destination for many of the world's workers, explosive growth in India, China, and a host of other developing nations has begun to entice the best and brightest to return home or not to leave in the first place. The flow of global talent is shifting, albeit very slowly. Africa, long the "lost continent," is rapidly being integrated into the global economy and into the global supply chains of the world's largest corporations, plugging the "last frontier" into the world economy.

Many in the West see all the above as a threat. This is not surprising; the status quo is in flux, and disruptive change is in the offing. The West no longer controls the global economic agenda. America has lost its ability to impose its economic will on the rest of the world; its ability to lead by example has been shattered by the U.S.-led financial meltdown of 2008. As discussed in Chapter 8, if the United States and the West resist and ignore the primary trends of the postcrisis world, the global economy will become fractured and fragmented—the economic cold war scenario.

THE THIRD AGE OF GLOBALIZATION

But the future need not be so bleak. In this alternate scenario, the West could face and embrace the broad macro trends confronting us today. These trends would be encouraged rather than discouraged. The West and the Rest can come to recognize their mutual interdependence and move down the path of mutual cooperation, not competition, on a number of fronts.

Against this backdrop, it is not impossible to envision the full bloom of the third age of globalization—with the world economy more integrated and interwoven than ever before. With an effective G-20 governing the global economy, with the United States and Europe accepting and adapting to their diminished role in the world, and with key developing nations becoming real global stakeholders, a new era of globalization is possible. Joint global stewardship will be required—not just between the United States and China, but also from Europe, Russia, Brazil, and key nations in Africa and the Middle East.

The end result would be an expanding global economy, with greater participation from states and regions heretofore long on the margins of the world economy. In the third age of globalization, central Asia, Africa, and various outlying Middle Eastern states would be pulled into the global fold by falling communication costs, advanced technology, and foreign direct investment from both the developed and developing nations. New trade routes would emerge and expand, promoting and thickening foreign direct investment and capital market ties between the West and Rest. Global competition would truly be global—pitting global leaders from the developed nations against their counterparts in the developing nations. The primary beneficiaries would be global consumers, enjoying more choices of goods and services at lower costs. Under this scenario, more women and more rural dwellers become global participants, adding more momentum to economic growth. An expanding economic pie, in turn, helps promote global cooperation in tackling urgent issues like global climate change, water scarcity, and other long-term challenges. This world is hardly perfect, but one where countries and their citizens come to recognize that a world more united than divided is the better path to follow.

The largest adjustment to this new era will fall on the shoulders of the United States. The world's last economic superpower needs to rethink how the world really works and then reset policies that build on America's strengths so that the nation remains one of the strongest in the world.

Answering this challenge, for starters, requires that America overcome two deficits: its knowledge deficit and its leadership deficit. The latter, the leadership deficit, speaks for itself. Washington is a house divided. Republicans and Democrats seem increasingly incapable and unwilling to work together in crafting bipartisan solutions critical to America's future. The to-do list, meanwhile, is only getting longer: immigration, America's mountain of debt, global climate change, military engagements in the Middle East, energy security—these issues can be tackled only if the nation's leaders work together, not apart.

By the knowledge deficit, I am referring to the fact that most Americans remain clueless to the world around them, oblivious to the fact that U.S. participation in the global economy is crucial to the economic well-being of every man, woman, and child in America. The last economic superpower needs the world more than ever before. Yet we as a country remain largely unaware of our rising foreign dependence on other people's resources, capital, and labor, and woefully misinformed about the rising global competition for such economic inputs. Similarly, America needs a better understanding of nations like China, India, Turkey, Brazil, and others like them. The prevailing consensus is that these nations are bound to succeed and that their success will come at the expense of the United States. Reality is far more complicated. America should worry more about China or India stumbling—failing rather than succeeding. Both Asian giants confront internal challenges as Herculean as those in the United States.

Each headline that speaks to the rise of China's or India's growing economic might is greeted with a mixture of fear and angst in the United States, leaving many Americans feeling less secure and confident about the future. These fears, ironically, would be justified if for some reason China or India decided to retreat and turn their back on the global economy, denying the world economy of new consumers, low-cost goods, and affordable labor among other things. The underlying health of the U.S. economy is increasingly intertwined with emerging consumers in Beijing, Cairo, Istanbul, and Delhi. Just ask U.S. automakers, who will be selling more cars in China than in the United States in the not-too-distant future. Or Procter & Gamble, General Electric, Boeing, and other U.S. multinationals whose future earnings are increasingly dependent on the developing nations. The more these firms succeed overseas, the better off the company's stakeholders—U.S. workers, shareholders, retirees, and local communities.

UNDERSTANDING WHAT'S
RIGHT WITH AMERICA

As part of America's knowledge deficit, many Americans need a better grasp of what is structurally right in this country. We are incessantly told what is wrong with the United States, so once in a while it is helpful to take stock of what is right and then go about making these positive building blocks even stronger.

For instance, nothing engenders more fear of the future than the alleged decline of U.S. manufacturing. The prevailing consensus is that America is not in the business of making "stuff." Manufacturing is the forte of Germany, Japan, and China, not the United States, with the past woes of Detroit and U.S. automobile manufacturers exhibit number one when it comes to the extinguished capabilities of U.S. manufacturing.

This is the consensus view—and a view that makes U.S. legislators, the media, and the average American worker defensive and antagonistic toward China, Japan, and other foreign manufacturers. A siege mentality has developed around America's "failing" manufacturing capabilities. But in reality the United States is a manufacturing juggernaut; we're still in the business of making "stuff" despite incessant media reports to the contrary. Indeed, no country manufactures more goods in a year than the United States, with America's share of global manufacturing output standing at 17.5 percent in 2008, according to figures from the United Nations Industrial Development Organization. America's share of global manufacturing is not far from where it was in 1980—roughly 20 percent. That means that U.S. manufacturers have held their own against intense foreign competition over the decades. Based on the last figures, of the 22 manufacturing industries identified by the United Nations, the

United States ranked among the top three in 19 categories. The United States was absent in just three sectors—apparel, tobacco, and leather. Meanwhile, the United States ranked number one in high-end manufacturing activities like medical/precision equipment and office and computing machinery.

What about China? The mainland ranks close behind the United States, with China's share of global manufacturing hitting 17.2 percent in 2008. However, the Chinese figures include mining and quarrying, and electricity, gas, and water supply in addition to manufacturing. The overall number is inflated, in other words. And besides, most of China's gains have come at the expense of Japan, South Korea, Mexico, and others, and not all that much from the United States in general. Japan was also well represented in the rankings, although the once-feared manufacturing juggernaut's global share of manufacturing output totaled 10 percent in 2008. Germany's global share was even less, 7.3 percent, well below America's share. America's global share of manufacturing in 2008 was larger than the combined total of Japan and Germany. The bottom line is that too many folks in the United States have equated the demise of Michigan and Ohio and the travails of U.S. automakers with the end of U.S. manufacturing. Nothing could be further from the truth.

Another key metric not well understood or appreciated by U.S. policy makers revolves around foreign trade. Contrary to conventional wisdom, the largest exporter in the world is neither Germany nor China. Rather, the world's top gun when it comes to global exports is none other than the United States. While China is the largest exporter of goods in the world, surpassing Germany in 2009, why count only goods? Why not count services? Thanks to falling communication costs and the ubiquity of the Internet, global service exports have soared in the past decade, with the United States in the forefront. U.S. exports of "other private services"—activities that include data processing, accounting, medical services, and telecommunications—totaled $252 billion in 2009. When goods and services are combined, U.S. exports top all others, totaling $1.5 trillion in 2009, or nearly 10 percent of the global sum. Germany, with 8.5 percent, ranked second. China ranked third, with an 8.2 percent share of total world exports.

Meanwhile, the United States remains the world's preferred destination for foreign multinationals. This fact runs counter to the common assumption that when firms decide to invest overseas, China is the first port of call. To the contrary, America has long trumped China for a variety of reasons, with the wealth and size of the U.S. market a key attraction to foreign firms. Cumulative foreign direct investment to China between 2000 and 2009 ($666 billion) was just a little more than one-third the total investment to America ($1.8 trillion) in the last decade. In other words, when it comes to attracting the foreign capital of Toyota, Siemens, Nestlé, and other corporate global giants, it is no contest—the United States wins hands down over China.

Hence, the noisy debate about U.S. outsourcing needs to be balanced with a more intelligent debate about U.S. insourcing. Thanks to the latter, some 5.5 million American workers were on the payrolls of U.S. affiliates of foreign multinationals in the United States in 2007, the last year of available data. Of this total, 1.7 million people were employed in various manufacturing activities; at last count, U.S. affiliates of foreign companies accounted for just over 12 percent of total manufacturing employment in this country, a sizable percentage given the steady decline in U.S. manufacturing employment over the past few decades.

In some states, the percentages are much higher. In South Carolina, for instance, nearly 22 percent of the state's manufacturing workforce is employed by U.S. affiliates of foreign companies. One of the largest foreign employers in the state is German car company BMW, with the premier global automaker investing over $4 billion into the state since the mid-1990s. The car company employs over 5,000 workers at its Spartanburg, South Carolina, plant, and has produced over 1.5 million vehicles since the first BMW318i car rolled of the assembly line in September 1994. In Kentucky, where many foreign automobile transplants are also present, foreign affiliates accounted for 19 percent of total manufacturing employment in 2007. In Ohio and Indiana, the percentages were 12.2 percent and 15 percent, respectively.

In the end, America stacks up quite well in critical activities like manufacturing, foreign trade, and foreign direct investment. This is a simple fact, yet it runs counter to the everyday narrative that America's manufacturing base has been allowed to wither, that U.S. firms are not in the business of exporting, and that U.S. foreign direct investment flows are one way—outbound. Against this backdrop, it is little wonder that average Americans fear the future. They are constantly told that everything is made in China, and there is no stopping the downward trend of U.S. manufacturing, and that white-collar service jobs are being outsourced to China and India. Playing on these fears, U.S. legislators rarely miss a chance to bash China when it comes to trade and remain anathema to various free trade agreements in the name of protecting U.S. workers and their standard of living.

America's general ignorance of its basic strengths threatens to undermine these very attributes. As the world's largest exporter, it behooves the United States to champion an open and free global trading environment and promote multilateral trading rounds like the Doha Round. Yet support for these endeavors has been lukewarm at best over the past few years. Indeed, there is very little support (or awareness) in the United States for the Doha Round of multilateral trade negotiations. This, despite the fact that a successful multilateral trade round that liberalizes trade in global services would be hugely beneficial to the world's top exporter of services—the United States. Meanwhile, three different bilateral free trade agreements remain in limbo in the halls of the U.S. Congress affecting U.S. commercial ties with Colombia, Panama, and South Korea. Finally, while President Obama has announced the lofty goal of doubling U.S. exports over the next five years, achieving this objective is not going to be easy if Congress does not grant the president fast-track trade promotion authority (TPA), which gives the president the right to negotiate trade agreements independent of congressional oversight. TPA expired under the Bush administration in June 2007. Since then, there has been very little talk of reviving a policy that has been notably successful in opening new foreign markets for U.S. goods and services in the past.

Perhaps there would be more urgency on the part of Congress if our elected officials realized that America is the world's largest exporter and therefore has a great deal to gain or lose when it comes to global trade. In a similar vein, perhaps many U.S. legislators and policy makers would be less fearful of and resentful toward U.S. companies that outsource—or move plants overseas—if they recognized the flip side of this process—insourcing. And given the benefits that flow from investment inflows—the creation of jobs, income, tax receipts, and the like—U.S. legislators should be crafting policies that aggressively encourage foreign direct investment, whether the investment is from Germany or China.

One of the best kept secrets in America is that when it comes to attracting foreign direct investment (FDI), nearly no one does it better than the United States. Foreign multinationals have long played a key role in the U.S. economy and promise to do the same in the future as long as U.S. policies do not result in investment protectionism. Finally, while America remains a manufacturing juggernaut, the manufacturing capabilities of the country need to be constantly nurtured. While the rise of China and other developing nations represents a key challenge to U.S. manufacturers, an even greater risk lies right here at home. The looming skilled labor shortage in the United States is right at the top of the list, a danger that requires the urgent attention of both Washington and corporate America. Without an educated, trained workforce, America's ability to compete in nanotechnology, aerospace, renewable energies, and other high-end manufacturing activities will be compromised. That's the real danger.

Yet against this backdrop—even though education remains a key building block to any economy—state and local expenditures on education in the United States have declined sharply over the past few years thanks to widening state budget deficits and the attendant requirement to balance state budgets. At precisely the moment when the United States needs a more educated and productive workforce, schools around the country are being shuttered. Many schools that have remained open are now holding classes four days a week instead of five. Numerous states are spending more on retirees (pensions, health-care benefits) than on education—or on the past rather than the future.

At the same time, fewer and fewer American students are actually graduating with a high school diploma. Up until recently, the consensus had long placed the high school graduation rate in the United States at 85 percent. That is hardly good, but the real number is thought to be even worse. According to research from the EPE Research Center, only about seven in ten students in the United States successfully graduate from high school each year. In many urban areas, the graduation rate is stunningly lower. In Philadelphia, roughly half the high school students do not graduate. In Baltimore, the percentage is even lower, with the city posting a graduation rate of just 35 percent. At the bottom of the list was Detroit—amazingly, the Detroit City School District graduates just one-quarter of its students. Overall, according to statistics from EPE Research Center, just over half (52 percent) of the students enrolled in high schools in the 50 largest cities in America complete high school and leave with a diploma.

Many Americans are aware of the shortcoming of the nation's public school system but are unaware of the magnitude of the problem, notably in America's urban centers, and the long-term ramifications for the future health of the U.S. economy.

Narrowing the knowledge deficit requires that the United States better understand its underlying strengths and set about fortifying the important building blocks of the economy. This will help bolster America's confidence in the messy multipolar world that is upon us. And a confident America, one ready to embrace and work with newly emerging powers, is a key prerequisite for the reincarnation of globalization.

Another prerequisite lies with emerging powers stepping up and doing their part to promote globalization. In this respect, China and its consumers are key. The Chinese consumer, in particular, needs to let loose and start spending more and saving less.

UNLEASHING THE CHINESE CONSUMER

Any first-time visitor to either Beijing or Shanghai cannot help but be impressed with the conspicuous consumption levels of China. Pick a product, and Chinese consumers want it. Automobile sales are among the strongest in the world. Over the past decade, demand has exploded for cell phones, computers, televisions, and other related goods, as more and more Chinese acquire the financial means to purchase Western staples. And it's not just the basics the Chinese are snapping up. China already ranks as the third-largest consumer of luxury goods in the world. More Bentleys are now sold in Beijing than in any other city in the world. Gucci's fastest-growing market is China, of course. The mainland has emerged as one of the fastest-growing markets in the world for just about everything. China is on course to have a million millionaires.

Contrary to the popular consensus, however, it is not all fast cars and fancy shopping malls for the average Chinese consumer. The importance of the Chinese consumer to economic growth in China has actually diminished over the past decade. While personal consumption accounted for nearly 80 percent of China's economic growth over the first half of the 1980s, consumption's share of gross domestic product (GDP) has actually declined over the past decade.

Growth in household consumption has lagged the underlying growth of the overall economy for the balance of this decade—even though household consumption outlays in China virtually doubled between 2000 and 2006. It has been investment and exports that have fueled China's boom of late, not the consumer. Household consumption as a percentage of GDP dropped from 46.4 percent in 2000 to just 35 to 37 percent in 2009. Among other nations in Asia, China has one of the lowest consumption-to-GDP ratios.

While supercharged levels of capital investment and exports have diminished the role of the consumer in driving growth, something even more fundamental is at work. The average consumer in China is not a credit card–touting shopper roaming the malls in search of fashionable jeans or a large-screen television. Despite the popular image portrayed by the media, the reality is quite different.

There is a great deal of economic angst affecting the average Chinese household, and China's extraordinary savings rate is one metric of this anxiety. The average Chinese household squirrels away a quarter of its after-tax income, one of the highest savings rates in the world. Why such a high level of savings? Prudence is one factor. Fear of the unknown is another.

While China's economic rise over the past three decades has been nothing short of spectacular, along with this phenomenal surge in growth has come wrenching social and economic change to China. The average Chinese household can no longer count on the guarantee of lifetime employment once provided by the Iron Rice Bowl cradle-to-grave social welfare programs of the past. Many of these social benefits have been scaled back or eliminated over the past decade, saddling the average Chinese consumer with the burden of paying for health care, pensions, education, and housing.

The share of health-care costs covered directly by the government dropped from 36 percent in 1980 to 17 percent in 2004. During the same period, the share financed by state enterprises fell from 43 to 27 percent. According to the Organization for Economic Co-Operation and Development, just half of China's urban population has basic health insurance, while even less is covered in the rural areas (less than 20 percent of the population). All tallied, China's total expenditures on health care are rather low relative to the rest of the world, averaging less than 6 percent of GDP.

Recognizing the shortcomings of its health-care system, the government has directed more state capital toward health care, expanding basic health-care coverage to nearly 85 percent of the population in 2008. The extent to which consumers have to pay out of pocket has fallen from the 2001 peak of 60 percent but still hovered around 45 percent in 2007, more than twice the share in 1978. By 2007, on average consumers were spending 4 percent of their outlays on out-of-pocket health spending, although the percentages were much higher in many rural areas of China.

While Chinese households have no choice but to save for unexpected and rising medical costs, the same holds true when it comes to retirement and expenses related to unexpected job losses. According to Chinese government statistics, only 16 to 17 percent of the population is covered under any basic government pension scheme; just 14 percent of China's workforce was covered by unemployment insurance in 2005.

Education represents another significant expense for the average Chinese family. According to Chinese government statistics, per capita expenditures on education account for around 8 percent of total consumption expenditures and continue to increase along with escalating expenses related to school. Households now confront rising fees for high school, traditional universities, as well as private colleges. Given that education is a national obsession in China, many parents find themselves financially strapped after paying for private tutors, extra classes, and other items related to producing the best and brightest in the family. For many rural families, student fees associated with school can be the equivalent of one year's income.

Add to the above soaring housing costs, which have increased as government subsidies on housing have declined. Taking care of the elderly is another financial burden confronting many households, with government expenditures relative to China's rapidly aging population inadequate for the nation's burgeoning elderly demographic. In the absence of government assistance, households have been left to take care of the elderly on their own.

In the end, the inconvenient truth is that Chinese consumers are not ready to drive the global economy. That is the bad news. The good news is that Beijing, albeit gradually, has begun to address the plight of the average Chinese household by raising public sector expenditures on health care, pensions, unemployment benefits, and other activities. These measures, in time, will free up some of China's excess savings for purposes of consumption, helping to rebalance the Chinese economy away from investment- and export-led growth and more toward consumption. In turn, a Chinese economy driven more by consumption would provide a substantial boost to global growth and trade and help thicken the webs of trade and investment with the mainland and various other parts of the world. It would also help dial back the anti-China protectionist rhetoric in the United States and Europe and lay the foundation for more bilateral cooperation between the United States and China in other strategic areas. All this will take time—years, if not decades. Patience will be required on the part of the United States. Yet, in the end, more balanced growth from one of the largest economies in the world is a prerequisite for the reincarnation of globalization.

EXPAND GLOBAL GOVERNANCE

Yet another requirement for the rebirth of globalization lies with the effective functioning of the G-20 and the reorganization of the world's existing multilateral institutions, primarily the International Monetary Fund and the World Bank.

As the world's new steering committee, the G-20 is now tasked with setting the global economic agenda and effectively running the global economy. But whether this diverse group, accounting for 88 percent of world output, can craft and coordinate global economic policies that are then followed by its various members remains to be seen.

In the wake of the financial crisis and the attendant global economic downturn, the G-20 presented a united front to the world, helping to stabilize the global economy and calm the nerves of investors. However, while all members of the G-20 pledged not to pursue protectionist measures at the first G-20 summit in Washington in November 2008, virtually all members have broken this promise in some shape or form over the past few years. In addition, while the G-20 spent most of 2010 crafting new policies that would regulate the world financial markets, various member states were busy doing the same thing, independent of the G-20. Against this backdrop, what could very well emerge is a global capital market wrapped in a patchwork quilt of regulatory frameworks that suffocates cross-border flows of capital. This runs counter, of course, to the reincarnation of globalization.

A revitalized global economy requires a G-20 with the credibility and clout to persuade various members to subsume their national interests for the good of the global economy. With 20 members, however, the temptation for powerful players like the United States and China to divide and rule, or create de facto alliances within the G-20, will be strong yet destructive. In this respect, the success or failure of the G-20 will largely hinge on how the United States and China, the world's two most powerful economies, conduct themselves within the group. To a large degree, the success of the G-20 depends on how well the so-called G-2, the United States and China, get along. The role played by emerging regional powers like Russia, Turkey, and Brazil will also be critical to the success or failure of the G-20. Each nation has emerged as a key regional power in its respective part of the world, with the trio less shy and more vocal on how the global economy should be managed.

While the G-20 is fairly representative of the new global order and gives the developing nations greater responsibilities and greater stakes in the global economy, the same cannot be said of the IMF and World Bank. Both institutions remain largely under the influence of the West, a situation that offends many developing nations and is anathema to globalization that is less Western-centric. The reincarnation of globalization will occur only if the developing nations feel they are real stakeholders in the global economy, having the influence to shape global economic policies. Toward this end, European representation at the International Monetary Fund should be further consolidated, going beyond the reforms agreed to at the G-20 summit in Pittsburgh. This step would give more quotas and voting rights to the developing nations, as well as increase their number of executive seats. The United States, for its part, should consider giving up its veto right, a move that would send a powerful signal to the rest of the world that the United States is willing to break from the past and ready to operate more in concert with the rest of the world. As a final move, the West should end the U.S./European duopoly on leadership of the World Bank and the IMF. For decades, since their inception, the World Bank has always been led by an American, while the IMF has always had a European at the helm. This arrangement, not surprisingly, is deeply annoying to the Rest and should be changed to include qualified candidates from any country in the world.

In the end, for globalization to be truly global, greater participation and greater buy in is going to be required of the developing nations. This can come about only if the G-20 does emerge as an effective governing body and only if the West is ready to give more say and sway to the developing nations in running the IMF, World Bank, and other Western multilateral institutions.

REFORTIFY THE WEST

Globalization cannot reemerge stronger and more inclusive without the participation and support of the West. Although the brand of the West has been devalued and while the collective global influence of the United States, Europe, and Japan has been eroded by the financial crisis of 2008, the West has to figure prominently in the reincarnation of globalization. By its sheer economic size, the West still matters, and in order for globalization to work in the future, the United States and Europe, in particular, must learn to live with more aggressive and powerful emerging nations like Turkey, India, Brazil, and China. The United States and Europe must also refortify and reenergize the transatlantic partnership, a partnership that remains vital to the future growth and management of the global economy.

Discussed in more detail in Chapter 6, the ties that have long bound the United States and Europe together are fraying. Many key issues threaten to divide the transatlantic relationship, with the U.S.-led wars in the Middle East, differences over global climate change, and the scope and scale of financial reform chief among them. Yet a productive relationship between the United States and Europe is required if the world is going to stand any chance of maintaining a free and open trading environment, stop the proliferation of nuclear weapons, answer the challenge of global climate change, and assist in raising millions of people out of poverty. That is just for starters.

Under the scenario of globalization reincarnated, the United States and Europe would work together to forge a more predictable and less messy multipolar world. Jointly, the United States and Europe take the lead in restructuring existing multilateral institutions like the IMF and the World Bank, giving more votes and chairs at the table to the developing nations. They also breathe new life into the Doha trading round by making key concessions, compromising on agricultural issues with the developing nations in order to push forward the talks over more liberal trade in services. The two parties also push on the frontier of renewable energies, and wherever possible, enlist the support and participation of India, China, Russia, and other emerging market stakeholders in such endeavors. The more the United States and Europe work together in tackling the pressing economic issues of our times, the more respect the Rest will have for the West, and by extension, the greater will be their willingness to cooperate with the United States and Europe.

Critically, the United States and Europe must also get their own economic houses in order, engendering confidence not only between themselves but also among the developing nations. The best way for the West to regain its credibility with the Rest is by implementing necessary but painful economic reforms at home. For the United States, that means drastically reducing the federal budget deficit to manageable levels and reducing the nation's dependence on foreign capital and oil. For Europe, that means fiscal restraint and efforts at boosting Europe's competitiveness, along with measures that create a more flexible and competitive labor market.

Of notable importance, legislators and policy makers in both the United States and Europe pledge to better inform and educate their respective populations/constituents of the benefits of greater cooperation and mutual coordination with the emerging markets. The mentality "they win, we lose" must be jettisoned for a more enlightened debate with the general population about the risks and rewards of participating in the new global economy unfolding. Pragmatism replaces dogmatism. The political courage is mustered to tell citizens the simple truth—that the economic future of the West is inextricably tied to the success of the Rest; the Rest's success, to a large degree, is our success.

Globalization can be reincarnated only if leaders in both the developed and developing nations educate their constituents of the benefits of cross-border flows of trade, capital, people, and ideas. In this world, more consumers and workers in the United States and Europe come to understand that their livelihoods are increasingly determined by growth in the developing nations. The prevailing consensus of yesteryear—that China's rise must parallel the decline of America and Europe—is turned on its head. And for their part, the developing nations strike a more conciliatory note with the West on key multilateral issues like global climate change, global trade, and nuclear proliferation. Rather than compete, China would cooperate with the United States in such fields as global climate change and energy security, and partner with the United States in boosting growth and ending misery in Africa. Under this scenario, Russia, Turkey, India, Brazil, and other newly emerging regional powers actively would work with the United States and Europe to overcome the world's most pressing challenges.

In the end, the mutual interests and goals of the West and Rest converge, and a more productive relationship ensues. The webs of globalization multiply and thicken.

IT IS DIFFERENT THIS TIME

The reincarnation of globalization requires that many things go right—that America refortifies its underlying economic strengths and regains its confidence when dealing with a more complex and diverse world; that China shifts its economic growth model away from exports and toward more personal consumption; that multilateral institutions, notably the G-20, succeed in guiding the world economy toward more equitable economic growth; and that the West comes together, confidently forging a more productive relationship with the Rest, as opposed to drifting apart.

All the above represents a tall order, and of course, must be accomplished in conjunction with other main actors on the global stage—India, Russia, Turkey, South Africa, Brazil, and China to name just a few. It will take every ounce of global leadership and courage to reincarnate globalization with non-American characteristics. For this to happen, it is critical that all key parties come to realize that, yes, this time is different.

The world has changed. The financial crisis of 2008 unleashed a seismic shift in the global economy. Free-market capitalism will survive but not in the unregulated and anything-goes environment of the past quarter century. The participation of the state in both the developed and developing economies is bound to become larger, not smaller. Around the world, the commanding heights have shifted from the private sector to the public sector. Regulated more at home and abroad, the ability of banks and nonbanks to push capital any place in the world at virtually any time is becoming more restrictive. It is the deglobalization of finance that threatens to unwind globalization as we know it.

The relative economic decline of the developed nations; the rising influence of the emerging markets in general and China in particular; the proliferation of regional trading blocs—these seminal trends were fast-forwarded by the crisis and have, in turn, accelerated the move toward a less U.S.-centric, more multipolar world. In the world of the future, there is no mistaking the fact that global power and influence will be more diffused among nations and regions, making it more challenging to coordinate and craft solutions to pressing global problems.

The new era will require far-reaching adjustments for those nations in decline and for those on the ascent. China remains coy and conflicted by its new global status, acting more like a reluctant stakeholder in the global economy as opposed to a willing leader. The developing nations in general are an incredibly heterogeneous bunch and may prove unable and incapable of leading the global economy forward.

Becoming more acclimated to a new multipolar world will be a notable and significant challenge to the world's last economic superpower—the United States. While America is expected to remain one of the most powerful nations in the world, its economic superpower status has been undermined by the Made in America global financial crisis and by America's profligate ways well before the crisis struck.

It is different this time for the United States: when America speaks today, the world is less inclined to listen, let alone jump to the tune of the United States. At the end of World War II, the United States largely dictated the global economic rules of the game to the rest of the world, which, with little resistance, accepted the American way of doing things. For over a half century, the rest of the world followed America's lead until the United States drove the entire world economy over the cliff in 2008. The world will never so blindly follow the United States again.

To this point, in most developing nations the standard economic medicine of the West is no longer accepted; there are alternatives, in other words, to the IMF and Washington consensus. Beijing has plenty of capital, as do other regional players like Middle East sovereign wealth funds, Russia, and Brazil. Today, when a developing nation finds itself in financial trouble, there are ways of working through the crisis other than humbly going hat in hand to Washington.

By various metrics (global output, trade, and investment), the economic gravity of the world is shifting from the west to east, or from the developed nations to the developing nations. Western multinationals no longer rule the world and now confront serious competitive challenges from emergent corporations in China, India, Russia, and other nations. While still one of the largest economies in the world, the U.S. economy has never been more dependent on foreign natural resources, foreign capital, and foreign labor. Under current circumstances, America is rapidly losing control of its own economic fate.

Since there is no turning back, the world's last economic superpower would do well to heed its own advice. On the first page of the State Department's National Security Strategy report, released in May 2010, the opening paragraph states the following: "To succeed, we must face the world as it is."

No 10 words better underscore the challenge before the world's last economic superpower. The world is messy and complicated, to be sure, but also brimming with opportunities for the United States and the world at large. The paths before us— an economic cold war or globalization reincarnated—could not be more different. With a little luck and massive doses of leadership, the multipolar world unfolding before us could be the start of another golden era of globalization, bringing success to all nations.

Notes

CHAPTER 1

1. Daniel Yergin and Joseph Stanislaw, *The Commanding Heights: The Battle between Government and the Marketplace That Is Remaking the Modern World*, New York: Simon & Schuster, 1998, p. 60.
2. References in quotes from the writings of Thomas Friedman. "Road kill" is a popular refrain of Friedman's when describing those resisting the forces of globalization.
3. Martin Wolf, *Fixing Global Finance*, Baltimore, MD: Johns Hopkins University Press, 2008.
4. U.S. Census Bureau, www.census.gov/foreign-trade/statistics/historical/gands.txt.
5. Wolf, *Fixing Global Finance*.
6. International Monetary Fund, "Globalization in Historical Perspective," Annex to World Economic Outlook, Washington, DC, May 1997.
7. John Micklethwait and Adrian Wooldridge, *A Future Perfect*, New York: Crown Business, 2000, p. 51.
8. Peter Drucker, "The Global Economy and the Nation-State," *Foreign Affairs*, vol. 76, September/October 1997, p. 162.
9. David Smick, *The World Is Curved*, New York: Portfolio, 2008.
10. Figures for world direct investment are sourced from the United Nations and various publications of the "World Investment Report," an annual report that is produced by the United Nations Conference on Trade and Development, or UNCTAD.
11. Smick, *The World Is Curved*.
12. Charles Krauthammer, "The Unipolar Moment," *Foreign Affairs*, vol. 70, 1990–1991, p. 24.
13. Charles Krauthammer, "Democratic Realism: An American Foreign Policy for a Unipolar World," Irving Kristol Lecture on Foreign Policy and Democratic Globalism, American Enterprise Institute for Public Policy Research, Washington DC, February 10, 2004.

CHAPTER 2

1. Mark Zandi, *Financial Shock*, Upper Saddle River, NJ: FT Press, 2009, p. 59.
2. Carmen M. Reinhart and Kenneth S. Rogoff, *This Time Is Different*, Princeton, NJ: Princeton University Press, 2009, p. 207.
3. Joseph Stiglitz, *Freefall: America, Free Markets, and the Sinking of the World Economy*, New York: W. W. Norton, 2010, p. 14.
4. Testimony of Federal Reserve chairman Ben Bernanke before the Joint Economic Committee, U.S. Congress, March 28, 2007.

5. McKinsey Global Institute, "Global Capital Markets: Entering a New Era," September 2009.
6. Ibid.
7. Kevin Phillips, *Bad Money*, New York: Viking, 2008, p. 107.
8. McKinsey Global Institute, "Global Capital Markets."
9. Figures are from the Federal Reserve—Flow of Funds data, a quarterly series of financial statistics produced and published by the U.S. Federal Reserve.
10. Paul Krugman, *The Return of Depression Economics and the Crisis of 2008*, New York: W.W. Norton, 2009.
11. Harold James, *The Creation and Destruction of Value*, Cambridge, MA: Harvard University Press, 2009, pp. 120–121.
12. International Monetary Fund, "Globalization in Historical Perspective," Annex to World Economic Outlook, Washington, DC, May 1997.
13. The World Bank, "Preventing and Minimizing Crises," *Finance for Growth: Policy Choices in a Volatile World*, World Bank Policy Research Report, June 2001.
14. Martin Wolf, *Fixing Global Finance*, Baltimore, MD: Johns Hopkins University Press, 2008.
15. Stiglitz, *Freefall*, p. 20.
16. Ian Bremmer, *The End of the Free Market: Who Wins the War between States and Corporations?*, New York: Portfolio, 2010, p. 67.
17. Laura Mandaro, "China's Wen Urges U.S. to Keep Deficit at 'Appropriate Size,'" MarketWatch, November 8, 2009.
18. Wolf, *Fixing Global Finance*.
19. Barry Eichengreen and Michael D. Bordo, "Crises Now and Then: What Lessons from the Last Era of Financial Globalization," Boston, MA: National Bureau of Economic Research, January 2002.
20. Joseph E. Stiglitz, *Globalization and Its Discontents*, New York: Norton, 2002, p. 69.

CHAPTER 3

1. Andrew Ross Sorkin, *Too Big to Fail: The Inside Story of How Wall Street and Washington Fought to Save the Financial System—and Themselves*, New York: Penguin, 2010.
2. Bank for International Settlements, 79th Annual Report, June 29, 2009.
3. McKinsey Global Institute, "Global Capital Markets: Entering a New Era," September 2009.
4. Ibid.
5. Julia Werdigier, "Will ECB Review Its Policy after Fed Cut?" *International Herald Tribune*, January 22, 2008.
6. Daniel Hamilton and Joseph Quinlan, *The Transatlantic Survey 2009*, Baltimore, MD: Johns Hopkins University Press, 2009.
7. Bank for International Settlements, 79th Annual Report, June 29, 2009.
8. Martin Wolf, *Fixing Global Finance*, Baltimore, MD: Johns Hopkins University Press, 2008.
9. "The Uncertainty Principle," *Wall Street Journal*, July 14, 2010.

10. "Experts Grade the Legislation," *Wall Street Journal,* July 16, 2010.
11. Philip Stephens, "Three Years On—and the Markets Are Masters Again," *Financial Times,* July 30, 2010; also see Floyd Norris, "In Basel, Eternal Work in Progress," *New York Times,* July 30, 2010.
12. World Bank, "Global Development Finance: The Role of International Banking," 2008; a paper produced by the staff of the International Bank for Reconstruction and Development/World Bank.
13. Ibid.
14. See Simon J. Evenett et al., "The Fateful Allure of Protectionism: Taking Stock for the G8 and Broken Promises," a G-20 Summit Report by the Global Trade Alert, Centre for Economic Policy.
15. World Trade Organization, Report to the TPRB from the Director General on the Financial and Economic Crisis and Trade-Related Developments, July 15, 2009.
16. Keith Bradsher, "Foreign Companies Chafe at China's Restrictions," *New York Times,* May 16, 2010.
17. Geoff Dyer and Guy Dinmore, "GE Chief Gives Vent to Frustration over China," *Financial Times,* July, 2, 2010.
18. European Chamber Business Confidence Survey, 2010; published by the European Union Chamber of Commerce in China, in partnership with the Roland Berger Strategy Consultants.
19. Anthony Faiola and Lori Montgomery, "Trade Wars Brewing in Economic Malaise," *Washington Post,* May 15, 2009.
20. "World Investment Report, 2010: Investing in a Low-Carbon Economy," United Nations Conference on Trade and Development, New York, July 2010.

CHAPTER 4

1. Floyd Norris, "After Jerky Swings, the Economy Begins to Look Nice and Boring," *New York Times,* March 6, 2010.
2. Katrin Bennhold and Alison Smale, "In Davos, Signs of Shift in Global Power," *New York Times,* February 19, 2010.
3. Bob Davis, "IMF Says Financial Revamps Could Thwart Global Deal," *Wall Street Journal,* April 23, 2010.
4. Philip Stephens, "Splintered Solidarity Has Put Global Governance in a Spin," *Financial Times,* July 2, 2010.
5. Jeffrey Sachs, "America Has Passed on the Baton," *Financial Times,* September 30, 2009.
6. "Leviathan Inc," *The Economist,* August 7, 2010.
7. Ibid.
8. Ibid.
9. Ian Bremmer, *Foreign Affairs,* May/June 2009.
10. Jennifer Hillman, "Saving Multilateralism," Brussels Forum Paper Series, The German Marshal Fund of the United States, 2010.
11. Abraham F. Lowenthal, "Obama and the Americas," *Foreign Affairs,* July/August 2010.

12. Ibid.
13. "Asia's Never-Closer Union," Banyan column, *The Economist*, February 6, 2010.
14. C. Fred Bergsten, speech delivered to Asia-Pacific Regional Economic Integration and Architecture, March 25, 2010, Auckland University, New Zealand.
15. "Riches in the Near Abroad," *The Economist*, January 30, 2010.
16. "New Silk Roads," Banyon column, *The Economist*, April 10, 2010.
17. See Jagdish Bhagwati, *Termites in the Trading System: How Preferential Trade Agreements Undermine Free Trade,* Council of Foreign Relations, New York: Oxford University Press, 2008.
18. John Prideaux, "The World in 2010," *The Economist* special edition.
19. "Getting It Together at Last," *The Economist*, November 12, 2009.
20. David Gardner and Delphine Strauss, "South-South Diplomacy Put to a Test," *Financial Times*, May 19, 2010.
21. John Pomfret, "China Invests Heavily in Brazil, Elsewhere in Pursuit of Political Heft," *Washington Post*, July 26, 2010.
22. Sewell Chan, "U.S. and Brazil Reach Agreement on Cotton Dispute," *New York Times*, April 6, 2010.
23. Martin Jacques, *When China Rules the World*, New York: Penguin Press, 2009, p. 168.
24. Xubei Luo and Nong Zhu, "Rising Income Inequality in China: A Race to the Top," World Bank Policy Research Paper Series, August 2008.
25. "Red Mist," *The Economist*, February 4, 2010.
26. "The Panda Has Two Faces," *The Economist*, March 31, 2010.
27. Kishore Mahbubani, *The New Asian Hemisphere: The Irresistible Shift of Global Power to the East,* New York: PublicAffairs, 2009.
28. David Pilling, "China Will Not Be the World's Deputy Sheriff," *Financial Times*, January 28, 2010.
29. The World Bank, "Emerging Stronger from the Crisis," World Bank East Asia and Pacific Economic Update, 2010, p. 21.
30. "Comparing Global Influence: China's and U.S. Diplomacy, Foreign Aid, Trade and Investment in the Developing World," CRS report for Congress, August 15, 2008.
31. Jacques, *When China Rules the World*.

CHAPTER 5

1. "A Citizen's Guide to the 2008 Financial Report of the United States Government," U.S. Department of Treasury, Washington, DC, 2008.
2. David E. Sanger, "Deficits May Alter U.S. Politics and Global Power," *New York Times*, February 1, 2010.
3. The figures cited in this section come from the U.S. Congressional Budget Office, January 2010, and the annual Economic Report to the President.
4. "A Double-A U.S.A.?" *Wall Street Journal*, Opinion Journal, February 5, 2010.
5. John Fund, "Warning: The Deficits Are Coming," *Wall Street Journal*, September 5–6, 2009.

6. Figures come from the Center for Media and Democracy, which publishes Source-Watch; www.sourcewatch.org.
7. Figures are from various reports from the Congressional Budget Office.
8. Figures are from various reports from the Congressional Budget Office.
9. Amy Belasco, "The Cost of Iraq, Afghanistan, and Other Global War on Terror Operations since 9/11," Congressional Research Service, September 28, 2009.
10. Ibid.
11. Stephen Daggett, "Costs of Major U.S. Wars," Congressional Research Service, Washington, DC, June 29, 2010.
12. Christopher Drew, "High Costs Weigh on Troop Debate for Afghan War," *New York Times,* September 15, 2009.
13. Joseph E. Stiglitz and Linda J. Bilmes, *The Three Trillion Dollar War,* New York: W.W. Norton, 2008.
14. Ibid, p. 71.
15. Linda J. Bilmes and Joseph E. Stiglitz, "The $10 Trillion Hangover," *Harper's,* January 2009.
16. Gregg Zoroya, "Mental Care Stays Are Up in Military," *USA Today,* May 16, 2010.
17. Gregg Zoroya, "Military's Health Care Costs Booming," *USA Today,* April 25, 2010.
18. Stiglitz and Bilmes, *The Three Trillion Dollar War.*
19. "Total Wall Street Bailout Cost," www.sourcewatch.org.
20. David Francis, "The Bailout's Costs Are Big—but Falling," *The Christian Science Monitor,* May 10, 2010.
21. Sewell Chan and Javier C. Hernandez, "Bernanke Says Nation Must Take Actions Soon to Shape Fiscal Future," *New York Times,* April, 8, 2010.
22. Ibid.
23. Ibid.
24. David M. Smick, *The World Is Curved,* New York: Portfolio, 2008, p. 51.
25. Edmund L. Andrews, "Federal Government Faces Balloon in Debt Payments," *New York Times,* November 23, 2009.
26. Figures are from the Congressional Budget Office.
27. Figures are from the Office of Management and Budget.
28. Keith Bradsher, "China Grows More Picky about Debt," *New York Times,* May 21, 2009.
29. Brad Setser, "Sovereign Wealth and Sovereign Power," Council on Foreign Relations, September 2008.
30. Geoff Dyer, "China's Dollar Dilemma," *Financial Times,* February 23, 2009.
31. Swell Chan, "Bernanke Says a Plan to Address the U.S. Deficit Could Keep Rates Down," *New York Times,* April 15, 2010.
32. Harold James, *The Creation and Destruction of Value: The Globalization Cycle,* Cambridge, MA: Harvard University Press, 2009, pp. 209–210.

CHAPTER 6

1. David Pilling, "The Looming Influence of the East," *Financial Times,* January 31, 2010.

2. Figures are from the International Monetary Fund.
3. See Daniel Hamilton and Joseph Quinlan, *The Transatlantic Economy 2010* and various annual surveys published under the auspices of the Center for Transatlantic Relations, The Johns Hopkins University, Washington, DC.
4. "The Cutting Edge," *The Economist*, February 24, 2001.
5. Figures on world foreign direct investment are sourced from the United Nations Conference on Trade and Development (UNCTAD) and various annual World Investment Reports, New York.
6. Figures are from the Bureau of Economic Analysis, U.S. Department of Commerce.
7. United Nations Conference on Trade and Development, World Investment Report, various annual editions.
8. Jean-Marie Colombani, "We Are All Americans," *Le Monde*, September 12, 2001.
9. Robert Kagan, *Of Paradise and Power: America and Europe in the New World Order*, London: Atlantic Books, 2003.
10. Robert Kagan, "Power and Weakness," *Policy Review*, June/July 2002.
11. See various reports and publications from Daniel Hamilton and Joseph Quinlan, the Center for Transatlantic Relations, The Johns Hopkins University, Washington DC.
12. Andrew Grice, "Financial Crisis Caused by White Men with Blue Eyes," *The Independent*, January 27, 2009.
13. Bertrand Benoit, "U.S. 'Will Lose Financial Superpower Status,'" *Financial Times*, September 25, 2008
14. David Pilling and Ralph Atkins, "A Quest of Other Ways," *Financial Times*, March 16, 2009.
15. Steven Erlanger, "Germany Asserts Its Interests as Greek Debt Crisis Unfolds," *New York Times*, April 13, 2010.
16. Anthony Faiola, "Greek Debt Crisis Merely Adds to List of Issues Dividing the European Union," *Washington Post*, March 21, 2010.
17. Gideon Rachman, "Long-Term Survival Strategies," *Financial Times*, January 25, 2010.
18. Brian Knowlton, "Gates Calls European Mood a Danger to Peace," *New York Times*, February 24, 2010.
19. National Bureau of Asian Research, policy report No. 3, April 1998.
20. "Stuck in Neutral," *The Economist*, August 15, 2009.
21. Hiroko Tabuchi, "Japan Unveils a Plan for Growth, Emphasizing Free Trade in Asia," *New York Times*, December 31, 2009.

CHAPTER 7
1. Ronnie Chan, "The West's Preaching to the East Must Stop," *Financial Times*, January 4, 2010.
2. Kishore Mahbubani, *The New Asian Hemisphere: The Irresistible Shift of Global Power to the East*, New York: PublicAffairs, 2008.
3. "Rising in the East," *The Economist*, January 3, 2009.

4. Andrew E. Kramer, "Russia's Evolution, as Seen through the Golden Arches," *New York Times*, February 2, 2010.

5. Patti Waldmier, "Office Girls Lead Charge to Boost Spending," *Financial Times*, January 17, 2010.

6. Charles Clover, "Russians' Appetite for Bling Put to the Test," *Financial Times*, January 19, 2010, p. 5.

7. Richard Freeman, "The Great Doubling: The Challenge of the New Global Labor Market," August 2006, available at http://emlab.berkeleyedu.

8. World Bank, Global Economic Prospects, 2010, Washington, DC.

9. World Bank, Global Economic Prospects, 2009, Washington, DC.

10. "Who's in the Middle?" *The Economist*, February 14, 2009.

11. World Bank, Global Economic Prospects, 2009, Washington, DC.

12. David Hensley and Joseph Lupton, "EM Consumers: Engines of Global Growth," Economic Data Watch, J.P. Morgan Chase, December 4, 2009.

13. "Two Billion More Bourgeois," *The Economist*, February 14, 2009.

14. "More Millionaires," *The Economist,* July 2010.

15. Ian Bremmer, "The End of Free Markets?" *Foreign Affairs,* May/June 2009.

16. Tina Rosenberg, "The Perils of Petrocracy," *New York Times Magazine,* November 4, 2007.

17. BP Statistical Review of World Energy, 2010; available on line at www.bp.com/statisticalreview.

18. Ibid.

19. Ibid.

20. Congressional Research Service, "Comparing Global Influence: China's and the U.S. Diplomacy, Foreign Aid, Trade, and Investment in the Developing World," report for Congress, August 15, 2008.

21. "An (Iron) Fistful of Help," *The Economist*, June 6, 2009.

22. Various World Bank publications.

23. Barry Popkin, "Will China's Nutrition Transition Overwhelm Its Health Care System and Slow Economic Growth?" *Health Affairs,* vol. 27, no. 4, July/August 2008.

24. Figures come from the U.S. Treasury Department.

25. Figures are sourced from the Bureau of Economic Analysis.

26. Ibid.

27. Alexei Barrionuevo, "Brazil Moves for More Control of Oil Wealth beneath Its Sea," *New York Times,* August 18, 2009.

28. U.S. Department of Commerce and other government data.

29. Dexter Roberts, "China: Closing for Business?" *Bloomberg Businessweek,* March 25, 2010.

30. Dewey & LeBoeuf LLP, "China's Promotion of the Renewable Electric Power Equipment Industry," the national foreign trade council, March 2010.

31. Albert R. Hunt, "Trade Villain of Its Own Making," *New York Times,* April 4, 2010.

32. Natasha Singer, "Drug Giants Lag Where Sales Boom, Study Says," *New York Times*, April 16, 2010.

33. "They Might Be Giants," *The Economist,* May 15, 2010.

34. Amelia Gentleman, "Brain Gain for India as Elite Return," *The Observer,* April 20, 2008.

35. Zhu Shen, "Life Science Blossoms,"TheScientist.com; available at www.the-scientist .com/templates/trackable/display/supplementarticle.jsp?name=china&id=56195.

36. Vivek Wadhwa, "Is the U.S. Experiencing Its First Brian Drain?" *New America Media,* March 31, 2009; also "Framing the Engineering Outsourcing Debate," a report developed by graduate students of Duke University's Master of Engineering Management Program under the guidance of Dr. Gary Gereffi and Vivek Wadhwa with consulting assistance from Katzenbach Partners LLC, December 2005.

37. Vivek Wadhwa, "A Reverse Brain Drain," *Issues in Science and Technology,* Summer 2009.

38. Hal Weitzman, "Concerns as Baby Boomers Prepare for Retirement," *Financial Times,* February 28, 2010.

39. Ibid.

40. Figures come from the U.S. Bureau of Labor Statistics.

41. "Innovation in Emerging Markets: New Masters of Management," *The Economist,* April 15, 2010.

42. "The College Completion Agenda 2010 Progress Report," College Board Advocacy & Policy Center, July 2010.

43. Mahbubani, *The New Asian Hemisphere.*

CHAPTER 8

1. Edward Luce, "The Crisis of Middle-Class America," *Financial Times,* July 30, 2010.

2. David Barboza, "China Says It Will Tighten Controls on Rare Minerals," *New York Times,* June 3, 2010.

3. U.S. Government Accountability Office, "Rare Earth Materials in the Defense Supply Chain," Briefing for Congressional Committees, April 14, 2010.

4. Ibid.

5. Asian Development Bank Report, "Water Rights and Water Allocation: Issues and Challenges for Asia," August 2009, and other annual and periodic publications from the bank.

6. Stanley A. Weiss, "Water for Peace," *New York Times,* July 13, 2009.

7. Sudha Ramachandran, "India Quakes over China's Water Plan," *Asia Times,* December 9, 2008.

8. Ian Bremmer, *The End of the Free Market,* New York: Portfolio, 2010, p. 140.

9. Martin Jacques, *When China Rules the World,* New York: Penguin Press, 2009.

References

Barbara, Robert J., *The Cost of Capitalism: Understanding Market Mayhem and Stabilizing Our Economic Future*, New York: McGraw-Hill, 2009.

Bernstein, Peter L., *Against the Gods: The Remarkable Story of Risk*, Hoboken, NJ: John Wiley & Sons, 1996.

Bhagwati, Jagdish, *Termites in the Trading System: How Preferential Trade Agreements Undermine Free Trade*, New York: Oxford University Press, 2008.

Bonner, Bill, and Addison Wiggin, *Empire of Debt: The Rise of an Epic Financial Crisis*, Hoboken, NJ: John Wiley & Sons, 2006.

Bremmer, Ian, *The End of the Free Market: Who Wins the War Between States and Corporations?* New York: Portfolio, 2010.

Chanda, Nayan, *Bound Together: How Traders, Preachers, Adventurers, and Warriors Shaped Globalization*, New Haven, CT: Yale University Press, 2007.

Dicken, Peter, *Global Shift: Reshaping the Global Economic Map in the 21st Century*, New York: The Guilford Press, 2003.

Duncan, Richard, *The Dollar Crisis: Causes, Consequences, Cures*, Singapore: John Wiley & Sons (Asia) Pte Ltd, 2005.

———, *The Corruption of Capitalism*, Hong Kong: CLSA Books, 2009.

Eichengreen, Barry, *Globalizing Capital: A History of the International Monetary System*, Princeton, NJ: Princeton University Press, 2008.

Eichengreen, Barry, and Michael D. Bordo, "Cries Now and Then: What Lessons from the Last Era of Financial Globalization," Boston: National Bureau of Economic Research working paper, January 2002.

El-Erian, Mohamed, *When Markets Collide: Investment Strategies for the Age of Global Economic Change*, New York: McGraw-Hill, 2008.

Engardio, Pete, *Chindia: How China and India Are Revolutionizing Global Business*, New York: McGraw-Hill, 2007.

Ferguson, Niall, *The Ascent of Money: A Financial History of the World*, New York: Penguin Press, 2008.

Friedman, Thomas L., *The World Is Flat: A Brief History of the Twenty-First Century*, New York: Farrar, Straus, and Giroux, 2006.

Gilpin, Robert, *The Challenge of Global Capitalism: The World Economy in the 21st Century*, Princeton, NJ: Princeton University Press, 2000.

Greenspan, Alan, *The Age of Turbulence: Adventures in a New World*, New York: Penguin Press, 2007.

Gross, Daniel, *Dumb Money: How Our Greatest Financial Minds Bankrupted the Nation*, New York: Free Press, 2009.

Halper, Stefan, *The Beijing Consensus: How China's Authoritarian Model Will Dominate the Twenty-First Century*, New York: Basic Books/Perseus Books Group, 2010.

Hamilton, Daniel, and Joseph Quinlan, *Globalization & Europe: Prospering in the New Whirled Order*, Center for Transatlantic Relations, Washington, DC: The Johns Hopkins University, 2008.

———, *The Transatlantic Economy Survey 2010*, Center for Transatlantic Relations, Washington, DC: The Johns Hopkins University, 2010.

Jacques, Martin, *When China Rules the World: The End of the Western World and the Birth of a New Global Order*, New York, Penguin Press, 2009.

James, Harold, *The Creation and Destruction of Value*, Cambridge, MA: Harvard University Press, 2009.

Jonsson, Asgeir, *Why Iceland? How One of the World's Smallest Countries Became the Meltdown's Biggest Casualty*, New York: McGraw-Hill, 2009.

Kagan, Robert, *Paradise & Power: America and Europe in the New World Order*, London: Atlantic Books, 2003.

Karabell, Zachary, *Superfusion: How China and America Became One Economy and Why the World's Prosperity Depends on It*, New York: Simon & Schuster, 2009.

Kennedy, Paul, *The Rise and Fall of the Great Powers: Economic Change and Military Conflict from 1500 to 2000*, New York: Random House, 1987.

King, Stephen D., *Losing Control: The Emerging Threats to Western Prosperity*, New Haven, CT: Yale University Press, 2010.

Krugman, Paul, *The Return of Depression Economics and the Crisis of 2008*, New York: W.W. Norton & Company, 2009.

Lowenstein, Roger, *The End of Wall Street*, New York: The Penguin Press, 2010.

Mahbubani, Kishore, *The New Asian Hemisphere: The Irresistible Shift of Global Power to the East*, New York: PublicAffairs, 2008.

Meredith, Robyn, *The Elephant and the Dragon: The Rise of India and China and What It Means for All of Us*, New York: W.W. Norton, 2007.

Micklethwait, John, and Adrian Wooldridge, *A Future Perfect: The Challenge and Hidden Promise of Globalization*, New York: Crown Business, 2000.

Mishkin, Frederic S., *The Next Great Globalization*, Princeton, NJ: Princeton University Press, 2006.

Morris, Charles R., *The Two Trillion Dollar Meltdown: Easy Money, High Rollers, and the Great Credit Crash*, New York: PublicAffairs, 2008.

Phillips, Kevin, *Bad Money: Reckless Finance, Failed Politics, and the Global Crisis of American Capitalism*, New York: Viking/Penguin Group, 2008.

Pozen, Robert, *Too Big to Save: How to Fix the U.S. Financial System*, Hoboken, NJ: John Wiley & Sons, 2010.

Prestowitz, Clyde, *Three Billion New Capitalists: The Great Shift of Wealth and Power to the East*, Charlotte, NC: Baker & Taylor, 2006.

Quinlan, Joseph, *Global Engagement: How American Companies Really Compete in the Global Economy*, Lincolnwood, IL: Contemporary Books, 2001.

Rajan, Raghuram G., *Fault Lines: How Hidden Fractures Still Threaten the World Economy*, Princeton, NJ: Princeton University Press, 2010.

Reinhart, Carmen M., and Kenneth S. Rogoff, *This Is Different: Eight Centuries of Financial Folly*, Princeton, NJ: Princeton University Press, 2009.

Ritholtz, Barry, *Bailout Nation: How Greed and Easy Money Corrupted Wall Street and the World Economy*, Hoboken, NJ: John Wiley and Sons, 2009.

Rivoli, Pietra, *The Travels of a T-Shirt in the Global Economy: An Economist Examines the Markets, Power and Politics of World Trade*, Hoboken, NJ: John Wiley & Sons, 2005.

Roubini, Nouriel, and Stephen Mihm, *Crisis Economics: A Crash Course in the Future of Finance*, The Penguin Press, New York, New York, 2010

Sachs, Jeffrey D., *The End of Poverty: Economic Possibilities for Our Time*, London: Penguin Press, 2006.

Sieff, Martin, *Shifting Superpowers: The New and Emerging Relationship between the United States, China and India*, Washington, DC: Cato Institute, 2009.

Stiglitz, Joseph, *Freefall: America, Free Markets, and the Sinking of the World Economy*, New York: W.W. Norton, 2010.

———, *Globalization and Its Discontents*, New York: W.W. Norton, 2002.

———, *Making Globalization Work*, New York: Penguin Books, 2006.

Stiglitz, Joseph, and Linda J. Bilmes, *The Three Trillion Dollar War*, New York: W.W. Norton, 2008.

Sirkin, Harold L., James W. Hemerling, Arindam K. Bhattacharya, *Globality: Competing with Everyone from Everywhere for Everything*, New York: Business Plus, 2008.

Smick, David M., *The World Is Curved: Hidden Dangers to the Global Economy*, New York: Portfolio, 2008.

Sorkin, Andrew Ross, *Too Big to Fail: The Inside Story of How Wall Street and Washington Fought to Save the Financial System from Crisis—and Themselves*, New York: Viking, 2009.

Starobin, Paul, *After America: Narrative for the Next Global Age*, New York: Viking, 2009.

Steingrat, Gabor, *The War for Wealth: The True Story of Globalization, or Why the Flat World Is Broke*, New York: McGraw-Hill, 2008.

United Nations Conference on Trade and Development, "World Investment Report, 2010, Investing in a Low-Carbon Economy," July 2010, New York.

Wessel, David, *In Fed We Trust: Ben Bernanke's War on the Great Panic*, New York: Crown Business, 2009.

Wiggan, Addison, and Kate Incontrera, *I.O.U.S.A.: One Nation. Under Stress. In Debt.*, Hoboken, NJ: John Wiley & Sons, 2008.

Wolf, Martin, *Fixing Global Finance*, Baltimore, MD: The Johns Hopkins University Press, 2008.

Yergin, Daniel, and Joseph Stanislaw, *The Commanding Heights: The Battle Between Government and the Marketplace That Is Remaking the World*, New York: Simon & Schuster, 1998.

Zakaria, Fareed, *The Post-American World*, New York: W.W. Norton, 2008.

Zandi, Mark, *Financial Shock: A 360° Look at the Subprime Mortgage Implosion, and How to Avoid the Next Financial Crisis*, Upper Saddle River, NJ: Financial Times Press, 2008.

Index

Abbas, Mahmoud, 107
Account deficit (*see* Debt)
Afghanistan, 101
  cost of war in, 124–125, 128
  war in, 40, 82, 123, 164
Africa, 6–7, 25, 48, 85, 102, 109, 115
Ahmadinejad, Mahmoud, 107
AIG (*see* American Insurance Group)
Almunia, Joaquin, 60
American Insurance Group (AIG), 56,
  92, 129
"Americans Are from Mars and
  Europeans Are from Venus"
  (Kagan), 154
Anti-immigration laws, 231
Argentina, 76, 98, 116
  financial crisis in, 43, 51
  G-20 and, 87–88, 91
ASEAN (*see* Association of Southeast
  Asian Nations)
Ashton, Catherine, 162
Asia, 18, 21, 54, 71
  economic cohesion in, 100–103
  financial crisis in 1997, 8, 87
  (See also specific countries in Asia)
Association of Southeast Asian Nations
  (ASEAN), 97, 99, 166
Australia, 32, 87–88, 99, 143, 188
Automobile industry, 36, 165, 247
  globalization's influence on, 16–17,
    151, 179–180, 193, 200, 246, 250
  protectionism in, 74–75, 77–78, 92

Bad Money (Phillips), 34
Bank for International Settlements, 55, 62
Banks/banking:
  bailouts, 59, 74, 93
  collapse of European, 7, 36, 56
  in developing nations, 12–13,
    202–203
  Islamic, 71
  lending in housing boom/bust, 19,
    30–31, 57, 64
  regulation of, 34–35, 67–69, 70,
    94–95, 157

Banks/banking *(cont'd)*:
  restrictions, 11–12
  shadow banking system and, 34–35
  subprime crisis and fallout with, 32,
    56–60, 66–72
Barofsky, Neil, 129
Bear Stearns, collapse of, 54, 55
Beijing, 18, 47, 49, 94, 110, 115, 137
Belgium, 32, 161
Bergsten, C. Fred, 100
Berlin Wall, fall of, 5, 21
Bernanke, Ben, 31, 39, 132, 141, 187
Bhagwati, Jagdish, 102
Bhasin, Parmod, 143
Biden, Joseph, 225, 226
Bilmes, Linda J., 126, 127
Bixby, Robert, 134
Bond markets, 13, 14, 30–32
Bordo, Michael, 50
Boutros-Ghali, Youssef, 90
Bovespa, 105
Brazil, 16, 65, 94, 98, 102, 118, 133,
  142, 260
  economic and political emergence of,
    6, 103–110
  financial crisis in, 59, 61
  G-20 and, 87–88
  oil in, 106
Bremmer, Ian, 95, 236
Bretton Woods system, 13, 19
  end of, 9–10, 11, 14–15
  expansion of financial globalization
    after, 14–15, 19
  proposals for new, 67, 156
Brown, Gordon, 36
Bruederle, Rainer, 160
Buffett, Warren, on derivatives, 34
Bush, George H., 23
Bush, George W., 53, 87, 109, 154, 251
"Buy American" provisions, 78–79
"Buy European" law, 79

Canada, 16, 22, 32, 78, 98
  fading global influence of, 143
  G-7, G-8 and, 86–87

Capital controls, 12, 70
Capital flows, global:
    China to U.S., 46–50
    global trade dwarfed by, 32–37
    unleashing of, 12, 13–15
    (*See also* Cross-border capital flows)
Cardoso, Fernando Henrique, 104
Carter, Jimmy, 2, 3
Cash:
    as China's top export to U.S., 46–50
    computer technology and global flow
        of, 14
    (*See also* Capital flows, global)
Castro, Fidel, 105
Celtic Tiger, 36
    (*See also* Ireland)
Chan, Ronnie, 173
Changyou Chen, 205
Chavez, Hugo, 103, 105
Chiang Mai Initiative Multilateralism
    (CMIM), 97–98
China, 5, 7, 9, 17, 22, 24, 25, 44, 59, 61,
    63, 64, 65, 67, 81, 85, 86, 87–88,
    90–91, 94, 95, 97, 99–100, 101,
    102, 122, 133, 142
    cash as top U.S. import from, 46–50
    consumers unleashed in, 253–257
    economic and political emergence of,
        110–118
    education in, 256
    energy deals with, 183–184
    health care in, 255–256
    as new global power broker, 176–180
    obesity rate in, 186
    oil in, 112, 181–184
    as primary U.S. creditor, 136–137
    protectionism in, 75, 76–77, 79
    soft power and, 116–117
    as sugar daddy to U.S., 48
    SWF in, 187–188
    U.S. Treasuries held by, 47, 135,
        138–140, 187
    water shortages in, 112
Climate change, 85, 104, 144, 219
Clinton, Bill, 92
Clinton, Hillary, 216
CMIM (*see* Chiang Mai Initiative
    Multilateralism)
Cold War, 42, 86, 125, 145
Cold War, economic:
    aftershocks, 238–240
    battle over nontraditional energy
        sources and, 221–225
    choosing sides and, 236–237
    coming, 211–240
    ending reign of U.S. dollar and,
        232–234

Cold War, economic *(cont'd)*:
    investment protectionism and,
        234–236
    migrant workers and, 229–231
    preparing for, 216–221
    scenarios, 213–216
    unemployment and, 225–229
*The Commanding Heights: The Battle
    for the World Economy* (Yergin and
    Stanislaw), 1
Computer technology, 14, 16
Consumers:
    in developing nations, 190–194
    unleashed in China, 253–257
Cross-border capital flows, 4–5, 9, 11,
    71
    between developed nations, 149–151
    plummeting, 58–59
    uphill, 41–46
Currency, 11–12
    EU and creation of single market
        and, 23
    proposal to eliminate U.S. dollar as
        world reserve, 49, 156
    (*See also specific currencies*)

DAX, 65
Debt, 121
    as American way of life, 27, 29,
        37–41
    cost of servicing U.S., 134–135
    current U.S., 38, 92, 120–122, 124
Deng Xiaoping, 22, 110
Deregulation, 4–5, 7
Derivatives, 67, 69
    financial globalization and, 12, 13, 14
    as weapons of mass destruction, 34
Developing nations, 14, 45, 46, 63, 66, 70
    banks/banking in, 12–13, 203
    cold reception toward Western
        nations by, 198–204
    coming war for talent with, 204–209
    competition for natural resources and,
        180–186
    middle class in, 178, 180–181
    as new global power brokers,
        173–210
    new world and faultlines with,
        209–210
    rise of, 85–118
    tables turned for consumers in,
        190–194
    U.S. investment too little, too late in,
        195–198
    workforce in, 177–178
    (*See also* Brazil; China; India; Middle
        East; Russia)

Dollars, end reign for U.S., 232–234
Dot-com meltdown, 27, 50–51, 52
Drucker, Peter, 12

East Asian Free Trade Agreement
    (EAFTA), 100
Economic Consequences of the Peace
    (Keynes), 6–7
The Economist, 92, 93, 100, 113, 148, 181
Economy, global, 1–3
    freefall and collapse of global, 19–20,
        55–66
    G-7/G-8 as outgoing stewards of,
        86–87
    new stewards of, 86–91
    primacy of transatlantic, 146–152
Education, 208, 252–253, 256
Egypt, 90, 94–95, 165
Eichengreen, Barry, 50
The End of the Free Market (Bremmer),
    236
Energy sources, battle over, 221–225
EU (*see* European Union)
Europe, 5, 10, 12, 13, 14, 54, 62, 64, 75, 93
    first age of globalization and, 6–7
    rebuilding of post-WWII, 1–2
    twilight of Japan and, 143–171
European Union (EU), 16, 22, 23, 59, 146
    antidumping investigations and, 79
    G-20 and, 87–88
Euros, 37, 137–138
Evenett, Simon J., 73
Exchange rates, floating, 12

FDI (*see* Foreign direct investment)
Federal Reserve System, U.S., 22, 27,
    55, 56, 59, 93
Financial globalization:
    accelerating pace of, 13–15
    influence of, 19–20
    retreat of, 66–72
Financial Shock (Zandi), 28
Financial Times, 53, 77, 115, 162, 216
Food, global demand for, 186
Ford, Gerald, 3
Foreign Affairs (Krauthammer), 21, 95
Foreign direct investment (FDI), 15
    growth of, 8, 17–18
    trade figures for, 148–149
Foreign exchange trading, world trade
    vs., 33
Fortis, 56
France, 32, 65, 67, 74–75, 89, 153
    first age of globalization and, 6–7
    G-7, G-8 and, 86–87
    protectionism in, 75, 77–78, 93
Fraud (*see* Housing boom)

Freefall (Stiglitz), 31
Freeman, Richard, 176
Free-market capitalism, 4–6, 8–9
Fukuyama, Francis, 9

G-7 (*see* Group of Seven)
G-8 (*see* Group of Eight)
G-20 (*see* Group of Twenty)
Gallatin, Albert, 119
Gates, Robert, 164
Germany, 12, 61, 63, 65, 75, 79, 101, 110
    first age of globalization and, 6–7
    G-7, G-8 and, 86–87
    Greece's financial crisis and, 159–161
    short selling of stocks banned in,
        67, 68
Global Trends 2025 (National
    Intelligence Council), 211
Globalization, 8
    cracks in foundation of, 152–155
    dominance of U.S., 20–24
    expanding governance with, 257–259
    first age of, 6–7
    historical backdrop for rebirth of, 1–6
    Nixon as founding father of, 9–13
    reincarnated, 241–265
    second age of, 7–9, 18–19
    third age of, 244–246
    of trade and investment, 15–20
    West refortified and, 260–262
    (*See also* Financial globalization)
Gold standard, 9–13, 72
    (*See also* Bretton Woods system)
Gorbachev, Mikhail, 5
Government:
    loss of faith in U.S., 2–3, 4
    state capitalism and, 93–95
    (*See also* Protectionism)
Great Depression, 11, 35, 65, 72, 83,
    93, 226
Greece, financial crisis in, 114, 132–133,
    158–161, 168, 170
Greenspan, Alan, 22, 24, 27, 31, 39, 52
Gross, Bill, 68
Gross domestic product, global, 13–14
    global financial assets *vs.*, 33
    postwar peak of, 8
Group of Eight (G-8), 86–87, 88
Group of Seven (G-7), 86–87
Group of Twenty (G-20), 68–69, 114–
    115, 118, 244, 257–259
    reneging of no-protectionist pledge
        and, 72–73, 80, 88
    rise of, 87–91

Hamilton, Daniel, 154
Hatoyama, Yukio, 169

HBOS, 56
Health care, 126–127, 255–256
Hillman, Jennifer, 96–97
Homes, net equity extraction from, 28–29
Housing boom:
    actions of mortgage companies during, 30–31
    banks/banking and lending practices in, 19, 30–31, 57, 64
    collapse of, 57, 82
    net equity extraction during, 28–29
    subprime crisis triggered by, 31
    Wall Street's dealings during, 30–32
    warning signs during, 29–30, 52
Hu Jintao, 214
Human rights issues, 23

Iceland, financial crisis in, 35, 36–37, 56, 57
IMF (see International Monetary Fund)
Immelt, Jeff, 77
Immigration (see Migrant workers)
India, 6, 7, 16, 18, 25, 65, 76, 81, 94, 101, 102, 174
    antidumping investigations and, 79
    banking regulations in, 94–95
    financial crisis in, 61, 63–64
    G-20 and, 87–88
    oil in, 185
    technology industry in, 204–205
Indigenous innovation, 200
Indonesia, 12, 76, 116
    financial crisis in, 43, 63–64
    G-20 and, 87–88
Interest rates, 11, 39–40, 59, 121, 134–135
International Monetary Fund (IMF), 10, 12, 59, 69, 71, 85, 98, 257
    Brazil and, 103
    G-20 and, 88–89, 90
    Greece's financial crisis and, 159
    regionalism vs. multilateral system and, 96–97
Internet, 39, 200
Iran, 48, 101, 115, 116, 184
    revolution in 1979, 3
    sanctions against, 107
Iraq, 23
    cost of war in, 124–128
    war in, 40, 82, 123, 153, 154, 171
Ireland, 32, 35, 36, 56, 63
Israel, 107
Italy, 32, 75, 86–87, 93

Jacques, Martin, 111, 118, 239
James, Harold, 141

Japan, 1–2, 8, 12, 47, 86–87, 93, 100, 120, 133, 142, 169, 248
    aging population in, 167–168
    CMIM and, 97
    economic rise of, 10, 21
    financial crisis in, 59, 61, 62–63
    as next Switzerland, 165–170
    twilight of Europe and, 143–171
Japan, Inc., 165
Jefferson, Thomas, 119
Johnson, Lyndon B., 10
Juncker, Jean-Claude, 60

Kagan, Robert, 154
Kan, Naoto, 169
Kazakhstan, 101, 188
Kennedy, John F., 152
Keynes, John Maynard, 6–7, 11, 157
Kissinger, Henry, 161
Korea (see North Korea; South Korea)
Krauthammer, Charles, 21
Krugman, Paul, 35, 58

Labor pool, 17, 18, 204–209
Lagarde, Christine, 160
Latin America, 8, 13, 54, 115
    (See also specific countries in Latin America)
Lawrence, Robert Z., 109
Lehman Brothers, collapse of, 19, 55, 83, 129, 152
Lenin, Vladimir Ilyich, 4
Lowenthal, Abraham, 98
Lula da Silva, Luiz Inácio, 104–106, 107, 155–156
Luo Ping, 140

M&A (see Mergers and acquisitions)
Mahbubani, Kishore, 114, 173, 210
Malaysia, 17, 79
Manufacturing, 35–36, 223, 249–250
Marx, Karl, 156
McKinsey Global Institute, 32, 33, 58
Medicaid/Medicare, 82, 121, 123, 131, 132
Mercosur, 16, 76, 109
Mergers and acquisitions (M&A), 190–193
Merkel, Angela, 160
Mexico, 12, 16, 22, 106, 133, 248
    G-20 and, 87–88
    peso crisis in 1982, 8
Middle East, 23, 54, 102, 107, 115, 136, 260
    Islamic banking in, 71
    oil crisis and, 1–2, 3, 11
    oil in, 181
    savings rate in, 44–45

Migrant workers, 229–231
Misery index, 2, 3, 24
  (*See also* Unemployment)
Mortgage-backed securities, 13, 30–32, 33, 36
Myanmar, 101, 184

NAFTA (*see* North American Free Trade Agreement)
Natural resources:
  competition for, 180–186
  rare earth minerals and, 217–219
  used as political power, 217
Netherlands, 32, 65, 164
New Century Financial, bankruptcy of, 54
New Zealand, 99, 143, 188
Nikkei, 167
9/11, 23, 24, 52, 125, 128, 153, 216
Nixon, Richard, 3, 72, 81
  as founding father of modern globalization, 9–13
North American Free Trade Agreement (NAFTA), 22
North Korea, 48, 115, 166, 184
Nuclear weapons, proliferation of, 85

Obama, Barack, 59, 67, 68, 76, 119, 125, 216, 225, 232, 241, 251
  stimulus package and, 128
Oil:
  crisis, 1–2, 3, 11
  global supplies of, 106, 112, 181–185, 193, 198–199, 216–217, 224
  nationalized, 182
  (*See also* Natural resources)
O'Neil, Paul, 39
Organization of Petroleum Exporting Countries (OPEC), 2, 121, 137
Ozel, Soli, 108

Pangalos, Theodoros, 159
Papandreou, George, 159
Paulson, Hank, 67
Per capita incomes, global, 8
Peres, Shimon, 107
Pharmaceuticals, 202–203
Philippines, 12, 17
Phillips, Kevin, 34–35
Phones, mobile, 174
Pilling, David, 115
Pitt, Harvey, 67
Poland, 16, 22, 61, 149
Pollution, environmental, 112
Populations:
  growth in Asia, 219–220
  Japan's aging, 167–168

Populations *(cont'd):*
  moving out of poverty, 177
  U.S. and aging, 131–132
Poverty, 25
  global estimates for, 64
  populations moving out of, 177
Prince, Chuck, 53
Privatization, 4–5, 7, 16
ProPublica.org, 129
Protectionism, 79, 93
  automobile industry and, 74–75, 77–78, 92
  economic cold war and investment, 234–236
  G-20, no-protectionist pledge and, 72–73
  tariffs as, 76–77

Rachman, Gideon, 162
Railways, 101, 128
Rao, P. V. Narasimha, 16
Reagan, Ronald, 3, 4, 9, 92, 125, 131
Real estate:
  boom worldwide, 32, 36
  plunging global values, 58
  (*See also* Housing boom)
Regionalism, rush to, 95–103
Regulations:
  banking, 34–35, 67–69, 70, 94–95, 157
  financial, 67–68, 94
Reinhart, Carmen M., 29, 83
Renminbi, 49, 140
Rogoff, Kenneth S., 29, 83
Rosenberg, Tina, 182
Roubini, Nouriel, 68
Rumsfeld, Donald, 153
Russia, 101, 102
  G-8 and, 86–87
  globalization and, 22
  oil in, 181, 224
  protectionism in, 75, 76
  savings rate in, 45

Sachs, Jeffrey, 91
Sakakibara, Eisuke, 156
Sarkozy, Nicolas, 67, 78, 89, 156, 160
Saudi Arabia, 87–88, 91, 188
Savings and loans, 34–35
  (*See also* Banks/banking)
Savings rate, 44–45, 255
  in U.S., 28, 40, 62
  world's foreign exchange reserves and, 186–188
Schwarzenegger, Arnold, 222
SCO (*see* Shanghai Cooperation Organization)

Securities, U.S.:
  mortgage-backed, 13, 30–32
  "safe" reputation of, 46
Securities and Exchange Commission,
  U.S., 34, 67–68
Securitization, 57
  (See also Banks/banking)
September 11, 2001 (see 9/11)
Setser, Brad, 138
Shanghai Cooperation Organization
  (SCO), 101–102
Singapore, 101, 188
Singh, Manmohan, 241
Smick, David M., 15, 18–19, 133–134
Smoot-Hawley Tariff Act of 1930, 80
Social Security, 82, 121, 123, 131, 132
Sorkin, Andrew Ross, 55
South Africa, 87–88
South America, 16, 64, 98
  (See also specific countries in South
    America)
South Korea, 12, 75, 116, 165, 174–175,
    188, 248
  automobile industry and, 16
  CMIM and, 97
  financial crisis in, 59
  G-20 and, 87–88
Southeast Asia, 14, 101
Sovereign wealth funds (SWF),
    187–189
Soviet Union:
  economic restructuring in, 5
  fall of, 21
  globalization and, 25
Spain, 32, 63, 64, 65, 141
Spence, Michael, 216
Stagflation, 1
Stanislaw, Joseph, 1
Steinbrück, Peer, 61, 156
Stelzenmüller, Constanze, 160
Stephens, Philip, 90
Stiglitz, Joseph E., 31, 43, 126, 127
Subprime mortgages:
  banks/banking and, 32, 56–60,
    66–72
  fiasco, 29, 31, 36, 54, 56, 60, 82
  home buyers and, 34
  Wall Street, housing boom and,
    30–32
Subsidies (see Protectionism)
Summers, Larry, 119, 120
Superpowers:
  rise of developing nations as joint,
    173–210
  U.S., as last economic, 20–24, 82
  (See also Developing nations)
SWF (see Sovereign wealth funds)

Switzerland, 65
  Japan as next, 165–170
Taiwan, 133, 137
Terrorists, 23, 24, 125
Thailand, 42, 79, 133
Thatcher, Margaret, 4, 9, 92
This Time Is Different (Reinhart and
  Rogoff), 29, 83
The Three Trillion Dollar War: The True
  Cost of the Iraq Conflict (Stiglitz
  and Bilmes), 126
Too Big to Fail (Sorkin), 55
Trade, global, 7, 108
  agreement increases, 99–100
  barriers, 16, 74
  capital flows surpassing, 32–37
  investment and, 15–20
  regionalism's rise with, 95–103
Trade restrictions:
  protectionism and, 72–76
  safeguard initiatives and, 80
  tariffs and, 76
Treasuries, U.S., 13, 39, 41, 120,
    138–140
  China's holdings of, 47, 135, 138–
    140, 187
  Japan's holdings of, 47
Trust, erosion of, 57, 82
Turkey, 107–108, 260
  banking regulations in, 94–95
  G-20 and, 87–88
  protectionism in, 76

Unemployment:
  economic cold war and, 225–229
  global, 64, 226–227
  oil crisis of 1973 and U.S., 2
  in U.S., in 1982, 3
United Arab Emirates, 174
United Kingdom, 4, 32, 60, 63, 65, 162
  first age of globalization and, 6–7
  G-7, G-8 and, 86–87
  protectionism in, 75
United Nations, 16, 80, 85
United States, 4, 5–6, 10–11, 12, 17, 23,
    35, 86–87, 89, 90–91, 93, 182, 193
  automobile industry in, 36, 74, 92,
    179–180, 246–247
  cash as China's top export to, 46–50
  cost of financial crisis to, 128–130
  cost of future entitlements to,
    130–134
  cost of servicing debt owed by,
    134–135
  cost of war to, 124–128
  current debt in, 38, 92, 120–122, 124

United States *(cont'd)*:
 devalued global influence of, 143–171
 economic prosperity and good life in,
  24–25, 51–52
 economy in 1970s, 1–3
 education in, 252–253
 financial system's implosion in, 55–60
 financial war and probable outcome
  for, 136–142
 globalization and refortifying,
  260–262
 housing boom in, 27–32
 investments in developing nations
  too late for, 195–198
 as last economic superpower, 20–24,
  82
 perfect financial storm and, 123–124
 protectionism in, 74, 78–79, 92
 savings rate in, 28, 40, 62
 stock market crash, 7, 8, 50
 unemployment rate in, 24
 what's right with, 247–253
 from world's largest creditor to debtor
  nation, 37–41, 122–123
 worlds of change for, 262–265

Van Rompuy, Herman, 161
Venezuela, 98, 116, 188
Veterans, U.S., 126–127
Vietnam, 9, 10, 76, 79, 101

Wadhwa, Vivek, 205, 206
Walker, David, 123
Wall Street, 8, 13, 14, 39, 53, 62, 92
 housing boom, subprime crisis and
  dealings on, 30–32
 role in expanding global money
  supply, 19–20
 September 2008 panic on, 19, 53–55
Wall Street Reform and Consumer
 Protection Act of 2010, 68

War:
 in Afghanistan, 40, 82, 101, 123,
  124–125, 128, 164
 developing nations and coming
  talent, 204–209
 in Iraq, 40, 82, 123, 124–128, 153,
  154, 171
 U.S. and cost of, 124–128
 U.S. and probable outcome of
  financial, 136–142
Water shortages, 112, 219–221
 (*See also* Natural resources)
Wen Jiabao, 48–49, 110, 140, 220, 225
When China Rules the World (Jacques),
 239
White, Harry Dexter, 11
Wolf, Martin, 9, 50
Workforce, global, 176–178, 192–193,
 227–228, 249–250
World Bank, 10, 11, 43, 50, 69, 70, 71,
 73, 85, 257
 G-20 and, 88–89, 90
 poverty estimates by, 64
 regionalism *vs.* multilateral system
  and, 96–97
World Investment Report 2010 (United
 Nations), 80
World Trade Organization (WTO), 22,
 75, 80, 146
 Doha Round of, 85, 88, 89, 99, 115,
  163, 250, 261
 increase of regional trade agreements
  and, 99
 regionalism *vs.* multilateral system
  and, 97
The World Is Curved (Smick), 15, 18–19
Wuttke, Joerg, 77

Yen, 167
Yergin, Daniel, 1

Zandi, Mark, 28

About the Author

Joseph P. Quinlan is managing director and the chief market strategist for US Trust, Bank of America Private Wealth Management. He serves as a senior fellow at the Center for Transatlantic Relations, the Paul H. Nitze School of Advanced International Studies of The Johns Hopkins University, and as a transatlantic fellow at the German Marshal Fund, Brussels, Belgium. Quinlan lectures on global finance and trade at New York University and Fordham University.